Gentlemen and Jesuits

Glory and Adventure in the Early Days of Acadia

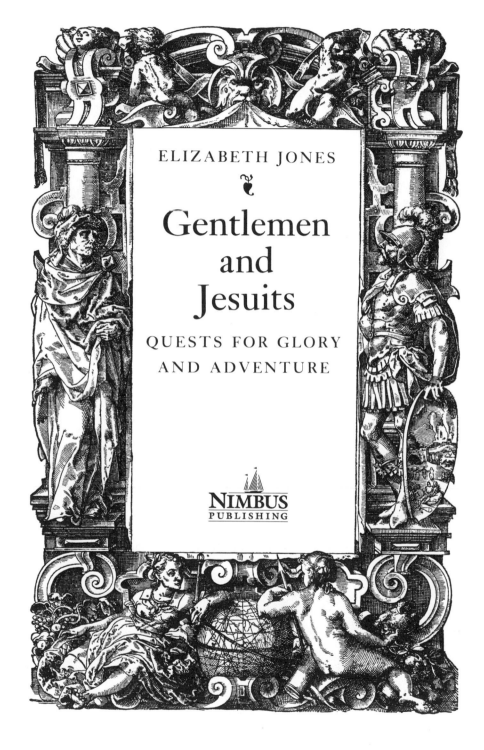

ELIZABETH JONES

Gentlemen and Jesuits

QUESTS FOR GLORY AND ADVENTURE

NIMBUS
PUBLISHING

Nimbus Publishing Limited
PO Box 9166
Halifax, NS   B3K 5M8
(902) 455-4286

Printed and bound in Canada

National Library of Canada Cataloguing in Publication

Jones, Elizabeth
Gentlemen and Jesuits : glory and adventure in the
early days of Acadia / Elizabeth Jones.

First published: Toronto : University of Toronto Press, 1986.
Includes bibliographical references and index.
ISBN 1-55109-367-7

1. Port Royal Habitation (N.S.). 2. Acadia—History. 3. Nova
Scotia—History—To 1784. I. Title.

FC2043.J66 2002   971.6'01   C2002-902031-X
F1038.J65 2002

The Champlain Society kindly gave permission to quote from and reproduce charts and
drawings from the Champlain Society edition of Champlain's *Works*. The Bibliothèque
Nationale of France authorized the reproduction of the portraits of Henri ɪv by Quesnel, of
Madame de Guercheville, and of a Jesuit priest (Escobar y Mendoza). Translation of
Lescarbot (p 80) from *Collected Poems*, by F.R.Scott. Used by permission of The Canadian
Publishers, McClelland and Stewart Limited, Toronto. The Nova Scotia Museum permitted
the reproduction of Mi'kmaq petroglyphs from Marion Robertson's *Rock Drawings of the
Micmac Indians* (Halifax 1973). These are redrawn from tracings of the originals made by
George Creed in 1887-8, the tracings being in the possession of the Nova Scotia Museum.

For my mother
Catherine Proksch
(an old Scotian)
who gave me a taste for history,
for Mary Jones,
and in very fond memory of
Bob Jones

CONTENTS

PREFACE

N COMING TO LIVE IN NOVA SCOTIA, I became intrigued, as so many other people have been, with the early French connection, the founding here of the first enduring European settlement north of Florida.* All Nova Scotian school children know something of the story. Almost four hundred years ago, Henri IV granted the monopoly of the fur trade to a company of French merchants who established a settlement first at Ste Croix in 1604 and then at Port Royal in 1605. After three years the monopoly was revoked and the interest of the leader, the sieur de Monts, and of his chief explorer and cartographer, Champlain, shifted to Quebec. However, a member of the lesser nobility, the sieur de Poutrincourt, held Port Royal as his fief. Between 1610 and 1613 he attempted to maintain the Habitation and to cultivate the land. He was also responsible for having a number of Indians baptized. In 1613 the Habitation was razed to the ground by a group of Virginians who considered the French presence a threat to English colonization of North America. School history books generally make mention also of the *Order of Good Cheer*, founded by Champlain at Port Royal during the third winter spent by the French in Acadia, and of the *Theatre of Neptune*, a masque written by Poutrincourt's lawyer friend, Marc Lescarbot, and the first theatrical performance to be given north of Florida.

* There is some controversy as to whether Port Royal rather than Quebec should be called the oldest European settlement north of Florida. I have preferred to describe it as the first enduring settlement, for though it endured, as we shall see, settlement was not continuous.

But the more I read about these settlements and the people involved in founding and maintaining them, the more summary such an outline seemed and the more fascinated I became. For, given the time and place, this was an exceptionally well-documented enterprise. Three authors, who were often eyewitnesses, have left fairly extensive though rather different accounts of discoveries and events. They are Champlain himself, Lescarbot, and the Jesuit priest, Father Biard, wished by the court upon the unwilling Poutrincourt and his son. While reading the works of all three, I found myself in the thick of their experiences, embarked on voyages with certain hopes and intentions only to find that some accident or conjunction of events brought an outcome quite different from what had been anticipated. Many characters, even those who make only a fleeting appearance, became amazingly alive, caught in a gesture or an attitude: one captain attempting to knife another when both ran the danger of being shipwrecked; an officious customs official stubbornly holding up a consignment of furs; an Indian chief magnificently casting all the trade goods he had obtained from the French into a canoe as a present to the chief of another tribe; Henri IV chastising Poutrincourt with all the valour of his lively tongue for being in Paris and not out at Port Royal converting the Indians; a Jesuit priest lying behind a chest in the captain's cabin and threatening to excommunicate anyone who should lay a finger on him; a Huguenot pilot anxiously skulking along the shore disguised as an Indian.

Yet few people I spoke to knew much about settlements and settlers beyond the usual brief outline. Hazy or inflated ideas of characters and events abounded. In several books I found many inaccuracies and misconceptions. It struck me that there was a place for a book of popular history, based on careful research, but intended for the non-specialist reader curious about these early settlements. This book is an attempt to fill the gap.

The question could be raised: why write the story of an endeavour that in terms of conquest or glory was not a conspicuous success? Indeed, the immediate outcome looked very like failure. And, given all the historical circumstances, it is unsure whether the French *could* have founded a flourishing settlement in Acadia in the early seventeenth century. Yet the story of their attempt to do so has a colour, a flavour, a texture all of its own. As it is so rich in human optimism, perverseness, error, folly, and endurance, it seemed to me well worth the telling.

Historical characters often become frozen into stereotypes: intrepid explorer, gallant nobleman, pious missionary, skilful artisan, evil traitor. The truth, in so far as we *can* come close to it by careful and sometimes intuitive reading of what documents there are available, is always more complex and more humanly interesting. It can be painful to realize that characters we have come to see in all the gloss of romance are less exceptional and more flawed than we like founders and so 'heroes' to be. But what we lose in flashy romantic colour we gain in nuance and understanding and so approach the density and bewilderment of real experience.

Often, too, there is a temptation when quarrels and tension arise among historical personages to plump for one side or the other and deliver very partial though would-be final judgments on the situation. Particularly in the dissensions between the Biencourt gentlemen and the Jesuits I have tried to show what lay behind both points of view so that the characters can be better understood rather than summarily blamed and dismissed.

My main aim then has been to tell a story and to involve the reader in events as they occurred. Yet in my presentation I have tried to weave some interpretation of characters and events into the narrative, often by dwelling on scenes and images and by implication rather than by direct exposition. So though this is essentially narrative history, I hope that the reader will not find an interpretative element altogether absent.

NOTE

No reference signals have been used in the text. Readers interested in general sources and particular citations will find them at the end of the volume under 'Sources' and 'Notes and References.' Page-by-page references to phrases and passages quoted are provided under the latter.

ACKNOWLEDGMENTS

I AM GRATEFUL for help from many sources. The Nova Scotia Department of Culture, Recreation, and Fitness gave welcome assistance. Dr John G. Reid, now in the History Department of St Mary's University, Halifax, read the first draft and made a number of very helpful suggestions, thus saving me from some glaring inaccuracies and omissions. For advice on matters of a technical nature I am indebted to several experts: C.R.K. Allen, that most whole-hearted of naturalists; M. Cechetto, home economist; Niels Jannasch, ex-Director of the Maritime Museum of the Atlantic; Dr Edwin F. Ross, surgeon, and Dr David Tindall, physicist. Responsibility for errors detected in any of their fields should be firmly laid at my door not theirs.

Elizabeth Fox produced a CBC documentary, 'Gentlemen and Jesuits at Port Royal,' that gave me interesting insights into the characters. M. Jean Estienne, a former archivist of the Somme, introduced me to Biencourt country by taking me to visit the ruined Poutrincourt keep. I would also like to thank Dr Michael Bishop and the French Department of Dalhousie University for their encouragement and assistance.

Edith Haliburton and Pat Townsend of the Watson Kirkconnell section of the Library at Acadia University were most helpful in bringing out books from 'the cage.' Librarians at the Killam Library, Dalhousie University, arranged for many inter-library loans.

I am also grateful to Frances Taylor, Winnie Horton, Rose Alphonse, and Anamaría Villalón, who, at different stages, turned versions and revisions into clear, efficiently typed manuscript. A.D. Wright was most helpful in checking the final version.

Wayne Daniels undertook to do the index, for which I am most appreciative.

It has been a pleasure to have the assistance and encouragement of Gerry Hallowell, history editor for the University of Toronto Press, and of Judy Williams, who edited the final manuscript with fine care.

Many friends over a number of years bore with me as I enthusiastically retailed the discoveries I was making myself while looking into the lives of explorers and discoverers. I couldn't possibly mention them all by name – they know who they are. I would, however, like to thank in particular David Jones for encouragement and support, and my daughters, Eleanor and Frances Royle, who read the manuscript and made their, as always, refreshingly candid suggestions and comments.

ELIZABETH JONES

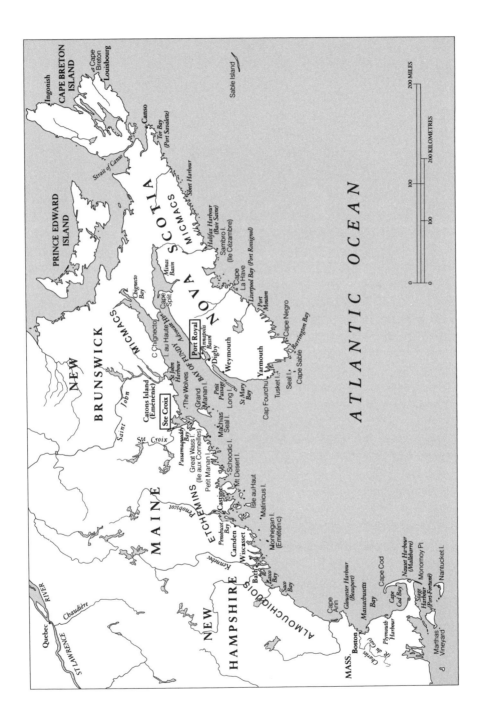

PART I

AN ENTERPRISE THE MOST VALIANT
AND LEAST ASSISTED

CHAPTER ONE

Towards the Countries and Confines of La Cadie

LE HAVRE, MARCH 1604: a place and a time for new starts. With the first hint of spring this Norman port rang with the cries and clamour of men putting out to sea. Three ships in particular caught the attention of harbour-watchers. Rumour had it that they were part of a French fleet going to help the Protestant Netherlands in their struggle against their arrogant Spanish overlords. But rumour was wrong. They were bound for the northern shores of the new continent across the Atlantic.

Around them as they lay at anchor was a bustle of sailors and workmen. They caulked, tallowed, rigged the ships, made them seaworthy for the long voyage, heaved the capstan round, and hauled provisions up on to the deck: barrels of ship's biscuit, salt beef, dried cod, rice, dried peas and beans, prunes, casks of wine, fresh water. And for the gentry: hams, spices, olive oil and vinegar, sugar-loaves, raisins, almonds, lemon peel, and other fruit that Marc Lescarbot later recommended as being

> Utiles en la marine
> Pour conforter la poitrine
> (Useful at sea
> To comfort the belly).

Also stored in the hold were an assortment of trade goods: glass beads, arrowheads, knives, and hatchets destined for the eager hands of tawny-skinned people across the water. In exchange for this glint of metal, white hands would reach out to grasp the gloss of furs. Space had to be found, too, for bleating sheep and hens clucking in their coops. Parts of a pinnace were carefully packed away. On arrival they would be assembled and the pinnace made ready for excursions close to the shore where the main ship could not venture.

It was not an unusual scene for a French seaport in early spring, though most of the ships would have been small fishing vessels. Even before Jacques Cartier's celebrated voyages in the 1530s, fishing smacks were making the hazardous crossing westwards, to return laden with cod. During the sixteenth century their numbers had increased, guaranteeing a ready supply of fish on Fridays so good Catholic countries could duly abstain from flesh without being famished. By 1604 over two hundred ships set sail in March every year for a six-months' season on and around the Grand Banks. So reckoned Father Coton, Henri IV's Jesuit adviser, who worried over the evil effects such a long absence from the sacraments must have on the sailors' souls.

But the curious could observe that more than barrels, hatchets, and fishing gear were being stowed away in two of the three ships. Lumber, trimmed and planed, doors, window frames, tables, and benches indicated that this was more than a summer excursion. At least some of the men going aboard with their chests or bundles intended to stay.

Supervising all this activity was Pierre du Gua, sieur de Monts. A gentleman in his forties, he had already made one voyage out to the New World. Though his name points to more southern origins, he was from Saintonge, that sadly luminous stretch of France south of La Rochelle and north of Bordeaux. Like many of the Saintongeois of the time, de Monts was a Huguenot. During the wars of religion that ravaged France between 1562 and 1598, he had fought bravely with the King on the Protestant side, and then remained loyal to him even when Henri had become a Catholic to smooth the way for peace. Now, as one of about 1,200,000 Protestants in a country of 15,000,000, de Monts benefitted from the Edict of Nantes, which marked the end of those vicious civil wars. This guaranteed Huguenot freedom of conscience and respect for their rights. France became the only country in Europe to tolerate two religions, the two warring ideologies of those times. The Huguenots retained their political organizations and a fair degree of independence in their 'places of security' or fortified towns. De Monts himself had been appointed governor of the town of Pons in Saintonge and received an annual pension of thirty-six hundred livres from the King in recognition of past services. (A maidservant in a bourgeois household received thirty livres a year besides board and lodging. A pilot could make sixty-six livres for a voyage across the Atlantic. A really splendid horse might cost three thousand livres. The Queen's allowance for lotteries and other 'small pleasures' was thirty-six thousand livres a year.)

And now in his sea-chest de Monts carried letters that distinguished him with yet other titles. One, signed by the King, began with a fine official flourish: 'To our dear and well-beloved sieur de Monts, Gentleman-in-Ordinary of the King's Chamber, Greeting.' Then followed the appointment, constituting him 'our Lieutenant-General, for to represent our person in the countries, territories, coasts and confines of La Cadie … from the 40th degree unto the 46th.' His main practical task was to found a colony and to settle Frenchmen in the New World. But the principal aim of colonization, so his commission ran, was to convert the benighted, barbarous Indians to Christianity, or, more specifically, 'to the belief and profession of our faith and religion,' which was, of course, Catholicism. This had been François I's official aim, too, when he had sent Cartier and Roberval out to the Great River of Canada in the 1530s and the 1540s. For Henri was anxious to prove to the world, and especially to the Spanish and Portuguese who jealously guarded their new possessions, that the Most Christian King was more interested in conversions than conquest. It was a stance all subsequent French monarchs who interested themselves in New France were to adopt. But de Monts' ships were not exactly laden with missionaries.

They were a motley assortment of characters, these colonists who were to prepare the way for the first enduring European settlement on North American soil. Nowadays such a group would be televised, photographed, interviewed. Much would be known about individual motives, hopes, ambitions. Without such documentation we can only focus on what written records remain and piece out the rest with our imaginings. We may wonder what de Monts made of the men climbing aboard the 150-tonner on which he himself was to sail. What comments might he have murmured to his secretary, Ralluau, standing by his side?

One man he already knew. He was to get to know him even better. This was Samuel Champlain, a trim, compact, sturdy figure, if we are to judge by a small drawing done some years later. This shows him in full armour, resolutely firing an arquebus while engaged in battle with one Indian tribe against another. In 1604 he was in his mid-thirties. His home town was Brouage, then an important port in de Monts' own Saintonge. From his childhood he had had experience of ships and the sea. A Catholic, he had fought for Henri IV in the five years between the King's conversion in 1593 and capitulation of the ultra-Catholic party in 1598.

Since then he had made two long voyages. The first was an extensive and exotic tour of New Spain and Mexico. On the second, made just the year before to the St Lawrence, he had found his true mission in life: the exploration of New France. It was on his return from this voyage that de Monts had made his acquaintance. De Monts himself had made a similar voyage in 1600 three years earlier. Comparing notes with Champlain, he was impressed with his quiet enthusiasm, his eye for coast and land, his ability to translate his observations into maps and sketches. For Champlain was a competent draughtsman. De Monts had also read the book Champlain had written about his experiences on this voyage: *Des Sauvages, ou, Voyage de Samuel Champlain de Brouage.* As he turned the pages, de Monts must have realized what an asset this soldier-navigator and mapmaker-author would be to his enterprise as explorer and recorder. Champlain's own great dream was to probe, explore, travel on, following rivers and seas westwards to where, he was sure, lay China and all the spices of the East. What de Monts saw of Champlain's character appealed to him: brave and adventurous but not foolhardy; honest, practical, reliable. It was the beginning of a long partnership between the two Saintongeois. Together they were to endure hardships, experience many disappointments. But they never lost faith in each other or in New France.

Also of the party were gentlemen of good birth. Like de Monts on his trip to the St Lawrence, they could have been there for 'pleasure,' as Champlain quaintly puts it, making us think of a leisurely summer cruise. Several of them intended to risk a winter in the New World, for Champlain mentions them on the plan of his first Habitation. So we can catalogue some resonant names: the sieur d'Orville, the sieur de Beaumont, Fougeray de Vitré, La Motte Bourgjoli, Genestou, Sourin. Of a certain du Boullay we learn that he had been a captain in the regiment of the most distinguished of the gentlemen, Jean de Biencourt.

The latter, generally known as the sieur de Poutrincourt, was an exceptionally tall man 'whose tallness becometh him very well.' He came of a noble family in Picardy that was bound by feudal ties to the powerful, ambitious House of Guise, the leaders of the Catholic League. As one of their faction, he had first fought against the King notably during the siege of Paris when Henri iv had appreciated him as a gallant adversary. After the King's conversion in 1593 he had taken his monarch's side against the Catholic extremists. These wars had not improved his fortunes. He was now entangled in lawsuits that had put him in touch with a lively lawyer from Vervins, Marc Lescarbot.

A definite purpose attracted Poutrincourt to the expedition. At the age of forty-seven, he was ready to start life over again, uproot his wife and family from their seigneuries in Picardy and Champagne and transplant them to a new one across the sea. He had some experiences of sailing, but was less interested in exploration than in the prospect of broad acres. On this voyage he intended only to survey the scene and choose his land; he would return later to found his settlement. A humanist education had given him a wide range of interests. He had a mathematical bent and also played, sang, and composed music. Besides, he had a certain practical knack. De Monts must have regarded him as a natural ally in schemes for colonization. But he might have noted in him a reckless streak, a thirst for renown. Vaulting ambition was certainly one spur to prick the side of his intent. As his friend Lescarbot put it, he 'had no mind to be the last that should follow and participate in the glory of so fair and generous an enterprise.' His immediate contribution to the expedition was seven hundred pounds of gunpowder. Defence had to be thought of as well as seeds of barley, wheat, and rye.

For the voyage itself mariners were needed. Captain Timothée was master of the largest ship, a 150-tonner on which most of the colonists sailed. Captain Morel commanded the *Bonne Renommée* of 100 or 120 tons. There was also a spare captain, Foulques. (The third ship was a small trading vessel that would sail straight to Tadoussac to engage in barter with the Montagnais.)

Morel's pilot was Guillaume Duglas, a seasoned sailor with thiry-five years' experience of transatlantic crossings. Two other pilots were Pierre Cramolet and Louis Coman. To the latter de Monts had, intriguingly, promised a hat as well as sixty livres in wages. And then there was Pierre Angibault, called Champdoré. He had a reputation as an excellent shipbuilder and carpenter, and would prove useful on voyages when pinnaces had to be put together or even built from scratch. And who knew what damage wild seas, hidden shoals, and rocks might do to the ship itself? But there were doubts as to his competence as a pilot and he was a stubborn man.

Men as well as ships are subject to accidents and might need attention and repair. Philippe Raybois, a surgeon, went out, but only for the summer. There was, however, at least one other surgeon on board, for later in the winter we catch the gleam of a dissecting knife. Also an apothecary, Henri Beaufort, twenty-one years old and still an apprentice. He must have been a considerate young man. Before sailing, he took care to make a will providing for his widowed mother, his sister and brothers.

For the spiritual health of Catholics and Protestants alike there were three clerics: two priests and one Protestant pastor. However, probably very few men on board, including the clerics, had much idea of spiritual health at all. France had indeed been racked and rent by the Wars of Religion, but, apart from the theologically minded, the vast majority of Catholics and Protestants had only very sketchy notions about the doctrines and tenets of their respective religions. Reform of Catholic seminaries, as advocated by the Council of Trent, had not yet got under way, so it is not surprising to find that the two priests on board were hardly imbued with those high sacerdotal ideals which, in the course of the seventeenth century, were to be increasingly known and cultivated. The cleric on this voyage we know most about was Abbé Nicolas Aubry, curious and elegant gentleman traveller. His very respectable Parisian family and friends, horrified to see how far a spirit of adventure was carrying him, 'sent expressly to Honfleur to divert him … and bring him back to Paris.' Somehow he shook off these messengers and went on to savour adventure to the full, if that is how almost starving to death in a wilderness can be described.

The other Catholic priest remains anonymous. All we learn of him is that he, like the Protestant pastor, knew enough of the rudiments of his faith to quarrel about it, and that he proved to be a bonny fighter, with fists as well as words. (Indeed, brawling priests who frequented fairs and taverns and lived openly with their concubines were a far from uncommon phenomenon at the time.) One can understand why, given a Protestant commander and such assistants, a certain scepticism was felt and voiced about the royal missionary zeal – though such comments usually came from hostile and jealous merchants. The Jesuits, the keenest and best-qualified missionaries of the day, were anxious to go to New France. But they were wary of this enterprise. It was led by a 'heretic.'

Then came the colonists, the men destined to clear the wilderness, build and maintain a settlement. They were artisans, mainly masons and carpenters. A forge at the Habitation indicates that one must have been a blacksmith or a maker of edge-tools. An oven and a kitchen point to bakers and cooks. But they were single men, or at least did not have their wives with them. The conditions of the country were as yet too little known to venture taking whole families across. Besides, French peasants, the people who had most experience of working the land and tending flocks and herds, were not interested in leaving France. At that time, they had more to gain by staying where they were. Sully, the King's chief minister, was the great champion of the peasant and his labours. 'Tillage and pasturage are the two breasts that nourish France' was his sententious way of putting it. And the King, so the story went, had said in his own down-to-earth way that he would like to see every 'labourer' (peasant, farmer) in his kingdom with 'une poule dans son pot' (a fowl in his cooking-pot). There was no need for country folk to look for a better life abroad.

With religious toleration guaranteed by the Edict of Nantes, there was no need, either, for the dissenting minority to seek in a new land a haven from harassment as the English Puritans were to do. In spite of heavy taxes France was altogether too comfortable for any but the adventurous or the desperate to want to emigrate. The King was aware of this lack of eager volunteers. A clause in de Monts' commission authorized him to recruit by force jailbirds, vagrants, and exiles. This commandeering of convicts and beggars dates back to Roberval's expedition in the 1540s, but there is no record to tell us whether some, or any, of de Monts' recruits were shaking off the dank smell of prison in the sea air. Yet, as he watched the men swagger and curse, shout obscenities, pugnaciously defend their small space around them, he knew that his experience as a military commander would not be lost. More disciplined, on the surface at any rate, were some Swiss mercenaries, enlisted for the defence of the new colony.

De Monts also needed interpreters, men who, when fishing or trading, had picked up some smattering of the language spoken by the Indians of the region. We know that at one time he had in his service a black man, Mathieu d'Acosta, who had been out with the Portuguese and knew the 'Acadian tongues.' In 1607 he was kidnapped from de Monts in Holland and became the subject of a long lawsuit between him and a merchant of Rouen. The sequence of events is such that, if d'Acosta did actually serve de Monts as an interpreter, and was not just a prospective employee, he too must have been on this voyage.

To help with search for mineral wealth went Maître Simon, a master miner. Perhaps also Maître Jacques, 'a native of Sclavonia.' But it is possible that his Croatian accent was not heard in Acadia, discoursing on copper and the workings of mines, until a year later.

One important member of the expedition was not on board the 150-tonner that carried de Monts. This was François Gravé, his lieutenant, who was to sail on the other large ship – the only one whose name we know – the *Bonne Renommée*. Gravé, sometimes known as sieur Dupont or Dupont-Gravé, was also a soldier who had turned mariner and trader. Not that he made a vast fortune in his ventures. In February that year he had borrowed three hundred livres from a bourgeois of Rouen to do some trading on this voyage, at an interest rate of 25 per cent – huge, but normal for the times and circumstances. Now fifty years old – Champlain was one day to remark that he respected him like a father – Gravé had already crossed the Atlantic several times. De Monts had first made his acquaintance on his journey to the St Lawrence in 1600; Champlain was with him there the year before. As a trader Gravé was somewhat unusual, for he was sympathetic to colonizers. Later he was to lend a helping hand at Quebec to the first priests there, the Récollets. One of their brothers, Gabriel Sagard, described him as jolly and jovial, always ready with a quip or a joke. But he was quick-tempered as well, and just as ready to join in a brawl or a bellowing match. Equipped with a fog-horn voice, he lustily used this to hail passing ships, shouting out greetings or inquiries. To 'the delight of his friends' he drank his liquor long and neat, but paid for it in his old age – at seventy he was still on the high seas – with painful attacks of gout. His full-blooded gusto made him the sort of legendary seafarer about whom endless stories are told below decks and in waterfront taverns.

On the 7th March de Monts' ship was ready to sail. Before leaving he consulted Gravé and they agreed to rendezvous at Canso on the east coast of the mainland of what is now Nova Scotia, across the strait from Cape Breton. The first to arrive was to leave a cross upon a tree or some other message. Canso was then a well-known fishing station and a convenient port of call. There, ships arriving from or returning to France could stock up on wood and fresh water.

So sails were hoisted and billowed in the wind as the ship moved out of sheltered waters into the open sea. There must have been a sense of relief that at last they were under way, a certain apprehension as to what lay ahead. Some may have wondered, and with good reason, if they were ever to see France again. The last land they sighted was the jutting-out point of Cap de la Hève. Three days later, on the 10th, the *Bonne Renommée*, too, swung away from shore, her beak-head pointing towards the ocean.

The invention of the telescope and Galileo's discoveries still lay a few years in the future. The earth, these men knew, was round. It was also, they believed, stationary. It would not have occurred to any of them to doubt that it was a moving sun they followed in its passage from east to west as they sailed for 'La Cadie.'

But what exactly was expected of these men? What powers did de Monts have? How was this enterprise financed? To understand and appreciate the achievement of de Monts and his men we need to know something of the background of this expedition.

For, despite high-minded talk of conversions, not only the Cross but also the lilies of France were to be planted in the new territories. Henri wished to see the French crown maintained there in its 'ancient dignity, greatness and splendour.' One of de Monts' duties was to establish the King's authority among the Indians, make alliances and treaties with them. For this he already had some encouragement.

The previous summer Gravé and Champlain had been to Tadoussac. This was then a recognized trading spot situated where the Saguenay joins the St Lawrence. There the Montagnais, who acted as middlemen for more distant tribes, brought furs every year from far west and north down rivers and over difficult portages. In his first published book Champlain had described how, after the trading, Indians and traders had 'made tabagie,' feasting on moose, bear, seal, and beaver. There was singing, dancing, and long speeches. An Indian who had visited France and returned with Gravé and Champlain addressed the assembled braves, described the welcome he had received in France, and spoke of the desire of the French to colonize the land. No mention, though, of the desire to colonize their souls! After a pause, during which the pipe of friendship was solemnly passed round, the grand sagamo replied that 'he was well content that His said Majesty should people their country and make war on their enemies, and that there was no nation in the world to which they wished more good than to the French.'

With the benefit of hindsight we can today take note of the fundamentally different attitudes of Europeans and Indians towards settlement. The Europeans, fully convinced of the superiority of their civilization, were quite sure that the Indians would want nothing better than to adopt European ways in order to improve their lot. The Indians, secure in their own culture and traditions, were interested in European settlers mainly as potential allies who could supply them with better tools and weapons with which to maintain themselves and their culture. This basic misunderstanding was to have many sad consequences.

Buoyed up with the grand sagamo's assurance, the King empowered de Monts in his commission to proclaim the royal authority in the new territories. He was to keep law and order and appoint the officers necessary to assist him. He was also to explore the country, seek out mines, and distribute lands and titles as he saw fit 'according to the qualities, conditions and merits of the persons of the same country and others.' Thus the grand sagamo at Tadoussac gives a diplomatic inch and His Most Christian Majesty takes an ell. It is difficult today not to smile a little cynically at the idea of de Monts investing an Indian in a title to land where his people had lived and hunted for centuries.

Another official piece of parchment de Monts carried was a commission from Charles de Montmorency, the Lord High Admiral of France. This appointed him Vice-Admiral, and authorized him to police and explore the seas and coasts of 'La Cadie.' The policing part was important. For the King had granted de Monts and his company exclusive rights to the fur trade for a period of ten years. As there was fierce competition for furs, de Monts would need all the authority he could muster to enforce this monopoly. But without it he could not afford to establish a colony. Ships, provisions, habitations, wages, all had to be paid for with profits from furs, the most valuable commodity North America then had to offer.

Fur as an article of fashion – it was warm, it looked luxurious – was in great demand. In terms of what the well-dressed gentleman was wearing, an elaborate beaver hat was becoming *de rigueur* to protect from inclement weather or to flourish in greeting. But European forests no longer bred enough of the wild creatures whose thick, glamorous pelts could be paraded in Court and town. Away across the Atlantic they roamed: foxes, martens, otters, beaver, and moose, hunted with skill and daring by the native Indians for whom they provided food and clothing.

For decades these Indians had shown their willingness to trade with the fishermen who were there for the summer, especially those who salted their cod on stages set up on the shore and dried them on pebbles and rocks. One can imagine the first shy meetings, the pointing, the dumb show, the realization that each had something the other would like, and then the bargaining. The Indians happily exchanged their fur garments for food, an occasional copper kettle and the metal tools that could be more efficient than their own beautifully made but blunter instruments of stone and bone. Europeans were quick to appreciate the worn skin of *castor canadiensis*, made suppler by Indian grease and sweat. One can see the furrier run his fingers over the dense, fine underfur, hint to his sailor supplier that he would not be unwilling to take more.

Huge profits could be made – from the European point of view. In 1602 two biscuits or two knives bought a beaver skin, which could then be sold to a merchant for just over four livres. (By 1610 the Indians' business sense had sharpened and a good beaver cost fifteen or twenty knives). With such an advantageous market, it is not surprising that merchants themselves began to organize special trading ventures along with the annual fishing expeditions. Often the two activities were combined. Towards the end of the sixteenth century such ventures were becoming more frequent and barter less haphazard as Indians and traders began to converge every year early in summer on places such as

Tadoussac. The fur trade began to feature large in French commerce. Fishermen and sailors might still supplement their wages by selling a few pelts on their return home. Merchants counted on making good profits by dealing in gross.

But foreign ships were beginning to encroach on shores that France had regarded as hers from the time the courtly Florentine explorer, Giovanni da Verrazano, had claimed them for François I in 1524. In particular the English had started to seize French ships with their cargoes of furs. It occurred to some that trading and territorial rights could be better established if a permanent, settled trading-post asserted the French presence.

Yet merchants were not very interested in colonization. As so often, it was a question of money. Though large profits could be made from the fur trade, outlay and risks were enormous. And settlement, what with buildings and maintenance, supplies, food, and salaries for the colonists, was an expensive business. Also, the danger of attack from possibly hostile Indians or rival Dutch and English traders demanded forts. This meant soldiers, cannon, gunpowder – all costly items. Besides, Cartier and Roberval had not been forgotten. The ghosts of their scurvy-ridden men, who had died in the horrifying and now legendary Canadian winters, haunted the seaports from which they had set out. The practical, hard-headed merchants of Dieppe, Rouen, St Malo, and La Rochelle invested in the fur trade for quick returns. Why sink good money in a doubtful colony? They were quite content, in the words of historian Marcel Trudel, with a trading counter.

And yet, Henri IV hankered after a colony. The bluff, reckless soldier of the civil wars was now hailed as the 'Gallic Hercules' and depicted as ushering in a golden age of prosperity. He had laid aside his white plumes and battered armour to govern as energetically as he had fought. Prolific of plans for the glory and good of France, he could not ignore the possibility of her expansion into the New World. Even so, royal encouragement was not backed by royal funds as in the days of François I and Jacques Cartier. Henri was notoriously stingy. And a new method was evolving in France and elsewhere by which a trading company bore the costs of colonization and then reaped the profits – if it could. The most that the shareholders asked of royal authority was the grant of a monopoly for trade to allow the company to cover the expense of maintaining a settlement. The French government tended to

Henri IV by Quesnel

favour such a plan. What did it cost but parchment, some wax, and a signature? But in France any talk of such an arrangement always provoked angry protests from merchants who would be cut off from the furs to which they felt they had a right.

It was their opposition that de Monts had faced ever since he had presented his proposition to the King early in November 1603, just four months before. In return for royal protection and exclusive rights to the fur trade, he offered to settle colonists. The fairly powerful lobby of merchants cried out that a monopoly granted to a particular company encroached on their immemorial rights to free trade. It would spell their ruin. And, as for trying to colonize Canada after the Cartier experience, *quelle folie!* Nonetheless, the King and de Monts, old brothers in arms, stuck to their guns. Other merchants were not automatically excluded from de Monts' company but rather invited to join in the venture. All had a chance of being shareholders. The enterprise was widely publicized and the books remained open long enough for those interested to inscribe their names. But to many the charge of one hundred colonists, later reduced to sixty, seemed too heavy, the chance of making a clear profit less likely. These merchants went on grumbling and did not join. Two rival factions took up their positions: Colonizers versus Free Traders.

For the moment, fortune, in the person of the King, favoured the Colonizers. On the 18th December 1603, a royal proclamation was issued in Picardy, Normandy, Brittany, and Guyenne. It forbade all trading in furs between the fortieth and forty-sixth parallels of the North American continent as well as in the St Lawrence area, unless the trader held shares in the new company. Those caught defying this order would have their ships and goods confiscated by de Monts. They were also liable to a stiff fine of thirty thousand livres.

While storing his precious parchments in his chest, de Monts may have reflected ruefully that both his commission and the proclamation were sealed with the Great Seal in yellow not green wax. For he knew that documents regarded as being of a permanent nature were sealed in ever-fresh green, those considered temporary in autumnal yellow. Protests continued. The King had a hard time getting the proclamation ratified, particularly by the Parliament of Rouen. (A French Parliament, of course, was not a legislative assembly but a legal body that gave the stamp of approval to royal acts.) Sully, Henri's right-hand man in plans and projects for French prosperity, was also hostile. Though a radical in religion, he was conservative by temperament and thoroughly disapproved of both the monopoly and the wild schemes for settlement. He scoffed at the sieur de Monts 'sailing off to people Canada,' quite against his warning that 'one never extracts much wealth from places north of forty degrees.'

One may wonder why the monarchy, in the teeth of such opposition, should champion the monopolists against the merchants. Obviously it was a question of honour and glory. But it was a question of international politics as well. Spain still dominated the New World. Flamboyant, fanatic, gorged with gold and silver from her colonies, she was the richest and most powerful monarchy in Europe. But she was weakening. The sumptuous galleon of her ship of state was beginning to look old-fashioned, top-heavy. And after the disaster of the Armada in 1588, the gilt had worn thin, her sails were decidedly tatty. Spanish interference in France, on behalf of the ultra-Catholics who had not wanted to accept even a converted Henri, ended with the Treaty of Vervins in 1598. A secret clause in this treaty further allowed France liberty of action in the Western Hemisphere above a fixed line that passed through the Canary Islands. From a Spain that had jealously guarded the lands and seas granted her by a stroke of the papal pen in 1493, this was a concession indeed. Colonies became possible. And now was the time to establish them. For the English and the Dutch were beginning to engage in mercantile adventures of their own far beyond European waters. Under the leadership of Sir Walter Raleigh, the English had already tried in 1585 to settle a colony on Roanoke Island off North Carolina. So it was clear that France must not lag behind, but should sail on to stake a real claim in the land Verrazano had named New France eighty years before.

Although de Monts might appreciate these larger political issues, his main concern had to be the practical task of organizing his company. On the 10th February 1604, just a month before he sailed, its articles had been drawn up and the terms of agreement signed. The capital invested amounted to ninety thousand livres. This was divided into five portions: two subscribed by merchants from St Malo; two more by merchants from La Rochelle and St Jean de Luz, a Basque town that specialized in whaling; and a fifth by merchants from Rouen, in which de Monts himself was principal shareholder. Profits were expected principally from the fur trade, for which they now held the monopoly. Macain and Georges, brothers-in-law from Protestant La Rochelle, contracted with de Monts to take one-third of the furs. They were to be associated with the fur trade in Acadia for many years. The shareholders also hoped to make money from fish, timber, and, in spite of Sully's tart scepticism, mines. But they agreed that no dividends were to be expected until the end of the second year. The first year's profits were to be spent on putting the new colony on its feet.

Five ships in all took part in the 1604 expedition: the three ships that had aroused comment in Le Havre, and also a whaler and a small trading vessel that set out from other ports. Of the three in Le Havre, the two larger vessels carried the men and supplies that we last saw following the sun westwards for 'La Cadie.'

CHAPTER TWO

Exploring the Coasts

HAT THEN WAS 'LA CADIE'? In 1524 Verrazano, Renaissance humanist as well as navigator, had named a part of the North Carolina coast Arcadie. Its lovely trees and peaceful beauty had put him in mind of the ancient Greek Vale of Arcady, that idyllic landscape where nymphs danced and shepherds piped. Subsequent maps pushed the name north-east until it came to designate the region that comprises today's Nova Scotia, New Brunswick, and part of Maine. And Arcadie had become Acadie, under the influence perhaps of the local Indian name for 'place,' *acadie*, as in Shubenacadie or Tracadie. De Monts' charter, however, covered a wider area than this. It gave him authority over coast and land right down to the fortieth parallel, where Philadelphia stands today. And in 1604 he had no rivals. The whole coast line from Florida north was bare of any European habitation.

So where in all this vastness should de Monts go? South-east certainly of the Great River, 'in order' wrote Champlain, 'to enjoy a softer and more agreeable climate.' Accordingly de Monts set his course for the south shore of Nova Scotia beyond Canso. From there they could explore.

For de Monts had already visited Tadoussac and had not been impressed by that icy spot, described by Champlain as 'a place the most disagreeable and barren in the whole country ... ' It was there that Pierre Chauvin, the merchant with whom de Monts had visited the St Lawrence in 1600, had made a half-hearted attempt to establish a settlement in return for a brief monopoly. De Monts had heard of the outcome of *that* enterprise. Chauvin had left sixteen colonists to winter in a shack at Tadoussac. Champlain's description of this venture is stiff with disapproval: 'It was like the court of King Petaud, each desiring to be leader; idleness and laziness along with the diseases that seized them unawares, reduced them to such straits that they were obliged to entrust themselves to the Indians, who charitably took them in.' It was a chilling object lesson in how not to colonize. The survivors were brought home. And Champlain criticized Chauvin for being keener on gain than settlement.

If history can be taken as an account of past mistakes the future should guard against, the brief history of French colonization held several warnings for de Monts. Besides Chauvin there had also been that extraordinary Breton gentleman who rejoiced in the name of Troïlus de Mesgouez and the title of Marquis de la Roche. In 1598 he had landed sixty 'mendiants veillants,' sturdy beggars – always the outcasts, the rejects – on foggy, desolate Sable Island, now famous or notorious as the ships' graveyard of the Atlantic. Every year La Roche sent out supplies, and sealskins and seal oil from the island were shipped back to France. But in 1602 no vessel loomed through the mist. Murder and mayhem ensued. The captain and his assistant were killed. Others disappeared in circumstances as murky as their fog-bound island. In 1603, when at last a ship arrived, only eleven survivors clad in sealskins, remained to tell a tale concocted to their own advantage.

And if de Monts, Champlain, Poutrincourt, and the other gentlemen were in a mood to sup full of horrors, they could have recounted what they had heard of the mid-sixteenth-century expeditions promoted by Admiral Coligny to settle Huguenots in Florida and Brazil. These had been bedevilled by greed, murder, rebellion, poisoning, treachery, starvation, and terrible trials at sea. Hundreds of Frenchmen had met horrible deaths at the hands of the Spanish and Portuguese. Still further back in time was the experience of Cartier's men, their ships and barrels seized in thick-ribbed ice, their legs swollen, their gums rotting with scurvy, the many desolate deaths.

This was not an encouraging record, yet de Monts could not afford to spend much time mulling over it. There were far too many present perils to think about. The ship had to thread her way through ice-floes while enduring the lash of equinoctial gales. One storm broke the ship's galleries. A joiner at work on these was 'carried away by a sea or flash of water to the next door of death – overboard' and, but for a frenzied clutch at some tackling, would have drowned. To danger and cold we can add the perpetual sickening pitch and toss of the vessel, the cramped quarters, the stench of bilge, and still have only a faint idea of the wretched discomforts of their life at sea.

On the 1st May, the day when the traditional volley was fired in the captain's honour, they sighted land through the fog. Excitement soon dissipated when it was discovered that the pilots had miscalculated. This was not the coastline of Acadia but ill-famed Sable Island. They were a hundred miles off course. The superstitious may have shuddered and crossed themselves at the thought of the ghosts of all the men murdered there two years before; Champlain, as geographer, noted the dimensions of the island. And he was interested to see the descendants of cattle left by the Portuguese sixty years earlier, the fine black foxes, and the seals, some of them the offspring of those whose skins had been cured and worn by the survivors of La Roche's settlement. Even so, no one wanted to linger there.

On the 8th May they at last sighted a prominent cape and in the joy of arrival named it Cap de la Hève (Cape La Have) after the last point of land they had seen on leaving home. The name, like a hyphen drawn all the way across the Atlantic, linked Old France to New. For four days they rode at anchor in nearby Green Bay while Champlain conscientiously took soundings, made notes and sketches for the first of his harbour charts, which are still admired by yachtsmen today. And though not quite accurate as to shoreline, they give a very fair idea of the lie of the land.

On the 12th they sailed south-west to another port. Here an unwelcome sight met their eyes. At anchor lay another French ship, the *Levrette*, and – there was no doubt about it – her crew were doing a brisk illicit trade in furs with some Indians. Fortified by the Lord Admiral's commission and the King's proclamation, de Monts ran out his cannon and ordered the ship to be seized, the furs confiscated, and the commander brought before him. The captain, Rossignol, sang out less sweetly than his namesake, the nightingale. He can hardly have considered it compensation when he discovered that the port was to bear his name. Later it became Liverpool. But Lake Rossignol in the region (the largest freshwater lake in Nova Scotia) and some local commercial enterprises still shadowily commemorate the furious captain.

The next day, still sailing south-west, they entered another port. There they decided to camp while waiting for news of Gravé. It was perhaps in the commotion of unloading that a panicky sheep jumped overboard and drowned, only to be quickly retrieved and eaten. In appreciation of the fresh meat someone dubbed the place Port au Mouton and Port Mouton (pronounced Matoon) it remains. Explorers, at the mercy of so many hostile forces, still have the sovereign edenic power to name.

Their anchorage was at Bull Point, situated at the entrance to the port opposite Mouton Island. It had a sandy beach, shady upland, and two ponds. After the crowded, smelly, rolling ship, this must have seemed a little paradise. Here in a light-hearted holiday mood they set up camp in little cabins they built themselves. The late maritime spring stirred in the woods. Buds and fresh green leaves unfolded among the dark evergreen; ferns uncurled in the undergrowth; shadbushes flung out white sprays of blossom.

The native inhabitants of this paradise appeared on the scene. This was the first time that most of the company had seen 'savages' close up, so they watched these men of the woods warily. De Monts and Champlain had, of course, seen Indians before, but this was their first encounter with members of the Souriquois tribe, a part of the Algonkian-speaking people. Then about three or four thousand strong – and some remembered the days when they had been much more numerous – they roamed in bands through what is now Nova Scotia, Cape Breton, and Prince Edward Island, and along the southern coast of the Gulf of St Lawrence. Later the French came to call this tribe Micmacs, the name by which they are now known.

From the first they were friendly, though they had good reason to suspect that it was white men such as these who brought with them the unknown diseases which, for many years now, had been striking them down and reducing their numbers. Summer was the time of year which drew them to river-bank and sea-shore. Food, in the form of fish and game, was plentiful. They swam or cleansed themselves in sweatbaths – one thinks of the now fashionable Finnish sauna – and then threw themselves into the water. And they traded. They knew what these men had come for in their ships and they knew what they wanted from them in return. Besides the usual metal goods there was all-important food to be had, especially ship's biscuit or bread. Here again, though, they would have reason for suspicions, as sailors sometimes fobbed off spoiled food upon them, and this the Indians regarded as an attempt to poison them. But they were happy to have blankets from which to make cloaks. Also old clothes: hats, shirts, handkerchiefs, and anything the women could use to clean their babies with. It is amusing to see the equivalent of diapers quite high on the list of desirable imports.

With their smooth, swarthy skins, dark eyes, and black hair, these Indians struck the French as a handsome race. The men were of medium height, their lithe muscular bodies almost entirely exposed to the summer air. Apart from a loin-cloth of supple skin, they wore nothing but a robe or cloak fastened at the neck and then thrown back, leggings, and moccasins. Even in the open air it took the French time to get used to the strong odour of animal grease the Indians exuded. Rubbed into their skin and hair, this protected them from blackflies, mosquitoes, and rain. As for the Indians, on looking at the white men, they thought again how ugly they found those thickets of hair that surrounded their mouths. The fat-bellied, hunch-backed, and snub-nosed aroused mocking comments the French could not yet understand. And the French, in turn, wondered at the paintings done in red and violet on the Indians' faces for special occasions.

While their men traded, the women worked. They set up the wigwams, lit fires, cooked, hunted for small game like porcupine, mended the light birch canoes with strips of bark, assiduously chewed fir gum to be used for caulking, and did a hundred and one other tasks. Some had babies on their backs, swaddled and strapped to a board that they suspended from thongs encircling their foreheads. If a baby cried, the mother sang and danced until the wailing stopped. With their other children too they were gentle, giving them everything they asked for, even the food from their mouths. In dress the women were more covered than the men, clothed in a sort of knee-length tunic made of skin worked to a beautiful softness and sewn down one side. It was held up by straps that went over the shoulder, and was belted, sometimes twice, once under the breasts and then around the hips. Like the men's robes these dresses were decorated with embroidery of brightly coloured porcupine quills called *matachias*. Both men and women, but especially the women, wore ornaments of this on their arms and around their necks. Girls brightened their finely sewn moccasins with it. Some also wore exquisite pieces of *wampum* made from small highly polished pieces of shell gleaming like porcelain. Among these, glass beads from France twinkled, strung together and mingled with tin and lead.

During their month's stay at Port Mouton, the French probably became acquainted with Messamouet, the sagamo or chief of the La Have area. He had, he said, been to France. So we get a tantalizing glimpse of his journey across the Atlantic in a Basque fishing-boat. In France he had stayed at the house of the governor of Bayonne, Philibert de Gramont, husband of 'la grande Corisande,' who, when a widow, became one of the most loved of Henri IV's many mistresses. Since 'savages' had a way of impressing Europeans with their innate courtesy and sense of ceremony, he had probably been well received there. Philibert de Gramont had died in 1580, so Messamouet must have made the journey more than twenty-five years before. But he still remembered in detail many of the things he had seen in France.

While trading with the Indians, some of the French no doubt learnt to smoke or 'drink tobacco' with them. There were pipes of different sorts to admire, some all of wood or stone. Others were ingeniously composed of a lobster-claw for bowl and a piece of whistle-clean alder for stem.

But if the French smoked it was for pleasure and not, as the Indians did in lean times, to keep hunger at bay. The stony, heath-covered soil swarmed with hares. The sea provided fish, the pond attracted waterfowl. There was always something to be roasted over the fires.

After the constant tensions and alarms at sea there was leisure, too, for talk and discussion – though the talk was not always of a leisurely sort. Debate turned to dispute. Father Aubry and a Huguenot held acrimonious exchanges about the merits of their respective faiths. Shore and woods, innocent until then of the theological disputes that bitterly divided the Old World, rang with words like Pope, Bible, transubstantiation, superstition, sacred image, and idolatry. Hardly an auspicious beginning for a group that was supposed to bring Christ to the heathen! It might well have been at this time that the other Catholic priest and the Huguenot minister started to come to blows. 'I do not know who was the stronger and gave the harder blow,' Champlain wrote much later when summing up the religious question in New France for Cardinal Richelieu, 'but I well know that the minister sometimes complained to the sieur de Monts that he had been beaten, and in this manner they settled their points of controversy. I leave it to you, if this was a pleasant sight? The Indians sometimes took one side, sometimes the other, and the French taking sides, according to their different beliefs, said everything that was bad of both religions, although the Sieur de Monts made peace as well as he could.' Champlain himself, not surprisingly, concluded 'that two contrary religions are never very fruitful to God's glory among infidels whom one wishes to convert.'

Fighting over the 'contrary religions,' the French do not then seem to have inquired very deeply into native religious attitudes. And even if the interpreters had been skilled enough linguists to question the Indians about religion, they would probably have come to the conclusion that these people of the woods, who seemed to live in such a random, haphazard way, just did not know what religious faith was. For Europeans generally took religion to mean a definite creed, an ethical code, preached by an organized body that insisted on certain communal as well as private observances. But for the Micmacs, as for all Amerindians, religion was not a dogma or a creed but rather a reverent sense of the numinous that permeated their lives. Everything in its way was sacred, was imbued with mysterious power (*manitou*, some called it): the elements, plants, animals, food, their tools, their weapons. Every act they performed was a recognition of the mysterious links between the seen and the unseen, the material and the spiritual, the natural and the supernatural. In the course of this history we shall see on what particular occasions the French got unsettling glimpses of Indian religious experience and how crudely they interpreted what they saw.

Though, for the moment, missionary work made no headway, exploration did. Bull Point was delightful as a summer camp, Port Mouton an excellent little port, but the poor soil made it quite unsuitable for settlement. On landing, Champlain was less concerned with religious bickering than with organizing an excursion. The eight-ton pinnace was assembled. On the 19th May, six days after arriving at Port Mouton, Champlain set out. With him were de Monts' secretary, Ralluau, and ten men, among them the miner, Maître Simon, and Poutrincourt's ex-captain, Du Boullay. They were away for nearly three weeks.

This excursion took them south-west and then north round the lower part of the Nova Scotian peninsula. First they sailed to Barrington

Passage and Cape Sable, then northwards among the islands that lie to the west off the coastline, past Yarmouth, on to Long Island, and so into St Mary's Bay. Here they explored the coves along Digby Neck as far as North Creek. They then headed back along the opposite shore of the bay, now known as the French shore because of its largely Acadian population. On the return journey they rounded the islands on the seaward side. Champlain was nothing if not thorough. The day before they reached Port Mouton a severe gale drove their pinnace ashore and they almost lost her; this, as Champlain drily remarked, would have placed them 'in dire distress.'

Fishermen had already given names to some of the places they visited: Cape Sable for example, which is not to be confused with Sable Island, and Long Island. But there were many others that Champlain and his companions had the joy of naming. Cape Negro received its name because of a rock in the distance, now Black Rock, which reminded Champlain of a negro's head. Perhaps it was the black interpreter, d'Acosta, of whom Champlain was thinking – that is, if he was with them. Also labelled for posterity were the Seal Islands, though only one of these is now known by that name. Again, the two parallel islands jutting out from Yarmouth looked like a forked cape, so they called the place Cap Fourchu. Yarmouth itself, until settled by the English, was known as Port Fourchu. St Mary's Bay also received its name at this time. Among other names given that changed with time and new settlers, the river now called Little River on Digby Neck was then named after Du Boullay, who was anxious for some credit in the work of exploration.

Everywhere Champlain made very careful notes on the coastline, the ports, their latitude, the navigational hazards and possibilities, the soil, the rivers and streams, the vegetation, and the wildlife. Each place that seemed suitable for cultivation is mentioned. The spot he most favoured was Port St Margaret, today's Weymouth. What also impressed him here was the quantity of shellfish: mussels, clams, and sea-snails.

But indeed wherever they landed he was amazed by the profusion of sea life. On one island they collected a barrel full of bluish-white cormorant eggs and nests squeezed one against another. On another there were so many gannets that the men could kill them with a stick. On yet another the shore was thick with seals, which they did not spare.

Near Port Forchu they made a good haul of cod. A practical man, Champlain always noted where a supply of food could be found. Neither was he averse to what he calls 'the pleasures of the chase.' But as a watcher as well as a hunter, he took delight in enumerating the many birds of different species. Three centuries of human greed, perhaps at times human need, have caused terrible depredations and vastly diminished their numbers. The cormorant, for example, has had to be declared a protected species.

The year before, while Champlain was on the St Lawrence, one Captain Prévert of St Malo claimed to have spent some time in these waters. The two had met at Ile Percée on the return voyage. Prévert regaled Champlain with stories of rich copper mines. So, on this excursion, Maître Simon was detailed to keep chisel and hammer at the ready in order to search for metal in the rocks. At what is now Mink Cove he reported 'a very good silver mine.' (Rocks here contain lead.) At Waterford, where 'the soil round about is red like blood,' he thought he detected an iron mine. So Champlain had much to relate to the sieur de Monts on his return to Port Mouton, though nothing particularly promising to suggest as a site for permanent settlement.

De Monts, too, had some news for him. In spite of all the fresh game, provisions had begun to run short during Champlain's absence. For this reason they started to draw on Rossignol's supplies. The holiday mood turned to one of anxiety as day after day went by and there was no sign of Gravé's *Bonne Renommée*, which carried supplies for the winter. Some who had already had their fill of adventure suggested a prudent withdrawal and return to France. At this Poutrincourt indignantly declared that death would be better than the dishonour of abandoning the enterprise; 'whereto' wrote Lescarbot, Poutrincourt's friend, 'the sieur de Monts conformed himself.'

About a week before Champlain's return, the worried de Monts asked some of their new Indian acquaintances to go up the coast towards Canso to look for Gravé. They agreed to do so on condition that the French fed their families during their absence. With them went a Frenchman carrying letters from de Monts. At the Bay of All Isles, near Sheet Harbour, de Monts' messenger sighted the ship he had last seen anchored at Le Havre. Gravé was enormously, exuberantly relieved. He was afraid that de Monts' ship had gone down among the icebergs. He was somewhat irritated. On arriving at Canso, he had looked in vain for their prearranged signs. There he too had had his troubles with illicit traders. He had seized four Basque ships from St Jean de Luz and confiscated their goods. Now he promised to send the masters of these ships on to de Monts, who, as Vice-Admiral, would know how to deal with them. Having read de Monts' letter, he and Captain Morel delivered a good part of the provisions. Their duty to colonization was almost done. The sailed on to Tadoussac to trade.

The picnic at Port Mouton was over. Orders were given to strike camp and board the ship. Rossignol's captured *Levrette* now went with them. Champlain and his ten men appeared in the nick of time. They had been given up as lost and the expedition was almost ready to set off without them. In such unknown territory a commander had to be prepared to cut his losses and continue. But, fortunately, there was Champlain to present his report, share his discoveries, and guide his companions round the coast. For the two vessels took the route that Champlain had just explored and came to anchor in St Mary's Bay.

A day or so later, about the 12th June, it looked as if the expedition had suffered its first casualty. Aubry, the Parisian priest of good family, went off with a group to roam the woods. While wandering through Long Island they came to a brook and knelt down to drink the clear water that they found so refreshing after the stinking slimy stuff in the ship's barrels. To free his hands, Aubry placed his sword on the ground and left it there when they all moved on. As they were making their way through the thick summer undergrowth back to the shoreline on St Mary's Bay, he suddenly remembered it and turned back. That was the last his companions saw of him. But it was not until nightfall, when they were all back on the ship, that his absence caused concern. Suspicious minds immediately leapt to the conclusion that the Huguenot he argued with so heatedly had killed him. One can imagine the thrill of alarm, the black looks, the accusations, the angry denials. On the shore they sounded a trumpet; from the ship they fired cannon shots. But no Aubry appeared. A very anxious de Monts asked the Indians to scour the woods for the priest. Even they could not find him and he was given up as lost. The forebodings of Aubry's friends seemed justified.

But there was still the question of a settlement to be considered. On a calm summer's day St Mary's Bay looked inviting with its blue shimmer of sea, the varied green of the coastline touched here and there with earthy red. But de Monts' practised eye soon noted that there was no place that could be defended from attack. And defence was *the* priority.

On the 16th June de Monts, with Champlain, Poutrincourt, Champdoré, Maître Simon, and some other men, set off to explore further. The two large ships remained in St Mary's Bay while they took the pinnace, which could be more easily manoeuvred. Through Petit Passage they sailed into the great flow and ebb of the Fundy tide. A 1541 map had represented this huge bay as *R. de fundo*. De Monts named it the Baie Française or French Bay. But whether because of 'fundo,' or as a corruption of *fond de baie* (end of the bay) or as a corruption of Cap Fendu (Cape Split), Bay of Fundy it has become.

Sailing along the Fundy side of Digby Neck, they came to the narrow passage between high cliffs now known as the Digby Gut. Here they entered what Champlain described as 'one of the finest harbours I had seen on all these coasts where a couple of thousand vessels could lie in safety.' Because of its regal dimensions Champlain called it Port Royal. (When Lescarbot later claimed that de Monts was the namer, Champlain stiffly corrected him.) This is now, of course, the Annapolis Basin, later called after an English monarch, Queen Anne. The explorers found much to exclaim at, as today's tourist can appreciate: the great, luminous stretch of water, the high surrounding wooded hills, the streams that glistened down them, the two islands, the wide rivers. They went a considerable way up the large river, now the Annapolis, that flowed east, naming it the Equille after the sand-eels they caught there. And they were equally delighted with the deciduous trees, the oaks and the ashes and the many meadows. At times these were flooded at high tide. Some decades later Acadian farmers dyked them to create the lush, leisurely pastures that we know today. Champlain acknowledged that 'this place was the most suitable and pleasant for a settlement that we had seen.'

As for Poutrincourt, the seeker of a new estate and fortune, he was quite enraptured. This was where his seigneury would be. Here was a good harbour, suitable sites for forts and a habitation, timber for construction, arable land, pastures, streams to turn mills – and game. On this occasion they hunted a moose that amazed them by swimming with great ease across the port. So Poutrincourt lost no time in asking de Monts to exercise, for the first time, his right to grant lands and make

Port Royal over to him. This de Monts promised to do, though the King would still have to ratify the grant when they returned to France.

Even so, now Poutrincourt could plan and dream. He could see himself as lord of his domain: trading for furs to maintain his settlement, hunting and fishing for food and sport, growing fine crops, the corn to be ground in his own mill. His family would be with him. They would establish friendly relations with the Indians, teach them to sow and plant. And they would prepare them to receive the Christian religion: how to make the sign of the cross, recite the prayers of salvation. He could compose liturgical music for them to sing. One must remember that most Frenchmen of the time had nothing but condemnation for the 'inhuman torments' that the Spanish inflicted on the Indians in their colonies. 'By their cruelties,' wrote Lescarbot, they 'have rendered the name of God odious, and a name of offence to these poor people ... Witness him that had rather be damned than go to the Paradise of the Spaniards.' And now Poutrincourt would show that French tolerance was a better way of winning souls than Spanish intransigence. It was a paternalistic attitude, to be sure, and one based on complete incomprehension of Indian culture, but not entirely ignoble for those times.

But his dreams – some would call them his delusions – were for the future. Champlain had yet to discover the mines of which Prévert had spoken. We may wonder at the persistence displayed by de Monts and Champlain in their search for mineral wealth. But if rich seams had been found, settlement would have been assured. They could go on to found a colony, even if envious merchants should cause their monopoly of the fur trade to be cancelled. No rock, so to speak, should be left unturned.

In this search the expedition left the hospitable basin. They sailed further up Fundy on past Cape Chignecto, named by them Cape of Two Bays because of its position between Chignecto Bay and the Minas Basin. At Port aux Mines, now Advocate Harbour in the Minas Basin, they discovered the copper that occurs in the trap rocks of that impressive site. Maître Simon pronounced it very good. Champlain was to return here on two other occasions. Champdoré noticed different glints and glitters and cut out of the rock a shining blue stone. This was amethyst, which is still fairly common along that coast. Back in France, Champdoré broke his stone in two, giving half to de Monts and the other to Poutrincourt. The two noblemen had their stones set in gold and Poutrincourt presented his to the King while de Monts' was graciously accepted by the Queen. So at least one semi-precious stone made its way from the wilds of Acadia to the court of France.

By now time was growing short and a site for settlement had to be chosen soon. On the 20th June they weighed anchor and set out again, westwards this time and round Cape Chignecto. On the 24th June they reached a large river, which they named the St-Jean in honour of St John the Baptist, whose feast day it was and who was also Poutrincourt's patron saint. It is pleasant to imagine the sailors celebrating it by lighting the traditional bonfire on the shore and jumping over it – an old pagan custom that had somehow survived into Christian times. And bonfires are still an important feature of the great St-Jean Baptiste festival in Quebec.

On the east side of the mouth of the Saint John River, they found some iron – but not enough to tempt them to stay. Though fascinated by the reversing falls, Champlain thought the river approach dangerous. Exploration of this magnificent waterway with its islands and fine trees was left to Ralluau and Champdoré four years later.

The 25th June was then considered Midsummer's Day, after which the days would be getting shorter. Again the voyagers felt the pressure of time as they continued south-west past the dark, rocky islands now ominously known as the Wolves. Here the ever-impetuous Poutrincourt was nearly lost when he left the pinnace for an island to capture some young sea pigeons then relished as a delicacy. But the boat went right round the island and he was sighted. Other islands could be seen in the distance, among them the long, dark bulk of Grand Manan. On the 26th or 27th June the pinnace turned into Passamaquoddy Bay and then up 'the river of the Etchemins.'

The French tended to call all the Indians living along the shore from Saint John down to Penobscot Etchemins. Later those in the Saint John valley came to be called the Maliseet, possibly because their area became a favourite trading place for ships from St Malo. Yet all these Indians, though they spoke different dialects, were part of the Wabenaki cluster, related to and friendly with the Micmacs.

As they sailed further up this river and then down again, de Monts and Champlain could feel their excitement rising. Right in the middle, below a point where three waterways met to form a Y-like cross, lay an island.

There is something remote and romantic yet satisfying about islands.

They stand mysteriously alone but they can be encompassed, contained. This one, of course, was not completely cut off or isolated in the middle of the ocean like barren Sable Island. Instead, on either side of the river lay the broad, well-wooded and well-watered shores of the mainland. Summer visitors today viewing the quiet charm of Dochet Island from either the New Brunswick or the Maine shore can understand how appealing it must have looked to voyagers anxious to settle down. Here, de Monts decided, they would stay. Because of the configuration of the waterways, he named the island Ste Croix, a name that was later extended to the river.

No one could then guess what a real cross this island would become. They happily pointed out to one another all its favourable features. It was easy to defend, since passing ships would come within range of the cannon they would set up on shore. It rose up steeply in ledges, so would have to be fortified in only one low place. There was good anchorage; hardwood trees as well as evergreens to supply timber for building; sand and clay for making bricks. No streams, but water could be fetched from one of the little rivers on the mainland where they might construct a mill. Only a few strokes of an oar and they could be on one side of the river or the other. The thick tall grass seemed to indicate fertile soil where crops should thrive. On the shores of the island itself there was a profusion of shellfish.

Champlain was hopeful: 'This place we considered the best we had seen, both on account of its situation, the fine country, and for the intercourse we were expecting with the Indians of these coasts and of the interior, since we should be in their midst. In course of time we hoped to pacify them, and to put an end to the wars which they wage against one another, in order that in the future we might derive service from them, and convert them to the Christian faith.'

It was an optimistic programme. We may note that he had not forgotten the terms of de Monts' mandate from the King. For there *was* material for conversion there: groups of Indians who came down to the shores of the river every summer during the fishing season.

The first job was defence. On an islet or nubble at the end of the main island facing towards Passamaquoddy Bay they erected a barricade which was to serve as a platform for mounting cannon. Everyone worked hard, though plagued by blackflies. Without Indian grease or the modern woodsman's repellents the faces of some of the men puffed up painfully about their eyes and almost prevented them from seeing.

Still, the barricade got built, after which de Monts sent Champdoré and some men off again in the pinnace. They were to tell the big ships still riding at anchor in St Mary's Bay to come to Ste Croix. Settlement, he could announce, was under way. Maître Simon went too in order to have another look at the mines and extract some samples. So Champdoré in the pinnace, having delivered his message, lingered on a little, while the ships hoisted sail for Ste Croix.

One day, the 28th or 29th June, he and some others went fishing near Long Island. A keen-eared man thought he caught the sound of a voice across the water. Could it be Monsieur Aubry? The others jeered. Did he really think Monsieur Aubry was still alive? But something stirred through the woods on the shore. White linen – a handker-chief? A plumed hat waggled on a stick. There was no doubt now. It was Monsieur Aubry, found sixteen days after he wandered away from his companions to look for his sword. 'Unused to long austerities' – Lescarbot is a little dry on the subject of this priest – he was weak with hunger. They were careful to give him only a little food at a time and joyfully took him along to Ste Croix.

Gradually his story was pieced together. Instead of turning towards the bay side of Long Island, he had walked in the opposite direction and had arrived at the other shore where there was no ship in sight. Not realizing where he was, he concluded that his companions had callously sailed away and deserted him. For the next sixteen wretched days he had fed himself upon sorrel and partridge berries found in the woods. But he kept near the shore hoping to see some sign of human life on the surge of the Fundy tide. At last he caught sight of Champdoré and his men fishing from the pinnace. He tried calling out but his voice had grown too weak to carry. This was before the days of survival kits. Baden-Powell, boy-scouting, and wood-lore still lay centuries ahead. What Monsieur Aubry did have, however, was a classical education. Some lines from Ovid pressed themselves upon his mind. What was it Ariadne had done when abandoned by Theseus?

> Candida imposui longae velamina virgae,
> Scilicet oblitos admonitura mei.
> (White garments to a long stick I tied
> To remind the forgetful I was still alive.)

Actually it is not clear whether Aubry thought of this classical allusion at the time, or whether it is Lescarbot who makes the connection between the quotation and Aubrey's very sensible action. But it could have been Aubry himself. His device worked and everyone was happy to see him again, particularly de Monts. It would have looked very bad indeed for a Catholic priest to disappear on an expedition led by a Huguenot. One wonders whether the Protestant accused of murdering Aubry received a due apology.

It took Aubry a long time to recover. Convalescing in the pleasant surroundings of Ste Croix Island, warmed by the summer sun, he might well give thanks to his Catholic God and his classical education. Around him rang the sound of axe on wood. Settlement had begun.

CHAPTER THREE

Settling In

ALL THROUGH JULY AND AUGUST sounds of axe and saw and hammer echoed around the island. Champlain had a sense of construction as well as the urge to explore, so was very happy when de Monts asked him to draw up a plan for the settlement. He examined the terrain and decided to group the various buildings round a central point: a shady tree that grew out of a flat, rocky ledge. This ledge and the space around it formed a public square, an important feature of towns back home in France. It was a place where men could gather when taking a rest, to talk, argue, boast, play bowls; a rallying point, too, if they should be attacked. Round this rose the large storehouse, de Monts' dwelling, a roomy barracks for the Swiss mercenaries, houses with mutiple doors and chimneys for gentry and artisans, a single house for the priest (so separated, we must suppose, from his sparring partner), a forge, a bakehouse, and a little chapel. Then there was a long covered gallery, an alternative public place where the men could meet either to work or relax when it rained.

It all looks very charming on Champlain's published plan of their island settlement. The storehouse and de Monts' lodging were particularly handsome, since they were built from sturdy frames, already prepared in France, and roofed over with good shingles. Another attractive feature on the plan is the gardens that the men planted in open spaces between the buildings and on the southward side of the island. But they are prettier on the plan than they were in reality. The seedlings drooped and withered under the hot sun as the soil proved too sandy for them to thrive, even though the men dug a well and watered them constantly.

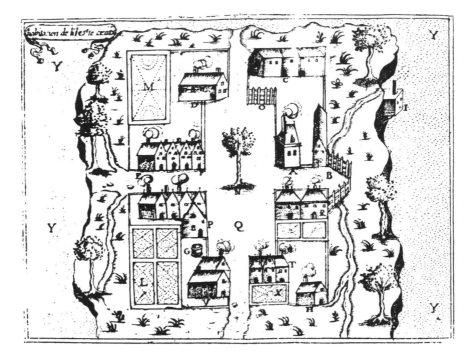

Champlain's plan of the Ste Croix settlement

A The sieur de Monts' lodging; B Public building for when it rained; C Storehouse; D Lodging of the Swiss; E Forge; F Carpenters' lodging; G Well; H Oven for baking bread; I Kitchen; L Gardens; M Other gardens; N Square with tree; O Palisade; P Lodgings of the sieur d'Orville, Champlain, and Champdoré; Q Lodgings of the sieur Boulay, and other artisans; R Lodgings of the sieurs de Genestou, Sourin, and other artisans; T Lodgings of the sieurs de Beaumont, La Motte Bourgjoli, and Fougeray; V Our priest's lodging; X Other gardens; Y The river surrounding the island

Once they had completed their lodgings, the men crossed to both shores of the mainland to make more gardens where the soil was good. Pale green shoots sprouting in cleared spaces below the dark fringes of the forest promised a fair supply of food for the future. Here some of the men built temporary cabins so they could give all their attention to these new crops. Already the disadvantages of an island settlement could be felt.

On the western shore, now the American side of the mainland, they chose a place for making charcoal. This would serve both for cooking and for warming the cabins when the weather turned cold. Here too they built a water-mill, as grinding wheat with the hand-mill proved a miserably slow job, one that everyone hated. But since they had a bakehouse, once the wheat was ground, they could enjoy fresh bread.

On the extreme eastern edge of the island stood the communal kitchen. It looks rather quaint on Champlain's plan, jutting out above the water with the smoke from its chimney unfurling over the ripples of the river. Yet the choice of site was not as odd as first appears. So placed, the kitchen was close to the storehouse, from which provisions were fetched, and near the covered gallery that might have served as a dining-hall. It has been suggested that its position, overhanging the river, made it very convenient for disposing of the garbage. Only at a later stage did the French accept the idea that they were on land, not at sea, and save refuse as fertilizer for their gardens.

An amusing tale of romance is attached to this kitchen, relating an event that gave the French some insight into Indian customs and traditions. The work of construction had not gone on unobserved, for a group of Indians had come to camp on the shores for their summer fishing season. These ancestors of today's Passamaquoddy Indians showed themselves to be friendly. Curious about these white men, they drew close. There was much to intrigue them: the fine timber from France, French building methods, their tools and weapons – and the food. French cuisine, even of the cruder, camping-out variety, proved so much to the taste of one particular young Indian, Bituani, that he settled himself in the kitchen. Here he did odd jobs in return for some of the dishes that simmered and roasted on the charcoal. But Bituani was a lover as well as a gourmet. He had his heart set on a certain girl. Her father, however, resolutely opposed the match and would not consent to the marriage. Was it while cleaning a fish or stirring a sauce that it occurred to Bituani simply to abduct her? For this is what he did, in violation of all tribal tradition.

The event threw the Indian encampment into a tremendous uproar and the girl finally had to return to her father. But the rebellious Bituani was not pleased. He made a great fuss among his people, told them he had complained to de Monts. This prompted the girl's father, ceremoniously attended by his friends, to visit de Monts in order to put *his* side of the case. It was a question, they made clear, of their marriage conventions. Indian custom demanded that a suitor should stay for a certain length of time – and in a state of continence – with the family of his wife-to-be, and go hunting and fishing for them. Bituani had not done this, had not proved he was capable of providing for a wife and family. He had spent his time hanging around the newcomers' kitchen instead of proving himself as a husband. A man's work was to catch the food, not cook it. De Monts disclaimed all responsibility for Bituani's presence in his kitchen, but praised him as a 'diligent fellow' ('un gentil garçon') and promised he should go hunting.

A mere promise from the French sagamo did not win over the ruffled father. Not until Bituani had been fishing and made a great haul of salmon was his bride returned to him.

This occasion must have prompted the usual ritual marriage celebrations: feasting and dancing that lasted all night, long speeches in praise of the groom's ancestors, and promises on the groom's part to excel them in prowess. But Bituani did not forget his new friends, and the next day, resplendent in his finest embroidered clothes, proudly brought his wife to visit them at the fort.

Poutrincourt relayed all this to his friend, for we have it from Lescarbot, who obviously enjoyed this little love story. From it, however, he drew the naïve conclusion that the Indians were willing and ready to recognize French authority, for 'they did make Monsieur de Monts judge of their debates, which is a beginning of voluntary subjection, from whence a hope may be conceived that these people will soon conform themselves to our manner of living.' We can now see that the last thing the Indians had in mind was 'voluntary subjection' to these white men who had left their own country for what they must consider a better land. They obviously did not resent the French for settling among them, but neither did they feel in awe of these foreigners. They simply and courteously let the French know what their customs were and showed their firm determination not to allow their young people to be seduced into strange ways. In fact, there is no knowing what might have happened if de Monts had been a different sort of leader, had shown less tact and good humour, and had peremptorily sided with Bituani. The proper conclusion to draw surely is that he was sensible enough to show his respect for tribal custom and *not* expect the Indians to 'conform themselves to our manner of living.'

The Bituani episode caused a ripple of interest and amusement in a settlement steadily going about the daily work of clearing, building, and planting. There were other diversions as well. De Monts had dispatched Captain Foulques in Rossignol's ship to Canso to meet Gravé and his *Bonne Renommée*, now returned from trading on the Great River. For the ship still carried in her hold certain supplies intended for the colony. Before Foulques had time to bring these back, de Monts received a visit from Duglas, Gravé's well-weathered pilot. He arrived in a little eight-ton pinnace, along with the glowering masters of the Basque vessels whose ships and furs Gravé had seized on first arriving at Canso. Champlain states that 'the sieur de Monts received them kindly.' Still, he could not let them go scot-free. Duglas was to take them and their captured ships to La Rochelle where the law would deal with them. The Basques later complained of unfair treatment. Enforcing the monopoly was to prove no easy business.

Still fascinated by the lure of copper, de Monts got the ever-ready Champlain to undertake another short voyage in the direction of Chignecto Bay. With Champlain and his sailors went Maître Simon and Messamouet, the La Have chief, who claimed to know the copper site well. Between the Ste Croix and the Saint John rivers they struck a small seam that Maître Simon declared to be reasonably good, for it would, he said, yield 18 per cent. But Messamouet proved to be a disappointing guide and could not lead them to the rich mines of which Prévert had made so much. Back to Ste Croix they went with Champlain determined to return again to make a more thorough search. Later, to his disgust, he learned that Prévert was a braggart who had never seen any mines himself. It was his sailors who had been into the Minas Basin and had returned with a few samples.

Champlain made this excursion towards the end of August. When he returned to Ste Croix, he found a stir and bustle about the two large ships. Chilly winds and some reddening leaves hinted at winter. It was time for those returning to France to embark. Ralluau, de Monts' secretary, left, charged with business matters concerning the voyage. There were furs to be sold, confiscated ships and goods to deal with, accounts to settle, and arrangements to make for the dispatch of next season's provisions. The company's shareholders would want a report. And Ralluau had one last commission. With him went a caribou which was to be delivered as a special gift from de Monts to the King. This poor creature survived stormy seas and finally joined the royal zoo at the palace of St Germain-en-Laye, where it caused a slight flutter of interest. But it was soon neglected and allowed to die 'for lack of water or other commodities' in the palace moat far from Acadian forests.

Still enthusiastic and hopeful, Poutrincourt sailed too. He had found what he wanted, a seigneury in the New World. All he needed now was the King's confirmation of de Monts' grant and – what was to prove far more difficult – the funds to start his own settlement. As a pledge of his continuing interest he left behind in the storehouse his seven hundred pounds of ammunition. Back home also went Monsieur Aubry to his concerned friends and family. Seven years later, according to Lescarbot, he was still making interested enquiries about settlement in the country where he had nearly perished. Captain Foulques, back from Canso, commanded Rossignol's *Levrette*, while that unhappy captain found himself on the ship commanded by Timothée. The pilots, Cramolet and Coman, returned, Cramolet promising himself to make the voyage again next season. Coman could look forward to sixty livres as wages and a further six livres to buy the hat de Monts had promised him. Some of the seventy-nine men who remained, watching the ships grow smaller and disappear in the mist down-river, must have wished they were aboard. Under a heavy sky the pinnace and the long-boat riding on the grey water seemed small, uncertain links between their island and the world they knew.

The weather was stormy. On the 2nd September Champlain, off on another exploratory jaunt, saw the big ships lying at anchor, waiting for calmer seas at the mouth of the Ste Croix River. On the 5th as he set his course south-west a thick fog rolled over to hide the homebound vessels from view.

The voyage back to France on Captain Timothée's ship was not uneventful. A secret tippler made his way below one night to have a go at a wine cask and found the hold rapidly filling with water from a leak in the keel. In mid-ocean a terrifying squall blew the ship over on her side. Only when a violent gust of wind tore the old sail to tatters was she able to right herself little by little. Then, when they were very nearly home, the pilots disagreed on how to round one of the Casquets, a dangerous group of rocky islands between England and France. Thick fog prevented them from seeing whether the tide was at ebb or flow. Suddenly they realized that they were running full tilt towards rock with 'no hope to save themselves.' Some panicked, some prayed and asked forgiveness of one another. But forgiveness was far from the mind of a desperate and enraged Rossignol. Drawing out a long knife, he lurched towards Timothée. This man, he screamed, had first ruined him and now wanted to drown him as well. Some men threw themselves upon Rossignol and pulled him away from Timothée. Others started stripping off their doublets in the hope of clambering on to the rock when the ship should strike. In all this confusion Poutrincourt tried, with some help, to change the sails. Somehow the dreaded crash was avoided. God, they all felt, must be on their side.

A few years later Rossignol must have felt that both God and French justice were on his. For in 1608 he won his case against de Monts by producing the licence he had been granted to fish off the coasts of 'Florida.' In his moment of triumph did he feel a twinge of gratitude for the men who had pulled him off Timothée, so saving him from a charge of homicide?

In due course after their return Ralluau made his report. Members of the company had every reason to feel optimistic after this first season. The fur cargo was valued at no less than ninety thousand crowns. There was fish to be sold as well as peltry, and the Basque whaler brought in further profits. But though furs meant money, the enforcement of the monopoly had caused tremendous ill will.

In the ports, Basques and Bretons had ugly things to say about de Monts and his captains. Why should these upstarts interfere with their freedom, prevent them from trading with the Indians? This was a right they had enjoyed for decades. They complained that de Monts' men had laid violent hands upon them, had harassed them even when they were going about their ordinary business of fishing. If the King did not cancel this monopoly, they would lose their livelihood – and here they became tearful – 'their wives and children would become poor and destitute, and be obliged to beg their bread.' This did not prevent at least eight contraband traders from being brought to book. Investigations led to the discovery that some of them had tried to escape recognition on the St Lawrence by flying foreign flags. The King issued further decrees that sternly upheld the rights of the company and threatened severe reprisals against those bent on defying the royal commands.

On yet another occasion the King stood firm behind de Monts and his company. A stubborn customs official at Condé-sur-Noireau in Normandy held up twenty-two bales of furs that were on their way to the hatters and furriers of Paris. One imagines this man as one of those functionaries bug-eyed with self-importance. These furs were foreign imports, he insisted, and duty would have to be paid on them. This prompted a stiff letter from the King who ordered him to let the furs through. New France, the letter emphasized, was not a foreign country but an extension of France. The royal displeasure bore down heavily on the officious official. He had prevented the company from using the profits from these furs on provisions for the new settlement. For the King's hopes were still high that the venture would prove successful, and that 'through the prudent conduct of the said Monsieur de Monts ... very great good may result to the glory of God, the salvation of the savages, the honour and grandeur of our estates and seigneuries.'

These were the very aims pursued by Champlain the previous September, when he set off south-west beyond the fog to explore and make alliances with the Indian tribes. He was away for a month and, on his return, could report some success. For during that time he sailed 150 miles along the rocky, indented coast of what we now call Maine, and then 50 miles up the Penobscot river where he did indeed meet an important chief. With him in his seventeen- to eighteen-ton pinnace went twelve sailors and two Ste Croix Indians as guides.

The first day's swift sailing took them as far as the Schoodic Peninsula. From there they sighted the high, shining bald peaks of 'L'isle des Monts-deserts' (Mount Desert Island), to which Champlain gave its name. As always when on his travels, Champlain delighted in name-finding, often fixing on a distinguishing feature. Typical are Isles Rangées (Ordered Islands) for the neatly aligned islands between Great Wass and Machias Bay; Isle aux Perroquetz, now the Machias Seal Islands, after the sea-parrots or puffins; Isle aux Corneilles (Rook or Crow Island), later renamed Great Wass Island. But the only names that stuck after this section of New France became New England were Mount Desert Island and Isle au Haut, first called Isle Haute. One may wonder what Champlain would make of today's Mount Desert Island, a fashionable summer resort with its elegant yachts, villas, cottages, hotels, motels, and gift shops. He would probably be gratified to note that one of the peaks bears his name, and that a protected area which extends over parts of that island, Isle au Haut and the Schoodic Peninsula, has been called Acadia National Park.

His first encounter with Mount Desert Island, however, was somewhat too close for comfort. Probably off Otter's Cliff the pinnace struck a rock, which made a hole in the keel. But this proved to be one of those accidents that have a lucky sequel. For while repairing the damage on shore the crew saw signs of human life. First smoke signals rose in the air some way off. Then two canoes approached, paddled by Indians who watched them warily from a safe distance. Champlain quickly sent his own two Indian guides off in a canoe to make friendly overtures, but the others pulled away. Their mistrust was short-lived, for the next day they were back. Champlain got his guides to offer them biscuit and tobacco and they returned the favour with a present of fresh fish.

This was just the sort of chance meeting Champlain had been hoping for. Yes, his interpreters told him, these Indians *did* have a chief. His name was Bessabez and he lived on the 'broader river,' the Pentagouet (Penobscot as the English called it). Would they lead the white men to him? They agreed to do so. Containing his excitement as their new acquaintances guided them on, Champlain kept a careful eye on the fascinating configuration of the coastline, on the many islands, the rocks, shoals, and sandbanks. When they reached the mouth of the wide, lovely Penobscot, he felt more than the usual prickle of curiosity. For here they were on the forty-fourth parallel. This river because of its latitude seemed to be the fabled Norumbega, a name that had been used for three-quarters of a century to designate the area, a particular place in the area, and then the river. Stories had arisen of a wealthy, sophisticated stone city whose inhabitants lived in round houses supported by pillars of gold, silver, and crystal. They wore sable cloaks, and men and women alike adorned their arms and legs with bracelets of gold and silver 'garnished with pearls, divers of them as big as one's thumb.' Champlain had heard that they sewed with cotton thread. But he was suspicious and sharpened his already keen senses to give the lie to tall tales.

Sailing upriver, they passed islands, and meadows, the Camden Hills, the harbours of Camden, Rockland, and beautiful Castine. With a mellow September sun catching glints of yellow and gold and scarlet among the green trees, nature might look magnificent. But there was no gorgeous stone city ahead raising its turrets into a blue sky and sparkling with precious metals. They saw nothing along the river, from the mouth to the spot where they anchored twenty or twenty-five leagues further up, except some conical birch-bark wigwams just like those of the Micmacs. The inhabitants painted their faces and sported *matchias* but were no more elaborately clad than the Indians they had already met. Champlain had been rightly sceptical about travellers' tales.

The French dropped anchor on the Kenduskeag near present-day Bangor. This spot became known to the French as Kadesquit. Champlain was delighted with the countryside and particularly impressed by a splendid stand of oak trees. (We shall see that, some years later, equally impressed Jesuit missionaries hoped to found a colony here.) But rocks and waterfall prevented the pinnace from sailing any further. So Champlain went off hunting after asking the guides to invite Bessabez, the great chief, and Cabahis, a lesser one, to come and visit him.

On the 16th September the parleys began. From their pinnace the French watched, with some apprehension, the arrival of these new Indians. How amenable would they prove to be? First about thirty Penobscot braves assembled on the shore. Then came Bessabez and his followers in six canoes, greeted rapturously with chants and high-leaping dances. Then, when the chief had landed, they all sat down in a circle on the ground.

A little later Cabahis and twenty to thirty of his followers arrived, perhaps intimidated, for they kept to themselves. Or they may have been a particularly retiring group, for it seems they had never seen 'Christians' before. Champlain, the explorer, always in search of the new, rather enjoyed being stared at and found a novelty himself. And if Mathieu d'Acosta, the black interpreter, was there, the Indians would have marvelled as much at the black Christian as at the white.

Champlain waited until all were assembled, then, together with his own two Indians and two of his companions, left the pinnace. He may have been somewhat dry-mouthed but he had taken precautions, instructing his crew to draw near the shore and keep their weapons ready in case of attack. This was the first large assembly of Indians that Champlain had had to face on his own as commander. But he had no reason to fear. Bessabez welcomed the advancing group with calm dignity, invited them to join the circle. The ritual smoking began. Champlain and his men received a gift of venison and waterfowl.

In his *Voyages* Champlain has left us with a detailed description of the proceedings. First he presented his message to his interpreter, who then passed it on to the two Indians. They, in turn, spoke to Bessabez and the assembly. The gist of the message was that the French had come as peacemakers and wanted nothing better than to be friends with Bessabez and his people and to reconcile them with other hostile tribes. However, the French also wanted to build a settlement – not, of course, in order to take the land away from the Indians but only to 'show them how to cultivate it, in order that they might no longer lead so miserable an existence as they were doing.'

The Indians, who enjoyed well-turned phrases and good rhetoric, courteously and lengthily declared themselves in favour of friendship, peace, and French settlement and then fixed on what they rightly saw as being the core of the question: trade. Once living at peace with their enemies, they would, they assured the French, be able to 'hunt the beaver more than they had ever done, and barter these beaver ... in exchange for things necessary for their usage.'

One of the interesting things that we today might note about this parley is that Champlain needs the help of the Indians but speaks with the voice of French patronage. In the name of de Monts and a King from over the water he has come to improve the lot of people who do not think it needs improving – apart from the acquisition of better utensils and tools. The Indians, however, view the alliance in terms of a fair, equal exchange. What they could not realize then was that hunting in order to trade rather than for their own needs would, in the long run, work a radical change upon them, alter the traditional rhythms of their life, and seriously affect the respectful regard in which they held animal life.

Champlain hoped to work other changes upon them, too, but for the moment did not broach the question of saving their heathen souls. But among the presents he handed out of caps, knives, and hatchets, he included rosaries – as outward signs of promised inward grace? Unaware then of the pious design upon them, the Indians gave themselves up to what the French might consider their happy pagan pleasures and danced and sang until dawn when the serious work of bartering began. Then Indians and French parted, the French, Champlain tells us, 'well pleased to make acquaintance with these people.'

Whatever the basic misunderstandings, the whole occasion marked the beginning of a good friendship between the French and the Indians that lasted as long as the French held Acadia. Just nine years later an unhappy group of Frenchmen attacked by the English were to receive compassionate offers of help from Bessabez and his followers.

Encouraged by this parley, Champlain was anxious to leave the Penobscot and sail to the Kennebec where he hoped to make a similar alliance with the Indians there. On his way down the river he stopped at Cabahis' encampment (on either the Orland or the Belfast river). If it was true that Cabahis had never seen Christians before, it must have been his first opportunity to see a sailing ship close up – and his first chance to sail in one. Champlain invited him on board the pinnace and took him twleve leagues down river. In exchange for the ride, as it were, Cabahis gave Champlain useful information about the sources of the Penobscot and pointed out a portage route to Ste Croix, as well as another via the Chaudière River to the Great River and Quebec.

They reached the mouth of the Penobscot, sailing along the western shore below the long ridge of the Camden Hills. But when his two Indian guides realized that Champlain was bound for the Kennebec, they made it quite clear they were no longer at his service, left the pinnace, and went off in their canoe. For they had no desire for an encounter with the Kennebec tribe, whom they regarded as great enemies. Undeterred by this, Champlain continued towards Muscongus as far as an island ten leagues from the Kennebec. This was to be named Georges Island the following year by the Englishman George Weymouth.

By now a fierce fall gale was blowing. The islands and reefs they passed looked dangerous. Food was in short supply. In this situation, the most sensible thing Champlain could do was return to Ste Croix and settle in for the winter. So caution overcame curiosity and, on the 2nd October, the French were back in their island habitation.

CHAPTER FOUR

Deaths and Discoveries

THEIR LOG CABINS LOOKED SNUG AND TIDY under a lowering sky and were certainly more comfortable than the pinnace in which Champlain and his party had spent the last month. Hardwood trees flaunted their brilliant fall colours among the evergreens. Then, suddenly, on the 6th October, four days after their return, white flakes began to fall from the sky. Snow muffled the ground, furred the dark branches of the trees, gleamed white among crimson leaves, lay in neat caps on the roofs of storehouse and lodgings. The new inhabitants greeted it with consternation, not with lyrical raptures. Had winter come so soon? They had spent five months in these novel surroundings. For most of the men it had been a busy and not disagreeable time: fishing, exploring, building, planting. True, they had been attacked by blackflies – but not by Indians. Now, as they looked around them and counted the months on their fingers, they realized, with sickening certainty, that nothing could change until March at least. Before them stretched six months of sheer endurance.

In summer the island had given them a sense of security, of cosy self-containment. In the winter they felt confined. In summer the shores of the mainland seemed to lie within easy distance. But now the settlers became very conscious of the fact that the river on each side of them was three times as broad as the Seine. Yet they were obliged to cross it frequently – and for very material, not just psychological, reasons. They needed water and wood. As there were seventy-nine men on the island, the small boat was in great demand and had to be reserved a whole day in advance. In their enthusiasm for building, they had practically denuded the island of timber. They had also thought that over October and November they would have time to stock up on logs and charcoal for the cold season, never dreaming it would be upon them so soon. Some cedars still remained standing on the northern shore of the island, but de Monts ordered that these be kept and not cut down. They provided some protection from the relentless and dreaded north-west winds and so proved more useful as a windbreak than as firewood.

With the wind came a freezing cold such as none of them had ever experienced before. As the winter progressed, it grew worse and worse. The wind shook and rattled their lodgings, blew through chinks and crevices, pierced them to the marrow as they sat miserably huddled over their small smoky fires. De Monts insisted that constant night watch should be kept for fear of the Indians who had set up camp at the foot of the island, or some other possible enemy. It was a wise but not a popular measure. Some of the watch, stamping and blowing on their hands, might have wondered what foreign vessels they could expect to see looming up-river through the blizzards.

Champlain mentions that there was very little rain that winter. This suggests that they must have known some of those bright days that we today, from the comfort of heated houses, describe as perfect winter weather, when the sky is a clear blue and the snow sparkles. According to a later visitor, the Jesuit Father Biard, there were some brisk sportsmen among de Monts' men: 'a jolly group of hunters, who preferred rabbit hunting to the air of the fireside; skating on the ponds, to turning over lazily in bed; making snowballs to bring down the game, to sitting around the fire talking about Paris and its good cooks.' It sounds a healthy, vigorous programme, but not one for which the hired men could feel much relish. What energy they had went on grumbling and bitterly wishing they had never let themselves in for this white hell.

On the 3rd December ice was seen floating down the river, swirling and heaving on the high tides. This put an end to the enforced exercise of crossing over to the mainland to collect wood and water. The men fell into a worse lethargy. There was little to drink. The well-built storehouse looked solid enough but it had no cellar and the air inside it was colder than that outside. The cider froze. To ensure fair distribution the man issuing the rations hacked and carved into the icy amber block and weighed it out by the pound since he could not measure it into bottles and pitchers. The Spanish wine did not freeze.

But as there was only a limited supply of this, it was not given out every day. The men took to drinking old dirty water and melted snow.

If Bituani was one of the Indians who lingered on in the region, he would have found cold comfort in the kitchen. With the shortage of fuel, most cooking was done on the little fires in the individual lodges. On these the hunters roasted their game. But most ate only salt meat and dried vegetables. As this inadequate diet left them weaker and weaker, grinding wheat with the hand-mill became an even more painful task. Fresh bread became rarer. And, of course, the outcome was inevitable.

In December some men began to feel their gums swell and flesh thicken in their mouths. It was the beginning of the dreaded scurvy that had proved so fatal in Cartier's time. Champlain gives a detailed account of the progress of the disease:

There was engendered in the mouths of those who had it large pieces of superfluous flesh (which caused a great putrefaction), and this increased to such a degree that they could scarcely take anything except in very liquid form. Their teeth barely held in their place, and could be drawn out with the fingers without causing pain. This superfluous flesh was often cut away, which caused them to lose much blood from the mouth. Afterwards, they were taken with great pains in the arms and legs, which became swollen and very hard and covered with spots like flea-bites; and they could not walk on account of the contraction of the nerves; consequently they had almost no strength, and suffered intolerable pains. They had also pains in the loins, stomach, and bowels, together with a very bad cough and shortness of breath. In brief, they were in such a state that the majority of the sick could neither get up nor move, nor could they even be held upright without fainting away.

The surgeons prescribed remedies – but to no effect. Indeed, they could not even treat themselves. De Monts and Champlain had read how Cartier's men had been helped by the wonder-working Annedda, dubbed the 'tree of life.' During the winter of 1535 the Indians on the St Lawrence had shown Cartier how to make an infusion from the ground-up bark and leaves of the Annedda steeped in boiling water. Those who drank this concoction experienced almost instantaneous relief. Centuries later we have learnt that the miracle tree was the white cedar, which has a high vitamin c content. It was, of course, the lack of this in fresh vegetables and fruit that brought on the scurvy. But the Indians at Ste Croix, when questioned, shook their heads. 'Annedda' meant nothing to them. Lethargy sank to despair as more and more men fell ill.

In January they began to die: masons, artisans, soldiers, though exactly who and how many of each trade we do not know. The atmosphere must have been nightmarish: the cold, dark huts lit and warmed only by a meagre fire; the chill stench of the bedridden bodies, their putrefying mouths; the sick unable to raise themselves while the less sick attempted to feed them liquid from straws. When the fierce north-west wind raged, they pulled their coverings more tightly around themselves. Many sank into a deeper depression. The very sick died. With death came confessions, and prayers, uttered by Catholic priest or Protestant pastor, summary last rites and a small hasty procession over the snow, beyond what had been the gardens, to the cemetery. Champlain says that the snow lay three feet deep all winter. One wonders if they simply buried the bodies under the snow and then interred them later when it thawed, as Cartier had been obliged to do.

And just as Cartier had done, de Monts asked the surgeons to dissect some of the corpses before burial in the hopes that this would help them diagnose the malady. They found the internal organs in a terrible state. But none the wiser after their grisly efforts, the surgeons assembled the anatomized corpses for decent burial. The wind blew and snow continued to fall.

Thirty-five men died in all. Lescarbot, who later had a chance to question the survivors, stated that 'the deadly season for that sickness is in the end of January, the months of February and March, wherein the most commonly the sick do die.' This means that on an average five men died every week over those months. And twenty more came close. One can imagine the pall of utter misery that hung over the habitation.

Only eleven men in all kept well and even these had some pains and found themselves short of breath. Champlain and de Monts were among those who remained active and comparatively healthy, as Cartier, in fact, had done. Still, they must have been bitterly disappointed that their lovely island should have turned into such a death-trap. But they now knew that only experience could prove whether a place was habitable or not. And they had, as they realized later, struck a particularly bad winter.

In March when the days were longer and the sunlight warmer, a group of Indians passed by. But though they wore good furs and had game to give the French in exchange for bread, Champlain did not consider that these Indians had anything to teach the French about survival tactics in winter.

Snow lay on the ground all April. But the worst was over. Fresh shoots appeared even through the snow. The fish began to run. As the food improved, the sick men started slowly to recover. Buds appeared on trees. It became possible to cross the mainland where the sharp raw smell of spring was in the air. In the early days of May they could stretch out their cold, cramped bodies in the noonday sun, feel the warmth penetrate to the long-chilled marrow of their bones. The birds returned. Every day the watch strained their eyes to see if they could make out the shape of a sail billowing on the river. For de Monts had asked Ralluau to send out fresh provisions and more men for the beginning of May. By the 15th there was still no sign of relief. Accidents were always possible. Ships, men, and supplies might have gone down among the ice-floes or in a storm. But the French could not possibly hold out another winter. De Monts decided to have two pinnaces built in which they could sail to Gaspé in search of a ship to take them home. (Such preparations, we shall see, became a frequent spring exercise for would-be settlers.) Champdoré, with his skill as a ship's carpenter, was in charge of this. For a month the sawing and hammering went on, the seventeen-ton pinnace that Champlain had used for his September exploration and the long-boat serving as a basis for the remodelled crafts.

Towards the middle of June they began to plan their departure. On the 15th Champlain was on night-watch. It was about eleven o'clock. Dark had just fallen and nearly everyone else had turned in for the night. A small shallop came into view. From it a well-known voice bellowed greetings. Gravé had arrived. The *Bonne Renommée* lay six leagues away from the island, but he had hurried ahead to let them know of her arrival.

There could not have been much sleep at the settlement that night. Gravé was the first white man they had seen for ten months. There were all the terrors of the past winter with which to regale their first visitor. He had arrived expecting to see a flourishing little colony and his own lodgings made ready to receive him. Instead, here were men pointing to spaces where their teeth had been and to the many humped graves in the cemetery which they had been lucky to escape.

The next day the *Bonne Renommée* sailed up the river. Cannon boomed and trumpets sounded a delirious welcome. Forty men arrived, a still larger audience for those who needed to talk of their sufferings. Gravé announced that yet another ship was on her way, the *St Etienne* of St Malo with more provisions.

Indeed, as far back as January of that year members of the company in France had been making arrangements for sending out men and supplies to the new settlement. Tillers, masons, caulkers, fishermen, and sailors had been engaged, many making an X on their contracts in lieu of signatures. Pierre Cramolet, the pilot who had been out the year before, signed on. So did another pilot, the Huguenot Israel Bailleul, whom we encounter again eight years later on the shores of Acadia disguised as an Indian. Another surgeon, too, had been hired, one Guillaume Deschamps. A document shows many of these men borrowing money, probably so they could do some trade on the side. The amounts range from thirty to eighty livres, about fifty livres on the average.

Encouraged by last season's profits, the company was confidently moving ahead. On its behalf Jean Macain of La Rochelle signed a charter-party with the master of the *Jonas*, a 150-tonner whose crew of thirty-six were to engage in whaling and trading. For the latter purposes she carried in her hold 31 barrels of wheat, 2 casks of prunes, 4,308 hatchets and 4 copper kettles.

De Monts felt assured then of continuing support for his settlement. If he had given up at that moment and returned to France, he would have been accused of being faint-hearted, a defeatist, disloyal to the King and the other members of his company. And, of course, it was in his own financial interest as a major shareholder to carry on. But it would be madness to risk another winter at Ste Croix. So he decided to go in search of a more suitable haven further south. Within a day of Gravé's arrival his mind was made up. The larger pinnace, in which the French were to sail off in search of fishing vessels to take them home, was already caulked and seaworthy. In it some of them could make a reconnaissance trip southwards beyond the coastline Champlain had explored in the fall. Once they found a more favourable site, they could dismantle the buildings at Ste Croix and transport them there. But it was important to get going as soon as possible. De Monts was concerned for the health of his men still convalescing, but he judged that his first duty was to ensure against another harrowing winter. Some days later, towards the end of June, the pinnace was off down the Ste Croix and out upon a summer sea.

With de Monts went Champlain, plummet and pen at the ready. Their pilots were Champdoré and Cramolet. Champlain also mentions some gentlemen; but apart from himself and the two pilots, there is no indication of who these might be. They had twenty sailors with them and an Indian guide, Panounias. And for the first time, there was a woman on board, their guide's wife. Panounias did not want to leave her behind and de Monts realized that she might come in useful as an interpreter and a token of French good will. For she was not an Etchemin like her husband, but an Almouchiquois from further south, the region they were going to explore.

The expedition lasted just over a month. The explorers sailed as far as Nauset harbour, which they called Mallebárre. In the course of this voyage they met a number of the native inhabitants. Champlain made rough charts and sketched, as they carefully examined the coastline and terrain and gave names to islands, capes, harbours, and bays. None of these names have survived. For nowhere on this attractive coast did the French choose to settle. Historians have speculated on how different the story of North America might have been if they had put down roots here. A closer look at some of their experiences might suggest why they did not.

The first area they explored was the Kennebec River. Here they encountered a group of Indians hunting birds then moulting and so unable to fly. Panounias' wife explained who the white men were and why they had come. Their new acquaintances guided them up the Black River channel to Wiscasset to meet their chief. Champlain gives his name as Manthoumermeer, but Champlain was notoriously bad at languages. So this Indian chief was probably the one Father Biard later met and spoke of as Météourmite.

The parley between French and Indians took place upon the waters, the chief addressing de Monts from his canoe, while ten other canoes containing his followers hovered in the background. Météourmite told the French that he was very willing to make an alliance with them, and would be happy to see them reconcile him and his enemies. He also promised to send word of them and their mission to two other chiefs, Marchin and Sasinou. And he graciously accepted de Monts' earnest of good will: ship's biscuits and dried peas.

The guides then took the French ship past Hockomock Point. Each left an arrow here to appease the guardian spirit of that rough, rocky place. When commenting on this in his *Voyages* Champlain showed himself no relativist in matters of religion. 'Such superstitions and likewise many others do they practise,' was his disapproving comment. (How many times a day, one wonders, did he make the sign of the cross?) They passed through the dangerous and dramatic tidal fall at Upper Hell Gate, but to do so had to tie a hawser to trees on the river bank and strain and heave to pull themselves through.

At Merrymeeting Bay they expected to meet chiefs Marchin and Sasinou. But these failed to turn up. So the French weighed anchor and returned to the mouth of the Kennebec, this time sailing down the main channel. De Monts was not tempted by this region. He had noted some pleasant grassy meadows, but the soil was poor, and rocks abounded. Champlain agreed that it was no improvement on Ste Croix.

As they sailed across Casco Bay, they caught sight of some high mountains towards the west – the White Mountains of New Hampshire. This, they were told, was the domain of an Indian chief called Aneda. Haunted by the recent horrors of the scurvy, Champlain gazed at them intently. Was that where the remedy lay? For he was persuaded that a chief called Aneda must know something of the 'annedda,' Cartier's wonder-working cure.

Spirits rose when they visited Richmonds Island. Here was a sight to delight French eyes: not only majestic oaks and nut-trees, but grape-bearing vines. It was their first glimpse of this fruit in Acadia. No other name would do for this place but one that conjured up dance, song, and sun-burnt mirth: the Island of Bacchus. Was this then the beginning of the warm south? Their next encounter seemed to suggest that it was.

For, a little way up the Saco River, they came across a settlement of Indians who tilled the soil and cultivated crops. They were the first non-nomadic Indians de Monts and Champlain had seen. Hordes of them dancing on shore greeted the explorers. Their good-looking young chief, Onemechin, at first cautiously circled round the pinnace in his canoe, then came on board to visit them. There was some trading on shore even though these Almouchiquois had nothing to barter but the clothes they had on, for they kept no surplus stocks for trade. Champlain observed their athletic bodies, their faces painted black and red, their high shaven foreheads, their long, elegantly twisted hair held in place by feathers. (Champlain seems to have been fascinated by hairdos. He always makes a special point of commenting on attractive coiffures, either male or female.) But – no parleys, for the French no longer had an interpreter. Her first mission accomplished, Panounias' wife remained behind on the Kennebec. So de Monts was unable to make a formal alliance with this tribe.

Still, the newcomers could use their eyes if not their tongues. They were curious to know what sort of crops these Indians planted, their methods of cultivation. De Monts and Champlain visited the gardens where corn sprouted from mounds surrounded by a few bush beans that kept the weeds from growing. The Indians fertilized the soil with shells of the 'signoc,' the curious horseshoe crab whose sharp tails went to tip the men's arrows. Both de Monts and Champlain were intrigued by this creature. De Monts gave a long detailed description of it and featured it as decoration on two of his maps.

Looking around them, the explorers were impressed by what they saw flourishing under the summer sun. The corn stood two to three feet high. The beans were in flower as were the many squash and pumpkin plants. Tobacco too was cultivated. Nuts lay on the ground. From the fine grapes, which the Indians, curiously, would not touch, the French made some much-appreciated juice. The river teemed with fish. Champlain was attracted by the easy profusion of good things here, the sense of settlement, the Indians' palisaded fort. At the mouth of the river was a little island suitable for 'the construction of a good fortress where one would be safe.' Another island? Ste Croix the year before had looked just as inviting. Champlain admitted that there was no knowing how cold it might turn in the winter. Hoping to find something better, they sailed on.

Between Saco and Cape Ann they saw nothing that particularly invited them to establish a settlement, though along the low, sandy shore they noted vines, nut-trees, lovely red-winged blackbirds. Goose Fair Bay swarmed with red currants and wild pigeons. At Cape Ann Champlain went on shore to speak to five or six dancing Indians. In exchange for knives and biscuits they danced some more, watched him draw a rough map of their surroundings with charcoal, then obligingly drew for him an outline of Massachusetts Bay, indicating with pebbles how many tribes lived round it and where.

From Cape Ann to Boston Bay Champlain was struck by the fine woods, the large areas of cultivated land. Great numbers of Indians danced on the beaches. In fact the French had never seen so many and probably felt somewhat overwhelmed. The English who settled in this region fifteen years later encountered very few Indians. For a great pestilence that raged in 1617 and 1618 silenced the dancers and left the land almost bare of inhabitants.

At Boston Bay the explorers again went on shore to meet the dancing inhabitants. Again they handed out knives and rosaries. Yet again the language barrier prevented them from making their mission known. Here they noticed that the canoes were not of the birch-bark but of the dug-out variety, the first sort they had seen. In Champlain's opinion they were tricky to handle and difficult to construct. The Indians worked laboriously with some stone hatchets to fell the trunks from which they were made. The few metal hatchets they had were of French make, obtained from the tribes further north in exchange for furs.

The Indians themselves, in the summer at any rate, wore clothes of grass and hemp. So furs here were not as plentiful as they were farther north. Is this the reason why de Monts showed little interest in the site that was to become the 'glorious city of Boston, home of the bean and the cod,' home too of generations of seafarers, merchants, revolutionaries, legislators, and intellectuals? Still, the eventual Charles River, which looked so broad from their position in the harbour, was thought important enough to be given de Monts' name and on Champlain's map appears as the Rivière Du Gas. Perhaps before his death in 1635 Champlain heard of the growing prosperity of Boston and remembered the day he had spent in the island-studded bay.

A couple of days later the French put into Plymouth Bay, so anticipating the Pilgrim Fathers by fifteen years. Here too the natives were exuberantly friendly. The French watched them fishing for cod with tree-bark line and a hook made of a harpoon-shaped bone tied tightly with hemp to a piece of wood. Champlain explored the area on foot and made a hasty sketch of the place. Again they lingered no longer than a day.

On the 20th July they entered Nauset harbour. But not with any great ease. Breakers crashing around them prevented them from sighting shoals and sandbanks. Mallebarre (Bad Bar) they decided on as an appropriate name for this port. It was the farthest south they were to go that season. De Monts realized he would have to make a decision soon and took a good hard look at this site. They were there four days from the 20th to the 24th July. The grass-clad, well-coiffed Indians, who were settled around the bay in circular wigwams thatched with reeds, seemed happy and friendly. They danced and bartered bows, arrows, and quivers for pins and buttons. De Monts, Champlain, and some armed men inspected the gardens and were impressed by their corn, beans, squash, tobacco, and the novel Jerusalem artichoke. The Indians dried their tobacco, cooked the corn in earthenware pots or ground it to flour to make cakes and biscuits. Wild grapes grew. De Monts had some preserved for the King so that His Majesty could sample fruits from his New France.

The French learned that, when the corn was ripe, wild turkeys would arrive which were very good to eat. The Indians communicated this to their visitors by means of cries and signs and by pointing to the turkey feathers on their arrows and in their hair. They were fairly resourceful, too, when it came to answering the main question the French had in mind: was there much snow in winter? They scooped up sand and let it fall through their hands, at the same time pointing to their visitors' large white collars to show they were talking about snow. Some indicated that it fell a foot deep, others less.

Champlain himself thought the climate would be temperate, even though during their stay a gale blew from the north-west, the sky grew grim and grey, and it became so cold that they had to search out and put on their thick winter capes.

On their fourth day there a disastrous incident occurred, much worse than a mere change in the weather. Some Indians had come aboard the pinnace while four or five sailors had gone off among the dunes to fetch water in large kettles. These were utensils that the Indians greatly admired and coveted. And Indians, as the French were to discover, had a much less highly developed sense of personal property than they did. A small group, expecting the sailors to pass by, ambushed them and snatched a kettle out of the hands of an unarmed sailor who had just filled his. Another sailor darted after the Indian who had taken the kettle but the latter proved too swift and got away. The sailors ran towards the pinnace calling on the French to frighten the many Indians on the shore with musket shots. The Indians on shore fled while those visiting on the pinnace dived into the water, all except one whom the French seized. When the Indians on shore saw the others swimming away from the pinnace, they must have suspected that the French were already taking their revenge. For they turned upon the man whose kettle had been stolen, shot arrows at him, then ran towards him and knifed him. He was a carpenter from St Malo, the first man to be killed by Indians since the expedition had landed in the New World roughly a year before. Champlain and others tried pursuing them with their muskets, but no European was a match for the fleet-footed Indians. On this occasion Champlain's musket exploded in his hands and 'nearly killed me,' he later recorded laconically.

Lescarbot, hearing the story from someone else, wrote that the enraged men were all ready to fire upon the Indians who were still in sight. But de Monts, seeing that the murderers had got away, told them to put down their weapons. Few leaders in his position, commented Lescarbot , would have shown the same restraint, 'grieved sore' though he was. He also ordered that the prisoner on the pinnace should be set free, since he could in no way be held responsible either for the theft or the murder. Along with Lescarbot one applauds such rational moderation. Champlain's version of the story shows that some of the Indians came to apologize, again using sign language. Shaking their heads, gesturing and pointing, they gave the French to understand that it was not they who had killed the sailor but others from further inland.

Still, it was a dispiriting experience for the French to find they had fallen among 'thieves' – and worse. There was no point in lingering here, suspicious of the Indians and shivering in the cold wind. De Monts decided to return to Ste Croix, for not one of the many sites they had visited did he consider suitable. But what about all those fertile fields where corn and vines flourished? We can only assume, along with the historians, that de Monts had come to prefer the devil of winter he knew to the swarms of Indians he did not. The elements are after all impersonal forces. One might learn how to deal with them. People can prove far more difficult. De Monts was a tried and tested soldier, but he wanted his new colony to develop peacefully. A contributing factor may have been that, further south, barter had brought in few furs. And it was on the fur trade that de Monts and his company mainly relied for profits.

On the 25th July the French left Mallebarre. And a 'Bad Bar' it certainly was. For it was on this bar that they nearly came to grief, as the pilots Cramolet and Champdoré had been negligent about buoying the entrance. We do not hear of Cramolet again but Champdoré stayed on to commit other navigational errors that were to exasperate and hinder Champlain.

On the return voyage the explorers stopped at Saco and made the acquaintance of chief Marchin, whom they had expected to see earlier at Merrymeeting Bay on the Kennebec. The French were most impressed by his handsome and dignified gestures. De Monts lavished presents upon him. Was it relief at being able to deal with an Indian whom he felt he could trust and respect? The chief returned the courtesy by handing over a young Etchemin boy whom he had captured in war. The French undertook to return him to his people. De Monts seems to have taken very seriously his role as peacemaker between Micmacs and the Etchemins on one hand and Almouchiquois on the other. It was certainly one of the reasons the French had for justifying their presence.

Sailing north-west, the French arrived at the Kennebec on the 29th. Here they hoped to meet Sasinou, the other chief they had missed at Merrymeeting Bay. Again he failed to turn up. But they obtained a few furs by barter from a chief called Abassou, who told them that white men had been fishing from a ship in those parts and had killed five Indians. From the description given, the French concluded they were English. And so they were. The ship was the *Archangel*, under the command of Captain George Weymouth. (This reconnaissance voyage had been launched under the patronage of Henry Wriothesley, the Earl of Southampton, better know to posterity because of his associations with the then busy and successful playwright/manager/actor Shakespeare.) For Virginia had not been forgotten. The English were still attracted to these parts. They came ready to trade but also with a view to settlement. Their intentions, like those of the French, were of the noblest: 'the sole intent of the Honourable setters foorth of this discovery' being 'a publique good, and true zeale of promulgating Gods holy church.' In early June they had kidnapped, not killed, the five Indians who, Weymouth hoped, could become their native guides once they had learnt English. So he took them back to England for a sort of enforced immersion course in the language. (We know that at least one of these Indians returned to his native haunts after they had all impressed the English with their ceremonious manners, bearing themselves 'with great civility, far from the rudeness of our common people.')

De Monts commiserated with the Indians over the loss of the five men and sailed on, happy in the knowledge that the French had found more favour with the native inhabitants of these parts than their English rivals. On the 2nd August the pinnace reached the western mouth of the Ste Croix. Anxious to be back at the settlement to see how the sick and the newcomers were faring, de Monts had himself rowed up-river in a canoe to the ill-fated but familiar island.

CHAPTER FIVE

First Winter at Port Royal

NEXT DAY CHAMPLAIN, PANOUNIAS, AND THE OTHERS arrived to discover another ship anchored off the island. This was the *Saint-Etienne*, a three-hundred-tonner, captained by des Antons who had brought the promised supplies from St Malo. The colonizers now had enough food to see them through the winter. But where should they spend it? Ste Croix was out of the question. Even on a lovely August day, with the corn they had sown the year before ripening under the woods, memories of the past winter were raw and cruel. De Monts consulted his chief officers. Thinking back on the explorations of the summer before, they remembered Port Royal with its wide stretch of shimmering water surrounded on all sides by hills. Surely they would be better protected there than on exposed Ste Croix Island. Besides, the sieur de Poutrincourt intended to settle there some day. This could be a start. De Monts ordered the Ste Croix lodgings to be dismantled. Masons and carpenters were busy pulling down every building except the storehouse, which was judged too large and solid to move. The woodwork was loaded onto two pinnaces that sailed to Port Royal with Champlain and Gravé in charge.

After coming through the Gut, they cast around for a suitable site. At first they were tempted by the place where the town of Annapolis Royal stands today. But they had second thoughts. Might not this be too far from the entrance to the port? So they chose a spot on the north side of the basin at Granville Ferry opposite present Goat Island. Carefully and consciously they tried to avoid previous mistakes. As the area was very thickly wooded, they could count on a plentiful supply of firewood. All around were marshes and springs so they would not have far to go for water. The long chain of high hills behind should protect them from the dreaded north-west wind. With fuel, water, and better shelter, they could hope to endure if not outface the winter.

Immediately the men set to work to clear the ground. The pinnaces shuttled busily between Ste Croix and Port Royal, transporting men, goods, and the rest of the finished timber to be used again for the new Habitation. Was it Champlain who planned the layout of this as he had done at Ste Croix? He did indeed make a careful sketch of it, which was later published in one of his books. (With this as guide the Canadian Government has built an impressive replica of the original. The replica may be grander, more carefully constructed and appointed than the Habitation that Champlain and Lescarbot knew. Still, it vividly conjures up the life of these early colonizers perched at the edge of a vast wilderness.)

Everything was more compact, more tightly pulled together than at Ste Croix. Instead of standing separately, all the buildings were joined together to form a rectangle around a central square. A new storehouse was built extending all along the east side with, this time, 'a very fine cellar some five to six feet high' so the cider would not freeze again. (Visitors to the Habitation may note how the cellar slopes from being five feet high at one end to six at the other.) Gentlemen's lodgings were to the north; the artisans' quarters lay along the west side; forge, bakehouse, and kitchen faced the port on the south. On the south, too, jutting out a little from the main rectangle and overlooking the water, they constructed a palisade on the east side and a platform on the west where four cannons were mounted. Defence and a careful watch were essential. Everyone must have considered it much more convenient having the cannon platform attached to the Habitation than way down at the tip of an island, as at Ste Croix.

The work went ahead quickly. When most of the fort had been built, the men turned to loading the ships. Gravé had told de Monts how unpopular the monopoly was in France. He had recounted the stories that circulated of de Monts' harshness, also the fishermen's complaints that they were faced with ruin, their wives and children with starvation. De Monts knew how faction and intrigue worked at court. He was aware that powerful Sully had set the seal of his disapproval on the enterprise from the start. News of the disastrous winter at Ste Croix was just the sort of ammunition that would be seized upon with glee by those hostile to the monopoly and colonization. Even people who had been favourably disposed might falter and admit that it looked as though New France was indeed uninhabitable. De Monts decided that he should return to France. There he could see the King, tell him exactly how things had turned out, and assure him that there was still hope a settlement could be established. In his place as commander he wanted to appoint the sieur d'Orville. But the latter was still sick from the effects of scurvy and declined the honour. Bluff, hearty Gravé accepted the command. It would be his first winter in the New World, to which he was by now a frequent summer voyager. De Monts expected to send another ship out from France the following spring. But, realistically, he instructed his lieutenant that if no relief had arrived by the 16th July, he was to get his people to Canso where they would find fishing vessels to take them home.

Most of the men who had survived Ste Croix longed to return home and thankfully sailed back with de Monts, leaving the new recruits in their place. But some stayed. Champdoré, necessary as pilot, was one. Champlain was another. The journey to Cape Cod had whetted his appetite for exploration. With de Monts' encouragement, he was now planning to sail down the coast as far as Florida. The young Breton nobleman Fougeray de Vitré, undaunted by the death of his cousin, René Noël, sieur de Bourgjoli, also remained. And it seems that the Catholic priest and the Protestant minister were still at it, snapping and sparring, endeavouring to score verbal – and physical – points off each other. Not even the grim spectre of death could induce them to relinquish their theological wrangles. Perhaps it simply conjured up further quarrels on the subject of heaven, hell, and their inmates.

Before leaving, de Monts assembled a small collection of curiosities for a sort of 'show-and-tell.' With this he hoped to awaken interest in a faraway land that most people would never visit themselves. The year before, Ralluau had taken back a caribou, whose sad fate we have already learnt. The seigneur de Peiresc, a noble and notable naturalist, has left a fairly detailed account of the caribou and also of the other exhibits de Monts brought back with him in the fall of 1605. The largest of these was a live female moose about six months old; the smallest, a humming-bird 'no bigger than an almond in its shell.' Peiresc gives the impression that the humming-bird was still alive when he saw it: 'it

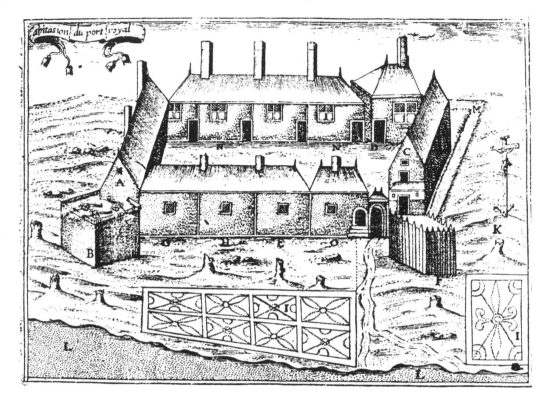

Champlain's plan of the Port Royal Habitation

A Artisans' lodgings; B Platform for cannon; C Storehouse; D Lodging of
Gravé and Champlain; E Forge; F Palisade of stakes; G Oven; H Kitchen;
I Gardens; K Cemetery; L Water of the basin; M Drainage ditch; NN Dwell-
ings (probably of gentlemen); O Small building for rigging of pinnaces

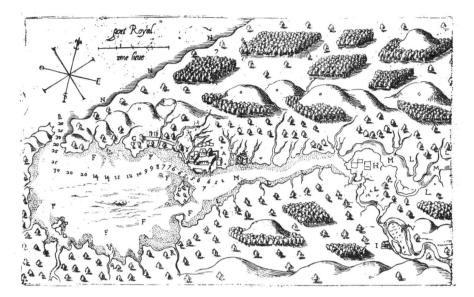

Champlain's map of Port Royal

A Site of the Habitation; B Champlain's garden; C Path through woods that the sieur de Poutrincourt had made; D Biencourt (Goat) Island; E Entrance to port (Digby Gut); F Shoals dry at low tide; G St Antoine (Bear) River; H Fields sown with grain (Annapolis Royal); I Mill that Poutrincourt had built (on Allens River); L Fields inundated at high tide; M Equille (Annapolis) River; N Seacoast; O Mountain slopes; P (Bear) Island; Q Rocky brook; R Another (Moose) River; S Mill (Allens) River; T A small lake; V Place where Indians fish for 'herring' in season; X Trout stream; Y Road through woods that Champlain had built flutters like a butterfly and lives only on flowers like bees.' But he could have got this by hearsay. For how could a humming-bird have been kept alive for thirty-one days on board ship, given the rate at which it needs to feed to keep humming? Other curiosities were the three horseshoe crabs, the largest of which was destined to be a present to the King. Also carefully packed went wide moose antlers, a moose's dewlap, a few dried-out muskrats, dead birds and their feathers or parts thereof: merganser, blue-jay, the red-winged blackbird seen further south. De Monts had pictures, too, of several other birds, probably drawn by Champlain, and some sketches of the greatest curiosity of all, the strangely clad 'Savages.' To illustrate how these hunted and fought and travelled, de Monts shipped bows 'taller than a man,' a hefty club, and a birch-bark canoe. The four-year-old Dauphin, the future Louis XIII, was taken to see the moose and to marvel at the 'incredible speed' of the light canoe as three sailors paddled it dexterously along the Seine.

And so de Monts departed with what could have been the nucleus of a natural history museum. Years later, viewing his souvenirs, he might think back on the fifteen months he had spent in Acadia, the wild coastline, the dense woods, the new, fascinating creatures – now just old feathers and fur. The country itself he was never to see again.

At Port Royal, Gravé kept the men busy completing the construction of the Habitation. Some prepared gardens, among them Champlain. Around his, he dug ditches in which he placed trout. For Champlain liked to combine the beautiful and the useful. In a spot near the seashore

completely surrounded by meadows ... I arranged a summer-house with fine trees, in order that I might enjoy the fresh air. I constructed there likewise a small reservoir to hold salt-water fish, which we took out as we required them. I also sowed there some seeds which throve well: and I took therein a particular pleasure, although beforehand it had entailed a great deal of labour. We often resorted there to pass the time, and it seemed as if the little birds thereabouts received pleasure from this; for they gathered in great numbers and warbled and chirped so pleasantly that I do not think I ever heard the like.

There was something of the homesteader in Champlain as well as the explorer, something of the naturalist as well as the hunter.

But he was too active to spend time only with the little birds. Once he had a lead, he liked to follow it up. He learned that Secoudun, the

Indian guide who had taken Prévert's men to the famous copper mine two years earlier, was chief of the Saint John River area. Together with miner Maître Jacques of Sclavonia, Champlain crossed the Bay of Fundy to visit him. Secoudun was happy to be their guide and once more Champlain sailed towards Chignecto. But the copper mine near splendid Advocate Harbour proved disappointing. There was some copper, but twice a day the high tides covered the rocks in which it was embedded. That put an end to dreams of great mineral wealth. Still, to take a Lescarbot-like view of things, the friendship of Secoudun and his people was at one juncture to prove more valuable to the French than a mine.

The colonizers had already become acquainted with the group that lived nearest them on St Mary's Bay and at Port Royal itself. The chief here was the remarkable Membertou, an exceptionally tall man, though not so tall, as Lescarbot was later to note, as his friend Poutrincourt. Among the smooth-cheeked Indians he stood out as having a beard. But then several Indian chiefs, it seems, grew beards as a sign of rank. Membertou's was streaked with white, though his hair was still black and his eyesight amazingly keen. He claimed to be over a hundred years old and to have seen Jacques Cartier. (But there are all sorts of ways that claim could be interpreted. How exactly, for example, did the Indians reckon years?) What *was* certain was his interest in the French. Perhaps, at first, it was merely politic on his part to become the staunch friend and ally of these newcomers with their efficient tools and weapons. 'He had,' Champlain declares, 'the reputation of being the worst and most treacherous man of his tribe.' Lescarbot corroborates this, and adds: 'which is the cause why he is said to have many enemies, and he is very glad to keep himself near the Frenchmen, to live in security.' But calculation does not necessarily cancel out affection. Genuine warmth was to develop between Membertou and the French. And if Membertou appreciated French firearms, the French were just as appreciative of prestigious Membertou's support.

On his return from the Minas Basin, Champlain found some men already down with scurvy, though not seriously. They braced themselves for another bad winter. Yet it turned out much milder than expected. It rained frequently but snow did not fall until just before Christmas, on the 20th December. Though the storehouse had a cellar, there were no drains, so water seeped in and under the floors and many men suffered from the damp. As yet they had no well and drank water from the nearest stream, less pure than fresh spring water. Wine was in short supply and by early spring there was none left. But they did have bread in spite of having to grind the corn laboriously with hand-mills. They received frequent visits from the Indians, who came from afar to barter moose, beaver, and otter skins for the usual knives, beads, and the occasional copper kettle. Others brought game on which they feasted. The French noticed how much the Indians liked the fresh bread. They could see, too, how strong and athletic they were, and suggested that they should grind the wheat in return for half of it. The Indians took a turn at the hand-mill and decided they would rather do without the bread.

In spite of the better diet, mouths again filled with superfluous flesh, legs swelled, and over the winter about twelve men out of the forty-five died. They were buried in the cemetery to the east of the Habitation. Among those who succumbed to the scurvy were the Sclavonian miner, Maître Jacques, and those two adversaries, the Catholic priest and the Protestant pastor. Years later the story went that the sailors 'laid them both in the same grave, to see if in death they would remain at peace, since, living they had been unable to agree.' This story is probably true, for we have it from Brother Sagard, the Récollet who got to know Gravé quite well at Quebec. It was obviously one of the stories in his large repertoire that gusty Gravé loved to tell – especially to clerics. So now the little community had to do without the consolations – as well as the quarrels of official religion. Like his predecessors at Ste Croix, Guillaume Deschamps, the surgeon from Honfleur, exercised his dissecting knife on some of the stricken corpses. But, like his predecessors, he could offer neither diagnosis nor cure.

Champlain, with time on his hands, plied the tools of his trade as cartographer, and worked on the outlines, sketches, and notes he had made over the summer. With scrupulous care he mapped the entrance to the Kennebec, Saco, Port St Louis (Plymouth), Mallebarre (Nauset), and Port Royal itself. He had already published a book two years before. Now he had ample material for a second and these charts would serve to illustrate and enhance both narrative and description. He also began work on a large general map of country and coastline. And what might he not discover next spring on the way down to Florida? A river, he hoped, that flowed westwards across the continent, leading eventually to a passage to the East.

So he was anxious to set sail early for the south. Just ten days after a fierce February gale, on the 1 March, Gravé gave orders for a pinnace to be fitted out. On the 16th he and Champlain, with Champdoré as master of the vessel and the usual complement of sailors, left Port Royal. All spring and summer seemed to lie before them. But they had reckoned without Maritime weather. A tempest arose and the pinnace was damaged. Though mightily battered, they still braved their way to the Ste Croix. There the snow lay piled high, head winds blew, fog was thick around them. On the 29th, Gravé, suddenly smitten with a sense of responsibility, decided to return to Port Royal to see how the sick were doing. He was not an abstemious man and the last two weeks had put a considerable strain on him. Back at Port Royal he had a heart attack.

On the 9th April, however, he was on board again, though still somewhat weak. But he, like Champlain, was anxious to explore the coast of Florida and thought 'that the change of air would restore him to health.' (Maritimers who flock to Florida in March will sympathize.) That night the pinnace lay just within the Digby Gut. Before daybreak Champdoré came to ask Gravé, who was sick and in bed, whether he should raise anchor. Yes, came the answer, 'if Champdoré considered the weather favourable.' It was dark, rainy, and very foggy. Nevertheless Champdoré gave orders for the pinnace to sail through the Gut.

It was a fatal mistake. The outgoing tide suddenly heaved them through the narrow passage and out towards the rocks. The sailors called out in terror. This brought Champlain, who was also in bed, staggering to his feet. There was little he could do now except watch helplessly as the pinnace crashed upon the rocks. But it did not disintegrate completely. The men set to and managed to get most of the supplies off the pinnace and onto the shore. A little later the Florida-bound vessel fell apart to become nothing but smashed planks floating on the Fundy tide.

Fortunately for the wrecked men, Secoudun and some of his people were encamped nearby. Out they paddled in their canoes to take the French and their salvaged goods back to the Habitation. This was surely one occasion on which the more stoical, impassive Indians might have wondered at the excitable French screaming their hostility and frustration at one of their own group.

For Champdoré, not surprisingly, was in everyone's black books. Champlain's verdict on him is severe: 'this was a great disaster and a lack of foresight on the part of the master, who was obstinate and little versed in seamanship, and would have his own way. He was a good carpenter, skilled in building vessels and careful in fitting them out with everthing needful, but he was in no wise qualified to navigate them.' Gravé, already shaken by his heart attack, was furious. Holding a summary inquiry, he judged Champdoré guilty of deliberately and maliciously wrecking the pinnace. (And Champdoré may indeed have expressed doubts about the voyage.) Then he sentenced him to be handcuffed and imprisoned until he could be brought before de Monts.

Poor Champlain was never to see the coast of Florida. There was another pinnace on the stocks but they had no time, they thought, to equip her before the arrival of a ship from France. Buds broke out on the trees, then leaves. Champlain could spend long hours listening to the warbling of his little birds. By the 15th June there was still no sign of vessels from home. Something would have to be done. Gravé released the skilful carpenter so he could finish the pinnace, and clapped the erring pilot in irons again when the work was done.

The 16th July arrived. Two pinnaces lay ready at anchor, one of eighteen and the other of eight tons. Much had to be loaded aboard along with the thirty-odd passengers and crew: food, merchandise, furniture. Two men volunteered to remain. Lescarbot salutes their courage by preserving their names for posterity: La Taille and Miquelet. Gravé promised them a hundred silver crowns each for their services. Membertou said he would care for them as if they were his own children.

On the 17th the two pinnaces sailed out of Port Royal. A couple of days later they ran into a summer squall which broke the rudder. The only person capable of fixing it was, of course, Champdoré. So Gravé again had his hands freed. Champdoré used them to such good effect splicing rope to mend the rudder that several men, including Champlain, pleaded that the charges against him should be quashed. Gravé reluctantly gave way.

On the afternoon of the 24th, when they were just off Cape Sable, they caught sight of a sail. It was a long-boat. They strained their eyes and, as they drew closer, made out that it was manned by Frenchmen. One familiar figure stood out among the rest. It was Ralluau, de Monts' secretary. The lonely coast reverberated with cries of greeting, relief, and delight. Ralluau announced that the work of colonization was to continue. De Monts had sent out a 150-ton ship, the *Jonas*, under the command of the sieur de Poutrincourt. With supplies and fifty men on board, the *Jonas* was on its way to Port Royal. Ralluau had come along the coast by long-boat, hoping to meet them, as he knew they had orders to leave if no ship arrived by the 15th July. So pinnace and long-boat together made their way back to Port Royal, which they reached at the end of the month to find the much larger *Jonas* already anchored in front of the Habitation.

In France de Monts had done his best to get the 1606 voyage off to an early start – in the teeth of considerable discouragement. The men he had brought back from Ste Croix had terrible tales to tell of cold, privations, sickness, death. The monopoly was as unpopular as ever. Expenses were enormous. Still he persisted, and on the 19th December, with the next voyage in mind, signed a contract with merchants from Rouen and St Malo as well as with Macain and Georges of La Rochelle. By February he had decided that his presence would be more useful to his company in Old than in New France. Gravé's term of office would be up. Who better to approach as his lieutenant and leader of the new expedition than Poutrincourt? The latter had already seen something of the country and was emphatic about his desire to settle there. In going to Port Royal he would be visiting the land de Monts had granted him, his own overseas estate as it were. De Monts himself still had hopes of settling a colony further south in a warmer climate. And then Poutrincourt was a known Catholic who spoke with some ardour of establishing the name of God among the Indians. His presence would lend colour to the King's claim that his main interest in New France was evangelical. So de Monts had dispatched a special messenger with a letter to Poutrincourt, then living at his seigneury of Guibermesnil in Picardy. Although entangled in lawsuits – he never really seemed to be free of them – Poutrincourt accepted the invitation. De Monts was arranging for the *Jonas* to leave La Rochelle early in April. Poutrincourt had a month in which to get ready. From the beginning he had wanted to involve his family in his New World venture, so on this occasion his son, Charles, aged fourteen, accompanied him.

Between the 15th and 20th March de Monts was busy in Paris signing contracts and interviewing artisans to be hired for the forthcoming year. Those engaged on this occasion were mostly men with some experience in construction: sawyers, masons, carpenters, joiners, locksmiths, a maker of edge-tools. There was also an apothecary and two tailors. Only some could sign their names. One locksmith, Jean Duval, who could write, placed a mark, approximately representing a key, before his signature. Just over two years later he was to achieve dubious distinction as the second Frenchman to be hanged in New France. (The first was one of Roberval's men hanged for theft in 1542–3. Duval's crime was to be the stirring up of a conspiracy to kill Champlain.) The wages agreed on ranged between 60 and 150 livres for the year, though provision was made in the likely event of the year's being extended. Most of the men received advance payment and were promised food and clothing as well. The tailors were at the lowest end of the scale with 60 livres each. The only man to receive 150 livres was François Guittard of St Germain-des-Prés, the maker of edge-tools. The services of his neighbour, the apothecary, were valued at 100 livres, which was the average wage for the masons. This apothecary was related by marriage to Poutrincourt through Poutrincourt's wife, Claude Pajot, who was of good Parisian bourgeois stock. His name, Louis Hébert, is still honoured in Quebec, of which he was to be the first real colonist. At this time he was already married to Marie Rollet, but she was not to see the new world for another eleven years.

Poutrincourt, too, was in Paris for the latter part of March. Protestant de Monts left it to him to look for a replacement for the pugilistic priest who, he surmised, would want to return after two years in the wilderness. They had no means of knowing that he was already dead. But it was Holy Week. The priests approached were busy with confessions, wanted time to come to a decision. And, in the light of subsequent events, one may wonder just how urgent Poutrincourt's search was for labourers in the Lord's vineyard.

He did, however, have a recruit of another profession. This was Marc Lescarbot, a lawyer then in his thirties whom Poutrincourt had met some years before. Lescarbot came from Vervins, a town just north of Rheims. It was a part of France that Poutrincourt knew, for his mother's family, the well-connected Salazars, had estates there. Vervins itself was the town where the important peace treaty between France and Spain had been drawn up in 1598. On that occasion Lescarbot had pronounced two Latin orations before the Papal Legate, later Pope Leo xi. For Lescarbot was a lawyer with literary pretensions, a confirmed scribbler who wielded a fluent pen. His wide education had given him a taste of scholarship (he knew Latin, Greek, and Hebrew) and had also alerted him to the fascinations of the world around him. He took a particular interest in medicine. At that time, however, he was experiencing a sense of disgust with his calling, as recently the courts had found against him – unjustly as it later turned out. Poutrincourt, knowing how intrigued he was by that largely undiscovered world across the Atlantic, suggested he should accompany him to Acadia. Lescarbot asked for a day's delay to make up his mind. Here unexpectedly offered him was a chance to see a new world for himself and flee a corrupt old one. It was an opportunity, too, to gather first-hand material for a book – though he did not then consciously plan to write one. So he agreed to go, and hurriedly packed clothes, paper, pen, ink, his Bible, and other books. As a result we have his *History of New France*, an invaluable source of information about those early days, written in a lively, vivid style. At times Lescarbot can be naïve, a little vain, blatantly propagandist in favour of his admired friend Poutrincourt, and maddeningly digressive when deploying his opinions and observations. But since he is so engagingly curious, he is not dull. Even his rather awful verse, decked out with all the rhetorical devices of the day, has a certain sprightliness.

He had no time to take leave of his mother but set out straight for La Rochelle. Later he wrote her a letter giving her the reasons for his abrupt departure. To reassure her he added that he was in the company of many 'men of honour in whose society I cannot but be edified.' Let us hope that mollified her!

Arriving at La Rochelle, he found de Monts and Poutrincourt already there. De Monts was obviously anxious to supervise the departure of the *Jonas* himself. Lescarbot had a little surprise for them, a poem he had composed on the journey entitled 'Adieu à la France.' De Monts and Poutrincourt were no doubt flattered, since what Lescarbot predicts for them is 'honneur,' 'gloire,' and 'immortelle vie.' It is they who are leading the way over rough seas and into an unknown land in order to 'jetter le fondement d'une Chretienne race' (lay the foundations for a Christian race). He found the clergy, 'the holy order,' lacking in zeal compared with 'l'ordre du mariage,' the married men. So Lescarbot, too, beats the salvation drum, insists that the main aim of these voyages is an altruistic one, the conversion of the savages.

How sincere was he? One answer might be that he was an enthusiast. His religion consisted of a not uninformed feeling for certain rites and beliefs. Rather than a dogmatic credo, it was this feeling for God's mercy and justice, symbolized by the Cross, that Lescarbot hoped would be communicated to the Indians, so their souls might be saved from hell. But with Lescarbot's sense of the sacraments went a certain lack of respect for those who conferred them. The Reformation had not left him untouched. Indeed it was quite usual at this time to find educated and fairly devout Catholics who were moved by the traditional rites, had no real desire to become Protestants, and yet were sceptical of much that concerned the Church. Besides, as a patriotic Frenchman, Lescarbot inclined to Gallicanism and state supervision of church affairs.

Religion and the glory of their enterprise were subjects Lescarbot would have touched on with his fellow voyagers. There is good reason to believe that among them were Claude La Tour and his son. Claude de Saint-Etienne de La Tour, as he liked to style himself, was an engaging adventurer of Parisian origins, who had charmed then married the extremely well-connected Marie de Salazar of Champagne, a close relative of Poutrincourt's own mother, Jeanne de Salazar. Marie by then was dead but had left behind a son, Charles, at this point about fourteen years old and some months younger than Poutrincourt's son, the other Charles.

The two boys may well have known one another from birth, since the La Tour domain that Claude inherited from Marie was near the St Just seigneury, which Jeanne was to leave our Poutrincourt. Indeed one of young Charles de Biencourt's titles was Baron de St Just. Of the two cousins it was the adventurer's son, every whit as charming as his father, who was to become famous in the annals of Acadia – far better known, in fact, than Poutrincourt or *his* young Charles. Here it might be observed that with the La Tours and Hébert, Poutrincourt's wife's cousin, it was quite a family party that the new commander of Port Royal had gathered together.

Another son was of the company, Robert Gravé, son of the redoubtable François. He was then about twenty-one or twenty-two and all set to launch upon an adventurous career. By every account he was favoured with a splendid physique, good looks, and an alert, practical intelligence.

Captain du Boullay, whom we have already met, was going out again to give support to his old commander. There was also a young man named Le Fèvre from Rethel near Rheims, probably another of Poutrincourt's Champagne acquaintances. All we learn of him is that he, like Poutrincourt, was terribly sea-sick on this voyage and did not emerge from his cabin until the ship reached the Grand Banks. Others that we know about are Ralluau, of course, the surgeon, Estienne, and Daniel Hay, a man who loved 'to display his courage among the dangers of the deep.' François Addendin, de Monts' personal servant, accompanied them. And there was a black man who could not, however, have been Mathieu d'Acosta, the interpreter, for he was to die and be dissected at Port Royal. The captain was the same Guillaume Foulques who had been out with de Monts in 1604 and had taken command of Rossignol's *Levrette* on the return journey.

Agents of the firm of Macain and Georges saw to the loading of the ship with food and supplies. Lescarbot, who liked his tipple, happily noted forty-five hogsheads of wine. With all the animals on board, the *Jonas*, at times, must have smelt and sounded like a farmyard. For there were pigs and a sheep, as well as fowls and pigeons securely caged to protect them from the gentlemen's dogs. In taking pigeons they were probably planning on building a dovecote for domestic use, of the sort that was then an important feature in farmyards. (A particularly fine example still stands today at the Hamel farm near the ruins of Poutrincourt chateau in Picardy, much as Poutrincourt himself must have seen it.)

While waiting for wind and tide, the gentry celebrated the end of Lent with copious feasting. Groaning, they declared they were looking forward to more meagre meals at sea. The workmen, recklessly lavish with their advance pay in their pockets, set up a merry din in their quarter of the town. Protestant La Rochelle was shocked. Sober officials clapped the unruly revellers into the town gaol until it was time to sail. Lescarbot, with the class consciousness of his age, conceded that some of the workmen were 'quiet and respectful.' Still, from his superior distance, he shook his head in bewilderment at their junketings: 'the common people is a queer beast.'

In the second week of April, just about the time that the pinnace, on her way to Florida, was wrecked off Port Royal, the *Jonas* lay at anchor outside the harbour of La Rochelle all ready for departure. But a violent wind rose at night and battered her against the ramparts. Next day the whole town turned out to see the frustrated gentlemen voyagers frantically pumping to save the ship from sinking altogether while most of the hired workmen, when called upon to help, shrugged their shoulders and laughed. It was not their enterprise after all – why should they worry? One begins to get a glimmer of one of the reasons why colonization took so long to get started in New France. The workmen, on whom so much depended, were paid underlings, not participants or even indentured men.

So the departure was delayed for another month. At great expense the ship went into refit. During this period of enforced idleness, Lescarbot turned his mind to religious matters. The Protestant ministers of La Rochelle, he heard, probably from de Monts, prayed every day for the conversion of the savages. Lescarbot reproachfully failed to note the same concern among the Catholics. Since there were a number of clerics in this seaport town, he thought that some of them 'would have been glad to sail the billows,' which they could see from the ramparts. But no priest could be found willing to make the journey. This required, he was told, 'an extraordinary zeal and piety.' Someone suggested he should apply to the Jesuits. But this, said Lescarbot hastily, 'we could not then do, our ship having almost her full lading.' It was an obvious evasion prompted by the one word, 'Jesuit,' which, for reasons we shall explore later, sent shivers down certain spines, Catholic as well as Protestant.

Finally, on the 13th May, the *Jonas* sailed. Despite being seasick at first, or in a characteristic phrase 'yielding up the tribute to Neptune,' Lescarbot seems to have enjoyed life on board. He got used to eating as plates and dishes slid violently to and fro on the table and learnt the trick of swaying to the movement of the ship while holding his wine glass firmly to his mouth. He admired the courage and dexterity of the sailors, made notes on winds and waters, mists and fogs, birds and fish; also on the anatomy of the porpoise which, he perceptively saw, had 'bones not in form of fishbones, but like a four-footed creature.' To while away the time when becalmed, they bathed in the sea, danced on deck, sang rounds. Lescarbot's breezy account of his sea voyage does something to offset, though of course it does not diminish, the horror that more usually characterizes tales of Atlantic crossings.

Two months after their departure, on the 15th July, they were at last off Canso. After a week of fog and bad weather the sun shone out suddenly, and the men on the *Jonas* saw two long-boats coming towards them with Indian men in one and Frenchmen in the other. The Indians arrived first, offering the ever-curious Lescarbot his first view of the 'savages' whom he was already predisposed to admire. He found them handsome enough but was somewhat disappointed that they were not attired in their best furs. While eating and drinking, these Indians were able to give them news of what had been happening at Port Royal. The other long-boat brought men from St Malo who were associated with de Monts' company. They were angry and frustrated. Those cursed Basques, they exclaimed, had again been bartering with the Indians and had got away with about six thousand skins! So much for the King's orders and de Monts' monopoly.

From Canso, Ralluau and a small company of men set sail in a long-boat to look for Gravé and happily encountered him as we have seen. On the 23rd July the *Jonas* put in at Port Mouton for wood and water. So Lescarbot was able to visit the very spot where the sheep had drowned. He noted the trees and plants and was enthusiastic about the beach peas they picked to take back to the ship. The cabins that Poutrincourt and others had built two years before were still intact. But they spent only two hours there, so had no time to go hunting for rabbits. Poutrincourt obviously remembered his first extended visit to Port Mouton and the sport to be had there with some nostalgia.

On the 27th the *Jonas* sailed through the Gut. Faithful to his promise to keep an eye on things, Membertou roused Miquelet and La Taille. Lescarbot heard how he 'came to the French fort ... crying as a madman, saying in his language: "What! You stand here a-dining (for it was about noon) and do not see a great ship that cometh here, and we know not what men they are."' He himself went out in a canoe with his daughter, and found, to his relief, that the newcomers were indeed friends. Miquelet and La Taille set the Habitation cannons roaring a welcome. The men on the ship returned the salute with cannon-shot, musket-shot, and trumpeting.

Four days later Ralluau arrived in his long-boat, and Gravé and Champlain returned in their two pinnaces. It was a joyful reunion, particularly, one might imagine, between Gravé *père* and his handsome young son. With lordly largesse Poutrincourt broached one of his own casks of wine for everyone to drink from. Some took full advantage of the invitation and drank, Lescarbot says, 'until their caps turned round.' Reproach was out of place. For a third winter in a row a colony of Frenchmen prepared themselves to outface cold, blizzards, and disease.

CHAPTER SIX

Beyond Mallebarre

AT FIRST THEY EXPECTED TO SEE THE WINTER THROUGH else-where than at Port Royal, for de Monts had instructed Poutrincourt to resettle the colony 'in a warmer country beyond Mallebarre.' But it was already August, and summer was nearly over. What should they do? There was little time left to explore. Poutrincourt consulted his chief officers, who all agreed that it was too late in the season to think of moving elsewhere. Instead it was decided that, in September, Poutrincourt should make a reconnais-sance voyage south. Then, having found, they hoped, a warmer and more suitable spot, the expedition would return to winter at Port Royal. Poutrincourt lost no time in getting some men to till and manure the ground. Although Port Royal was regarded now as merely a temporary site, it was Poutrincourt's domain and he was anxious to see how good the soil was for farming. The place he chose to cultivate was right at the mouth of the Equille (the Annapolis) River. (It was here that some decades later the French established a fort that the English eventually took over and named Fort Anne.)

In mid-August Poutrincourt's men made a second tilling and planted seeds. The rich earth responded beautifully. Within eight days little green shoots of varying shapes appeared above the ground, promising wheat, rye, hemp, flax, turnips, radishes, and cabbages. It seemed that crops could flourish as well here as in Poutrincourt's native Picardy. Seafaring Gravé was taken on a triumphant tour of the new fields so he could give a good report of agricultural possibilities in Acadia. Lescarbot was enthusiastic about the future. He accepted that the colony might go south, but for the moment rejoiced in Port Royal.

Might it not one day, with the importation of grapevines of course, become quite self-sufficient? For, Lescarbot was convinced, 'he that hath corn, wine, cattle, woollen and linen, leather, iron, and afterward codfish, he needeth no other treasures for the necessaries of life.'

On the 22nd August the settlers received a visit that brought them to the harsh realities underlying the pastoral dream. Fields could flourish only if subsidized by monopoly of the fur trade. And here was des Antons of St Malo, the captain who had brought the fresh supplies to them last year at Ste Croix, with the depressing news that several ships had been seen illicitly trading with the Indians at Cape Breton. One in particular was commanded by Boyer, a merchant from Rouen, guilty not only of disobeying the King but also of breaking his word. For Poutrincourt, while in La Rochelle, had released Boyer from prison on the merchant's firm promise not to sail out and engage in trade again. Gravé was all set to give chase. This was much more in his line of business than looking at crops. Besides, it was time for the *Jonas* to return to France. With Gravé went all the men who had wintered at Port Royal except three: Fougeray de Vitré, still undeterred by the harsh climate, Champdoré, and, of course, Champlain.

The departure for France of the *Jonas* inspired Lescarbot to further poetic utterance. Bidding his fellow Frenchmen farewell in his 'Adieu aux Français,' he delivered himself of the first poem written in the New World north of Florida. Not a masterpiece, alas! But then, he explains, he wrote it in the midst of the din made by men running around and hammering everywhere as they got their lodgings ready for the winter. Most of the 'Adieu' is devoted to rather laboured poetic praise of the beauties and promise of Port Royal. But he does not forget the colonizers, and Gravé, whom Lescarbot calls Dupont, receives a trumpet-toot of glory as outgoing commander of the fort:

> DU PONT dont la vertu vole jusques aux cieux
> Pour avoir sceu domter d'un coeur audacieux
> En ces difficultés mille maux, mille peines,
> Qui pouvaient souz le faix accravanter tes veines …

> (DU PONT, whose name is graven on the sky
> For having stood with matchless bravery
> Against a thousand ills, a thousand pains,
> Enough to crush the spirit in your veins …

The poem concludes with Lescarbot's consigning his 'généreux François' (Frenchmen of stout heart) to Neptune's care. And Neptune did indeed see the *Jonas* safely home over the Atlantic.

Lescarbot had farewells to make not only to the homeward-bound but also to those going on the reconnaissance voyage south. Poutrincourt ordered the eighteen-ton pinnace to be got ready. He himself was to be in command, with Champdoré reinstated as pilot. (Did Champlain raise a quiet eyebrow, or simply accept that there was no one else available?) Young Charles de Biencourt went with his father, also Louis Hébert the apothecary, Estienne the surgeon, Robert Gravé, and some sailors and workmen, among them the adventurous Daniel Hay and the locksmith, Jean Duval. After a couple of false starts the expedition finally got under way on the 5th September, leaving Lescarbot in charge at the Habitation.

Had one long sea voyage proved enough for Lescarbot? His activities suggest that he was delighted to be back on land again. For this rather literary lawyer had a natural love of gardening. True, he loved to cite resounding examples, both biblical and classical, of great men who had not disdained to till the soil: Noah, Cincinnatus ... But there was nothing affected about the sheer hard work Lescarbot was prepared to put into his garden. Before leaving, Gravé and his men must have mentioned the moisture that seeped through the walls in the winter, so Lescarbot now had a ditch dug all around the fort.

The workmen were required to spend only three hours a day on their various trades. They, too, learned to adapt themselves to different tasks. Masons successfully tried their hand at baking; a sawyer, turned charcoal-burner, produced a fair pile of fuel. And they still had plenty of time to go looking for shellfish, which they found everywhere: under the rocks and in the mud of the beach when the tide was low.

The Port Royal Indians, then and later, generously brought half their catch of fish or game to the Habitation. The remaining half they often bartered for bread. Addendin, de Monts' personal servant, gratefully remembered by gourmet Lescarbot, kept the gentlemen's table plentifully supplied with wildfowl: bustards, ducks, wild geese, and plovers. To wash all this down everyone received each day a pint and a half of 'pure and good wine.' This 'September liquor' Lescarbot considered 'a sovereign prophylactic against the ravages of scurvy.'

At night, while the men talked and argued and sang, Lescarbot would retire to his room to read, write, plan some other literary surprise. He did not feel he was exaggerating when he called Port Royal an 'Earthly Paradise, a Promised Land.' De Monts and Champlain had spoken of those fertile places farther south where the Indians tilled and hoed and produced fine crops. Lescarbot refused to believe they could be any lovelier than Port Royal.

Meanwhile, the exploration party on board the pinnace were on their way in search of a warmer paradise. On the 7th September they arrived at the mouth of the Ste Croix. Here the pinnace was nearly dashed to pieces against a rocky island. Champlain names the cause of this near-distaster with tight-lipped severity. Again it was 'Champdoré's obstinacy, to which he was very subject.'

There in Passamaquoddy Bay they met a number of Indians assembled in canoes. Among these were the two chiefs who had guided Champlain to the Chignecto Bay area in search of copper: Messamouet, the Micmac chief from La Have, who, it will be remembered, had visited Bayonne, and Secoudun, the Etchemin of the Saint John River, who had helped the French home when their pinnace was wrecked outside Port Royal. They were off on a good-will mission to the none-too-friendly Almouchiquois farther south.

Leaving the pinnace, Poutrincourt and Champlain went up river in a long-boat to Ste Croix Island. Poutrincourt visited and prayed over the graves of the men he had known on his first journey out. It was a sober reminder of what winter could bring. Both Poutrincourt and Champlain were curious to see how de Monts' crops had fared. Vegetables and grain, they were pleased to see, had come up thick and strong. Poutrincourt arranged for some of the wheat to be taken back to Lescarbot at Port Royal.

Back on the pinnace at the mouth of the river they had to come to a decision. Red leaves flared a warning among the dense green of the woods. Should they make straight for Cape Cod and explore below Mallebarre, or should they follow the coast? Champlain, eager to see more, was naturally in favour of sailing directly to Mallebarre. But Poutrincourt, the official leader, decided to skirt along the coast. It is quite possible that one of his reasons for doing so was that Messamouet and Secoudun had pressed for French support in their dealings with the Almouchiquois. De Monts had, after all, presented the French to the Indians as peacemakers. In such a dilemma – the delights of exploration versus duty to allies – Champlain would have felt torn. It was he who had successfully initiated diplomatic relations with Bessabez two years before, telling him that the French hoped to reconcile the hostile tribes. But later he was to regret Poutrincourt's decision and the wasted time.

More precious time was lost on the Penobscot where the pinnace had to be refitted. (This expedition was to prove more bedevilled than most by bad weather and accidents.) Fast currents then carried them on past the mouth of the Kennebec to Casco Bay, where Marchin, the dignified chief who had so impressed de Monts and Champlain the year before, greeted them with a loud and solemn 'Hé, hé.' The French-Almouchiquois alliance was renewed with a prodigality of presents: knives, hatchets, and beads for the Almouchiquois, moose meat for the French. From there they made their way to the Island of Bacchus first visited by Champlain in July the previous year when the grapes were still small. Now, in September, he found them 'ripe and fairly good' with 'a fruit as fine as those of France.'

On the 21st they reached Saco, to be greeted by the agricultural Almouchiquois with whom their Indian friends were hoping for a parley. Onemechin, the handsome young chief, handed over a Micmac prisoner to Poutrincourt. About fifteen canoes, full of painted warriors, circled round the pinnace. Then they came on board, to be treated to a spirited oration by Messamouet. For almost an hour he held their attention, gesturing dramatically as he made his bid for a friendly alliance. It was in their interest, he assured them, to join forces with his tribe against other enemies, and take advantage of the French desire to trade and explore. He himself had visited France and had seen what wonderful things the French had to offer. In a moment of magnificence, he cast into Onemechin's canoe all the kettles, hatchets, knives, red jackets, and food he had obtained by barter. The French looked on in amazement at such prodigality. In their reckoning, this one gesture cost more than nine hundred livres! Night came on and the visiting Almouchiquois returned to shore.

The next day Onemechin responded by sending out a canoe laden with presents for Messamouet: corn, tobacco, beans, and pumpkins. The Micmac chief was outraged. Onemechin had not even bothered to make a speech in reply to his impassioned oration and was now fobbing him off with a few vegetables. He left for La Have in high dudgeon. In terms of Indian etiquette this was a *casus belli*. There would be war yet.

Secoudun, however, remained with the French who went on past

Cape Ann to discover a fine harbour that Champlain, somewhat to his chagrin, had missed on the previous voyage. This now popular resort of Gloucester harbour the admiring French called Beauport (Fine Port). Here they were greeted by a band of dancing Indians who seemed as merry as they were numerous. Poutrincourt was especially intrigued by their musical instruments, pipes made from painted reeds. But his ear judged their music to be far less tuneful than the pastoral melodies piped by the shepherds of his native Picardy. There was the usual polite exchange of presents. The French noticed, however, that these Indians were not averse to helping themselves to knives and hatchets, which they adroitly slipped between their buttocks or shuffled under the sand with their feet.

But if the French considered these people thieves, what did the native inhabitants make of *them*? Thinking that de Monts might like to transfer his settlement here, Poutrincourt had some land tilled for future plantings. Did he, one wonders, ask permission? In the absence of interpreters that seems unlikely. Might not the Almouchiquois then have regarded these white men, confidently taking over their land, as a threat? They knew, too, that such foreigners brought with them diseases that had already considerably diminished the numbers of their northern neighbours.

A certain incident indicates that the French were indeed not welcome here. While the ship was being caulked, fifty armed warriors, moving in single file, silently advanced upon some men who were washing their clothes in a stream. The sight of Champlain alone on a causeway and a glimpse of Poutrincourt with eight musketeers watching them from the woods stopped them in their tracks. In one concerted movement they formed a circle, began to sing and dance. Some then went up to trade with the men at the stream. Not one hostile word was spoken but the air was thick with suspicion.

The next day it was even thicker. For who should come visiting the pinnace with the local chief but their good-looking acquaintance from Saco, Onemechin? He had promised friendship with the French, but how seriously had he meant it? What was he doing in league with these possible enemies? Poutrincourt pretended not to notice anything and presented Onemechin with a suit of clothes. But he found it too cumbersome and gave it away in parts, the doublet here, the hose there. Did he consider French friendship as superfluous as their finery?

The atmosphere at Beauport continued uneasy. Onemechin paid another visit to the pinnace, talked, dined, and announced the arrival the next day of a huge number of men in canoes – six hundred according to Lescarbot, two thousand to Champlain, so the sign language cannot have been altogether clear. By now it was the 30th September and time, the French wisely decided, to be off.

They sailed into Cape Cod Bay, then rounded Cape Cod. On the 2nd October, during a spell of bad weather, they anchored off Mallebarre. They had been voyaging for almost a month and Champlain was still no farther south than he had been the previous year. Then, when favourable winds *did* start to blow the pinnace southward, the rudder broke. The explorers managed to round the southern point of Monomoy (Cap Batturier – Reef Cape – to the French), and a local Indian, discovered by Daniel Hay, guided them into the welcome but somewhat shallow waters of today's Chatham Roads and Stage Harbour.

Here the explorers spent two weeks. They set up a forge on the beach so they could mend the rudder. An oven, too, so they could bake fresh bread. Champlain's general impression was very favourable. He liked the scenery, the cleared land, the little cultivated hills where the usual corn and beans grew. He was chiefly impressed by the fact that they stored corn for the winter, placing it in grass sacks and burying it four to six feet down in the sand. These were the first Indians he had come across who seemed more like the provident ant than the feckless grasshopper.

The French occupied their time here with characteristic pursuits. They made contact with the Indians in the usual way by trading, the Indians bringing them grapes in little reed baskets. Besides making notes on the native inhabitants and their ways, Champlain studied the terrain. Hébert, the plant-loving apothecary, uprooted some vines to take back to Port Royal, but eventually, much to Lescarbot's disappointment, left them behind. Poutrincourt went hunting and also put on something of a military display in order to overawe the inhabitants, whose large numbers and lack of respect for French property made the visitors mistrustful. The Indians may have been impressed by watching these newcomers flourish naked swords and pierce thick pieces of wood with their muskets. They cannot have appreciated being fired upon by these same muskets. Yet that is what one of the crew did on seeing an

Indian make off with a hatchet – not exactly a wise or diplomatic gesture.

By the 14th October the rudder was fixed, the ship ready to sail. On the shore the French erected a cross to indicate that Christians had been there. Poutrincourt, Champlain, and some of their musketeers made a last long excursion inland. They found the atmosphere strange and unsettled. Small armed bands lurked in the woods, hid in the grass. Women were packing up and moving off with the children as though they were being sent out of the way. Poutrincourt and Champlain steadily went on handing out presents to the Indians they encountered – trinkets for the women, knives and axes for the men – pretended not to notice any suspicious activities, and were careful not to be the first to attack.

Back on the beach Poutrincourt warned the men at the little encampment that there was trouble brewing. It looked as though the Indians might launch a surprise attack during the night. Though at night most of the men usually retired to the pinnace, some remained on land to guard the equipment it was inconvenient to shunt every day between ship and shore. Now, however, Poutrincourt ordered every-one to return to the pinnace. But there was still some bread baking in the oven. A few men stayed behind to see to that.

At midnight Poutrincourt realized they were still on shore and sent the long-boat with orders that they were to come aboard immediately. One of the men on shore was a swaggering young spark who 'played the cock and ringleader.' They had hot biscuits to eat, he called back, made at the same time as the bread. If the others wanted to drag him on to the boat, he swore they would have to get him drunk first. He laughed when the men in the long-boat pointed out that if they stayed on shore they risked being surprised by the Indians or punished by Poutrin-court. They could look after themselves, he shouted. They had swords, muskets, and just a few days before, they had fired twice at one of those thieving savages.

Spurred on by this bravado, some men from the long-boat joined the daredevils on shore, while one of these, Poutrincourt's personal servant, obediently returned to the pinnace with the rest. By the time they got back, Poutrincourt was asleep, never thinking that his orders had been disobeyed. He was not told that five men were still on shore, sitting by the fire, enjoying hot biscuits and savouring their recklessness.

By daybreak they had all fallen asleep except for one man who was supposed to be on watch. But even he did not hear the stealthy approach of about four hundred Indians creeping up over a little hill. A salvo of arrows whistled through the air. The men staggered up, called for help. The ringleader, Lescarbot relates, fell, 'face downwards, with a little dog upon his back, both transfixed and transpierced by the same arrow.' Another man, too, was killed almost immediately. A third reached the water's edge, then collapsed. A fourth was badly wounded. Jean Duval, the locksmith, with one arrow in his chest, escaped death this time – only to be hanged two years later. (Indeed his story reads like a cautionary tale: he started by thumbing his nose at authority and ended on the gallows for inciting his companions to put down tyranny and kill Champlain.) Once the arrows had hit, the Indians broke into loud, triumphant war-whoops.

Poutrincourt, Champlain, and others leaped up, still in their shirts, grabbed their muskets, jumped into the long-boat, and made for shore. But the swift-footed Indians fled and, from a safe distance, jeeringly danced and sang, while the French buried their dead beneath the cross they had set up the day before. Then, as the tide began to ebb, they returned to the pinnace.

The victorious Indians reappeared on shore, pulled down the cross and 'dug up one of the dead, took off his shirt and put it on, holding up the spoils which they carried off.' As if this were not insult enough, 'they also turned their backs to the [pinnace] and made mock of us by taking sand in their hands and casting it between their buttocks, yelping the while like wolves.'

Marooned on their pinnace, the outraged French redoubled fire from their little brass cannon. But the Indians simply threw themselves down upon the sand and let the shot fly over them.

The rising tide brought the angry, musket-armed French and Secoudun, their Etchemin ally, back to shore. Secoudun in great fury wanted to give chase and take them all on single-handed. The French managed to hold him back. Once again they buried the bodies and set up the cross. The scene of this misfortune – the worst that had as yet befallen them – they called Port Fortuné, probably reverse-naming out of superstition.

On the next day, the 16th October, they put out of this most unpropitious place and sailed along the southern coast of Cape Cod.

Champlain's plan of Port Fortuné (Stage Harbor);
several events superimposed

A Placc where Frenchmen were making bread; B Indians surprising the French; C Frenchmen burned by Indians; D Stricken Frenchmen making for pinnace ('D' omitted by engraver); E Troops of Indians burning the Frenchmen they have killed; F 'Mountain' overlooking the harbour; G Indians' lodges; H Frenchmen on shore charging Indians (tall figure Poutrincourt?); I Indians defeated by Frenchmen; L Shallop in which the French were; M Indians around the shallop; N The sieur de Poutrincourt's pinnace; O The harbour; P Small stream; Q Frenchmen fallen dead into the water; R Stream coming from certain marshes; S Woods through which Indians approached

They sighted Isle Douteuse – still doubtful, as we do not know whether this was Martha's Vineyard or Horseshoe Shoal. Then storms drove them back into Port Fortuné – at least it had a reasonable harbour. They saw no Indians.

On the 20th they were off again along the coast. Champlain gave his own name to the little Mashpee river, probably realizing by then that this was as far south as they were likely to get. The coast looked promising but was difficult to approach. For the third time they made for shallow but sheltered Port Fortuné.

It was decidedly an unlucky spot. Within a few hours of their arrival young Robert Gravé lost three fingers of a hand when firing off a musket, which exploded without, however, harming anyone else. Unfavourable winds kept them lingering there. Still smarting under the Indian victory, the French hatched a plan to get revenge. Poutrincourt's main aim was to capture some of this tribe and take them to Port Royal to cut wood and grind corn at the hand-mill, a task everyone loathed. But how to get near them? Poutrincourt had an idea. The French would have to dissemble, pretend they were still anxious to trade, and would like to smoke with the Indians. While luring them on towards the long-boat with offers of goods, ten of his strongest men were to throw rosary beads round their necks and lengths of 'match' round their waists, and then drag them onto the ship. ('Match' was a long string of tow, one end of which was kept smouldering so fire was always available.)

It was a complicated stratagem and clumsily executed. Startled, the Indians pulled away, but the French, as were their orders, had their swords at the ready. They stabbed and hacked at the Indians, who could not get away at their usual speed since their feet were in the water. Six or seven were killed and Secoudun made himself richer by several scalps. Now French and Etchemin might consider they had exacted their revenge, but some Frenchmen, too, were injured in this inglorious mêlée, and had to be helped back to the pinnace.

Not a pretty tale, this first recorded incident we have, from the time of de Monts' arrival, of French killing Indians. But though Poutrincourt's stratagem may strike us today as low and dishonourable, we should remember that such trickery was common both in European warfare and Indian blood feuds.

Over the next few days the Port Fortuné Indians tried to draw the

French onto the land. But any attempted retaliation dwindled into a strange game of hide-and-seek, with the Indians taking off when Poutrincourt, Champlain, and armed men approached their places of ambush.

By now everyone began to think longingly of Port Royal. The wounded badly needed attention, for the surgeon had not brought enough healing salve with him. 'This,' remarks Champlain severely, 'was a great mistake on his part, and a grief to the sick men as well as to us, inasmuch as the stench from their wounds in a small vessel like ours was so great that we could scarcely bear it.' Champlain rarely complains. The smell must indeed have been awful.

Champlain had another reason to be discouraged. In his commission to de Monts, the King claimed the coastline for the French from the fortieth degree to the forty-sixth. But on this voyage the French, much to Champlain's disappointment, had got no farther south than 41°31', only twenty minutes beyond the latitude reached the year before. This was the last occasion Champlain had to explore this coast, though of course he did not realize that then. It was soon to be claimed by France's northern neighbour, England.

For there, Weymouth's 1605 voyage and his kidnapped Indians had aroused the curiosity of merchants who proved to be far more enterprising than their French counterparts. In the summer of 1606 yet another English expedition had come out to explore the Kennebec–Cape Cod area – which the French still considered to be part of New France. And in April of that year, while de Monts and Poutrincourt were busy organizing the departure of the *Jonas* from La Rochelle, King James of England had granted a patent for the plantation of Virginia. Two companies were involved. The London Company was given rights to the coast between the thirty-fourth and the forty-first degrees. It was this company that was to settle Virginia itself. The other, the Plymouth Company, was granted the coastline between the thirty-eighth and forty-fifth degrees of latitude, a claim which gobbled up Acadia. Yet at this time the French made no remonstrance to the English. Henri's ambassador to the English court may not even have noticed the encroachment, the Netherlands then being the focal point of Anglo-French diplomacy. The English were in such a hurry to start their Virginian settlement that they set out in the depths of winter. On the 19th December three ships bound for the plantation of Virginia set sail with 105 men. It was an expedition that was to have vast consequences for world history. And the following year, 1607, John Popham and Raleigh Gilbert arrived to build a colony at the mouth of the Kennebec.

Unaware of these impending English settlements, Poutrincourt vowed he would return in the summer to explore beyond Mallebarre. But the French had lost their chance. In 1613, eight years later, Poutrincourt was to realize to his cost just how thoroughly New England had ousted New France.

The voyage back to Port Royal was long, stormy, and filled with alarms. Between Mount Desert Island and Great Wass the rudder broke again and they had to beach the pinnace on an island in order to fix it. Here some Etchemins came in a canoe to tell Secoudun that fellow tribesmen had made a raid on the Kennebec Indians, who were near neighbours and allies of the Almouchiquois. The Etchemins had killed some men and captured women whom they later put to death near Mount Desert Island. The injured Kennebec tribe, aided by the Almouchiquois, would surely seek reprisals. Secoudun's diplomatic mission south had failed. Nevertheless, he was in good spirits when, on the 10th November, the French put him on shore – with some supplies and his Port Fortuné scalps to hang about his neck, bite at during the victory dance, and flaunt as Europeans did their captured flags.

On the 14th November, after more storms, batterings, and another near-fatal accident right outside the port, they at last passed safely through the Gut. As they sailed towards the Habitation, Poutrincourt and Champlain might have reflected that all in all it had been a disheartening two months. They had lost men in an encounter with hostile Indians. And their efforts to mediate between Etchemins and Almouchiquois had come to nothing. Still, experience can always be put on the credit side even when it does not represent any concrete achievement. Since the expedition had survived so many perils, the French could console themselves with the thought that the saving hand of God must still be with them, encouraging them in all their endeavours.

CHAPTER SEVEN

A Winter of Good Cheer

HE PINNACE ANCHORED OFF THE HABITATION – a welcome sight on a stark November day. As Poutrincourt and the others lowered themselves into the long-boat, a curious mythological vision met their eyes. There in person was Father Neptune himself approaching in a small boat drawn by six Tritons. The tailors, turned costume designers, had been busy. The boat was draped with the sea god's colours; a blue veil fluttered round the deity's figure and his legs were encased in buskins, the elevated boots that denoted serious drama. His hair and beard flowed in long silvery locks. In one hand he held an imposing trident. (Had François Guittard been at work in the forge or was this a converted gardening fork?) Another canoe, containing four 'Indians,' followed. Neptune's 'chariot' drew alongside the long-boat, and both paused upon the waters. Then the sea god raised his hand in a gesture of command and addressed Poutrincourt in fluent though not particularly elegant Alexandrines:

> Arrête Sagamos, arrête-toy ici,
> Et regardes un dieu qui a de toy souci.
> Si tu ne me conois, Saturne fut mon père,
> Je suis de Jupiter et de Pluton le frère.
>
> (Halt, mighty Sagamo, no further fare!
> Look on a god who holds thee in his care.
> Thou knows't me not? I am of Saturn's line
> Brother to Pluto dark and Jove divine.

The marine member of the pagan Trinity then gave a resounding account of what mankind had achieved to date through the good graces of his oceans: travel to farthermost ports, transportation of exotic goods, adventure.

> Si l'homme veut avoir une heureuse fortune
> Il lui faut implorer le secours de Neptune.
> Car celui qui chez soi demeure casanier
> Merite seulement le nom de cuisinier.

> (If man would taste the spice of fortune's savour
> He needs must seek the aid of Neptune's favour.
> For stay-at-homes who doze on kitchen settles
> Earn no more glory than their pots and kettles.)

Brandishing his trident, Neptune swore to further Poutrincourt's noble designs. Had he not shielded him and his men time and again from the Fates? (This was truer than Lescarbot could then have guessed.) Destiny as well as Neptune favoured a flourishing French Empire. From the New World would re-echo

> Le renom immortel de De Monts et de toy
> Souz le regne puissant de Henry votre Roy.

> (Thine own, de Monts' and puissant Henry's name.)

At that point a trumpet sounded and the six Tritons raised to their lips the trumpets with which they had been furnished in lieu of conches. Poutrincourt unsheathed his sword and the Tritons proceeded, each in turn, to declaim variations on Neptune's theme of a triumphant New France. The fifth, however, interrupted these strains of glory to provide light relief with some amusing Gascon verses. (A comparable effect would be that of introducing a pawky ballad in Broad Scots into a flowery English oration.) Old Neptune, it appeared, had not been acting his age and had been caught philandering like some young gallant. These greybeards were not to be trusted. After flirting outrageously they would make off when they pleased. Was Lescarbot here risking a joking allusion to the King himself, a greybeard still notorious for falling in love far too often with far too many ladies? A word Lescarbot uses, 'bergalant,' is the Gascon form of Vert-Galant (fresh or evergreen gallant) – a name by which Henri is still remembered today. (Visitors to Paris may recall the Square du Vert-Galant below the equestrian statue of Henri on the Pont Neuf.) But if Lescarbot was introducing a light-hearted topical allusion into his solemn masque, he quickly corrected it with poker-faced propriety. The sixth Triton began with a more fitting salute:

Vive Henri le grand Roi des François

(Long life to Henry sovran King of France).

Neptune's chariot then gave way to the canoe, manned by 'Indians' who were obviously Frenchmen with painted faces and dressed in beaver cloaks and moccasins. The gifts they presented were of Indian origin: a quarter of moose, beaver skins, and wampum. But the speeches came straight from Lescarbot's study. The first Indian improbably insisted that he could hardly wait for Poutrincourt to introduce 'piété' and 'moeurs civils' (piety and civilized ways) into the wilderness. Another assured him that in New France, too, Cupid's burning arrow struck fire into the hearts of men. He had brought wampum made by his mistress' fair hands, and at her insistence. So

> She would be sad and in distress
> And lose her pretty playfulness
> If promptly and with nimbleness,
> I cannot speak of some kindness
> Conferred on me by your highness.

The fourth, who had no luck in the chase, swore he would abjure Diana and became a votary of Neptune's – that is, he would give up hunting for fishing. Meanwhile – the one real Indian touch – he asked Poutrincourt for 'caracona' – bread.

Poutrincourt obviously fell into the spirit of the thing. He thanked Neptune, and then the assembled company broke out in a four-part song, begging Neptune to grant that they might all meet again some day in France. So in all this brave talk of establishing New France, homesickness for the old one raises a nostalgic note. Then everyone, including some of the real Indians, made for the Habitation. The trumpet sounded, and the cannon boomed and re-echoed as if 'Proserpina were giving birth to a child.' (Lescarbot, like the Indians, loved these echoes and often mentioned them.)

As the returned travellers passed through the gate, they could see displayed upon it three coats of arms: the lilies of France, de Monts' three triangles or monticules, and the Biencourt lion rampant. Around them twined wreaths of laurel (indigenous bayberry) with Latin mottoes affixed below. However discouraging their voyage might have been, these emblems bore vivid witness to French perseverance in the New World.

Here at the entrance to the fort a 'fellow of merry humour' welcomed Poutrincourt, then, turning towards the courtyard, called on an unseen army of cooks and stewards to get the poultry on the spits and to pour the wine. For their good companions had returned 'as keen of tooth as kidney.' Bowing, he stepped aside to let them pass, inviting them first to sneeze away all the chill air and then fill their brains with the sweet fumes of wine. The masque ended in a veritable orgy of audience participation as everyone sneezed, laughed, and drank. It was a more cheerful return to the Habitation than any of them had anticipated. Even Champlain, who did not like Lescarbot very much, mentions these 'jollities' with approval.

So unfolded the first theatrical performance in North America, 'Le Théâtre de Neptune.' The historian Marcel Trudel quotes a contemporary of Lescarbot as saying that 'when the French settle somewhere, the first thing they do is set up a theatre; the English a shop and the Spaniards a convent.' But to offset this commercial image of the English, we may remember that this was the period of some of Shakespeare's greatest plays. *King Lear* was performed before James I the day after Christmas that very year, just six weeks after this masque upon the waters of Port Royal.

Lescarbot was quite conscious of the fact that his 'entertainment' was a curiosity rather than a work of art. He published it, he says, to show that their little colony 'vivait joyeusement' (led a merry life). But he also hints that the men at Port Royal became restless during Poutrincourt's long absence. If the explorers had met with some fatal accident, Lescarbot might well have had a mutiny on his hands. The preparations for the masque gave the men something to do, kept them hopeful about their leader's return. Lescarbot sometimes lets his little vanities loose to perform a naïve public jig. Yet here he is quite reticent about his resourcefulness in getting everyone involved in amateur dramatics to relieve the tension.

But now Neptune's season was over until next spring. After exploration by sea came cultivation of the land. Poutrincourt inspected the wheat sown before his departure and was encouraged to see that it was doing well. Champlain, Hébert, and others prepared ground for the small gardens each hoped to have in spring. They found the soil 'fat and sandy,' often with a substratum of clay. At Poutrincourt's suggestion, Hébert used the clay as a plaster for young Gravé's damaged hand. From it he also had bricks made for the building of chimneys. (Three hundred years later, clay from the same site went to the making of bricks for the reconstructed Habitation.)

On the banks of what is now Allens River, opposite the Habitation, some of the men prepared a quantity of charcoal principally for the forge. So François Guittard, the toolmaker, must have been kept busy over the winter months earning his 150 livres by shaping and sharpening weapons and tools for the settlement.

Shortly after their return the man wounded at Port Fortuné died. They buried him in the cemetery to the east of the fort.

A little later Membertou and his people, who had set up their wigwams about five hundred paces from the Habitation, had *their* funeral rites to observe. Panounias was dead. He was, we may remember, the guide with the Almouchiquois wife who had accompanied de Monts and Champlain the year before on their voyage down south. Late that fall he had gone trading down the coast with goods he had obtained by barter from the Port Royal storehouse. Somewhere off the Penobscot some Almouchiquois attacked and killed him and made off with his merchandise. This was no gratuitous murder inspired by greed but an act of vengeance for the deaths of the Kennebec men and woman whom the Etchemins had killed near Mount Desert Island a short time before. (Along with the settlers we begin to glimpse something of the workings of the Indian blood feud.)

Ouagimou, a chief from the Ste Croix region, managed to get possession of Panounias' body, dried it out and embalmed it. Then he brought it to Port Royal where the dead man's friends and family had settled in for the winter. Their faces painted black and their voices raised in loud wailings, they crowded around the body as it was carried on to the shore. Realizing that the noise might disturb the French, Membertou came to the Habitation to tell them that mourning usually went on for a month but that, on this occasion, they would limit it to a week. The mourners collected the dead man's possessions from his wigwam: his tobacco, beaver, skins, weapons, and his dogs, and burnt them on shore – 'to the end that none should quarrel over his succession,' assumed Lescarbot the lawyer.

While at the Habitation, Membertou begged Champlain to give him a handsome red coverlet to wrap the body in. Bound in this, and decorated with feathers and ornaments, the body was 'placed on its knees between two stakes, with another supporting it under the arms.' Membertou made a rousing funeral oration, calling on the men to avenge Panounias. They all vowed that, come spring, they would take to the war-path against the Almouchiquois.

After a solemn smoking session, they wrapped the body in a moose skin. Everyone brought presents to be buried with Panounias. At that time the French were not aware that this had a religious significance, was done so that his spirit might have the use of the spirits of weapons, clothes, and kettle in the other world. They were simply amazed and somewhat chastened by this lavish bestowal of valuable gifts upon a dead man. Later Panounias was taken to one of the secret burial islands where the Indians interred their dead so no enemy might disturb their bones.

But, besides funeral rites for the dead at Port Royal, there were also feasting rites for the living. Champlain had lived through two winters in Acadia and had learnt something about the techniques of survival. It was the active men, he had noticed, who were most successful at warding off scurvy. So he proposed his now famous Ordre de Bon Temps (Order of Good Cheer) to keep the colony hunting, healthy, and happy. Fourteen or fifteen gentlemen sat at Poutrincourt's high table. Each in turn became chief steward for the day and was responsible for the meals served. So each, two days before his turn, went off hunting and fishing to see if he could bring back something to surprise and outdo the others. This friendly rivalry meant that all members of the company had fresh fish or meat every day. (It was left to the workmen to find their own game, and some, it appears, were not as energetic as the gentlemen.) Meals at noon and night were served with ceremony. Once the cooks had set the food on platters, the procession formed. First marched the chief steward, a special chain of office around his neck, a napkin over his shoulder and a staff in his hand. Then came the others, each carrying a dish which they placed with due formality upon the table. The closing ceremony came at night, when, after grace, the chief steward removed the chain from around his neck and presented it to his successor. Then each drank to the health of the other. No doubt the toasts did not end there and the singing of madrigals, folk songs, and rounds continued far into the night.

They enjoyed the same good fare that Lescarbot had relished in the fall: wildfowl, sturgeon, moose. Winter brought more game: beaver, otter, wildcat, and raccoon. Lescarbot compared beaver meat to mutton, and bear flesh, 'very good and tender,' to beef. His favourite dishes, which he considered superior to anything to be had in the Rue aux Ours, then famous in Paris for its cook-shops, were 'tender' moose meat, 'of which we made good pasties,' and 'delicate' beaver's tail. With this there was of course wine, and the daily allowance, which was the same for everyone, of 'peas, beans, rice, prunes, raisins, dry cod, and salt flesh, besides oil and butter.' A speciality for dessert grew locally, 'certain small fruits like small apples coloured red, of which we made jelly' – the first cranberry sauce? (Cranberries have a certain vitamin c content. If the gentlemen also had lemon peel, they were well on their way to warding off scurvy.)

As audience and fringe participants, writes Lescarbot, 'we had always 20 or 30 savages, men, women, girls, and boys, who beheld us doing our offices. Bread was given them gratis, as we do here to the poor.' The visitors sat around the hall on their haunches, observing, commenting, and laughing.

Membertou, however, was always treated as an equal. He and other visiting chiefs sat at table eating and drinking with the gentlemen. Lescarbot remarked that they were more restrained in their table manners when with the French than among themselves, did not wipe their hands on their hair or their dogs and unconcernedly break wind. Membertou appreciated the good French wine and told Poutrincourt that it helped him to sleep more soundly and less fearfully at night.

There was quite a coming and going among the Indians of the Port Royal, Saint John, Ste Croix, and Gaspé regions. To avenge Panounias they were organizing a massive attack on the Almouchiquois at Saco in the spring.

When Ouagimou, the Ste Croix chief, came visiting, he obviously brought some of his family with him. The French were not slow in noticing that he had 'a very comely daughter of about eleven years of age.' Poutrincourt might have remembered that, at that age, his sister Jeanne had been appointed as an attendant on the young Mary Queen of Scots at the French court. And it was becoming almost customary for explorers to offer their sovereigns the opportunity of bestowing their regal condescension upon the people they took to be their New World subjects. Several times Poutrincourt asked Ouagimou to let him take his attractive daughter to France 'in order to present her to the Queen.' Royal favour, Poutrincourt assured Ouagimou, would ensure that he 'should never lack corn or aught else.' Ouagimou evidently was unimpressed by the honour or the bribe, and refused to part with his daughter. One cannot but applaud his decision. It is doubtful whether Marie de Médicis, a cold mother herself, would have wasted much affection on the little Indian girl. (French settlers and missionaries were to find, too, that Indians were prepared to exchange children but very unwilling simply to hand theirs over.)

Ouagimou's daughter might well have suffered the same fate as little 'Canada,' son of a Montagnais chief, whom Gravé had brought to France in 1603 at the chief's request. In May 1604 the little Indian was baptized. Then he fell ill and was taken to the Château of St Germain, where the royal children, legitimate and illegitimate, were brought up together. The Dauphin, later Louis XIII, who was then about two and a half, took quite an interest in poor 'Canada,' sent him soups, jellies, and fruit from his own table. But royal concern could not save this child of the wilds. He died in June. A year and a half later the Dauphin still remembered his 'Canada,' his quaint pronunciation, 'the colour of his blue coat and the shape of his bonnet.'

In histories of colonization there is always much talk of 'firsts.' That winter of 1606-7 was remarkable in being the first really satisfactory winter that the French spent in the New World. It was exceptional, too, in being the first time that Europeans and Indians had lived in such friendly proximity. Almost every day the Indians came to visit the French at the Habitation. Most would arrive giving their traditional greeting of 'Ho, ho, ho.' But some took to wearing plumed hats which they would doff when making a bow *à la française*. The Indians quickly developed a taste for wine, the French a taste for tobacco, those two much-questioned aids to conviviality. And indeed, if Lescarbot had been able to see into the future, he would have been horrified to learn what ravages wine and brandy were eventually to work upon the Indians.

One might hesitate to use the term 'separate but equal' in this context, but that is a pretty fair description of the relationship between Membertou's band and the little French colony. In the light of de Monts' commission, the French could not but look upon the land as theirs and upon the native inhabitants as potential subjects of the French King. But they had the tact not to urge this point of view upon the Indians. Membertou had no sense whatsoever of being Henri's liegeman. As sagamo, he claimed, according to Lescarbot, to be 'the equal of the King and of all his lieutenants, and often said to M. de Poutrincourt that he was his great friend, brother, companion, and equal, showing his equality by joining together the fingers of each hand which we call the index or pointing finger.' He also made quite specific demands as to the honour due a man of his rank. French captains visiting Port Royal were welcomed with salutes from the cannon. Each time he returned to Port Royal after an expedition away, Membertou expected to be greeted with the same ceremonious roar.

Some of the French were equally curious about Indian life and customs. On one occasion during this winter some of the French went to live for six snowy weeks with the Micmacs, slept on pelts on the ground, and ate only Indian fare. Neither Lescarbot nor Poutrincourt could have guessed then that in less than a decade this would become the normal way of life for Poutrincourt's son, Charles, and a handful of his followers. In just three years, too, Robert Gravé would be found living with the Etchemins. Later in New France, many young Frenchmen became impatient with the restraints of European civilization and threw themselves with great zest into the tough, precarious, nomadic Indian life. They became the famous 'coureurs de bois' – the very name evokes freedom and the wilds.

Lescarbot himself spent one memorable night about seven miles away from the Habitation. News came that a moose had been killed and left on the banks of the river that flowed into the south side of the port. Lescarbot promptly named this river Rivière de L'Orignal, and today it is still called Moose River. The Indians must have invited some of the French to come and sample the meat cooked in the traditional manner. First they ate some of it roasted over the fire, then they ate it boiled. Lescarbot found the manner of boiling water for the stew simple but ingenious. One man hollowed out the trunk of a tree to make a 'tub or trough.' Water was poured into this rough wooden kettle and a constant supply of red-hot stones lowered into it to keep the water at boiling point. Then in went the meat to stew until cooked. This was, of course, the way of doing things before the French had arrived with their copper kettles. Lescarbot was fascinated – and satisfied: 'We made ... a very dainty feast with this venison, the tenderness of which no words could express.' And there, under the cold winter stars, they 'passed the night, having swept away the snow for our camp.'

The curious Parisian lawyer was alert to learn all he could about and from the Indians. For he liked and respected them with a tolerance perhaps absorbed from Montaigne, whose *Essais* he had no doubt read. The manner in which Lescarbot compares Indian and European ways, not always to the advantage of the latter, is strongly reminiscent of Montaigne's in his famous essay on the 'cannibals' of Brazil. Lescarbot found much to praise in the Micmacs: their physical fitness, their swiftness and keen-sightedness, their skill in hunting. The men did not treat their women with all the chivalry the gallant Lescarbot could desire. Yet though the women ate apart, were excluded from feasts and councils, and did all the menial work, they were, he thought, not cruelly treated. They loved their husbands and cherished their children. Lescarbot took particular note of their practical and decorative skills in the making of wigwams, canoes, clothes, rush mats, baskets, dishes of bark, and ornaments: 'They also make purses of leather, upon which they work designs worthy of admiration, with the quills of porcupines coloured with red, black, white and blue, which are the colours they use, so vivid that ours seem not to approach them.' In museums one can see many such artifacts, some dating back to the eighteenth century. European fashions and requirements have obviously modified indigenous patterns and articles since 1607. But it is likely that the ancient and attractive double-curve motif was one of the designs Lescarbot found 'worthy of admiration.'

As for the Indians' moral qualities, Lescarbot had nothing but plaudits for their courage and generosity. Long before Rousseau, he described them as 'truly noble,' – though one is tempted to interpret 'noble' in the sense also that the men were 'gentlemen' because their chief occupations were hunting and war. He was struck, as were many other Europeans, by their kindness to other members of their tribe, their lack of 'ambition, vain-glory, envy, avarice.' In this they were very different from the competitive, quarrelsome, 'Christian' French. Chiefs were respected but restricted and could not rule as tyrants.

Lescarbot did feel, however, that they might lead a less precarious existence if they organized their lives better, settled in a fixed spot, and developed his own very pronounced taste for agriculture. But his main reproach was that they were too vengeful, too anxious to hit back at an enemy when they considered themselves slighted or wronged. One particular execution surprised and shocked him, probably because it involved women – and some good-looking women at that. An Almouchiquois woman prisoner had helped a fellow prisoner to escape, so the women of Membertou's group put her to death, a good distance, Lescarbot noted, from Port Royal. The French, he says, 'reproved them sharply for this cruelty, whereof they were all ashamed, and durst not show themselves anymore.' But, with characteristic fair-mindedness, Lescarbot adds, 'This is their form of justice.' Mindful of the European rack and wheel and many other infamous devices, burnings, hangings, and disembowellings, Lescarbot might well have asked himself whether French justice was any less cruel.

Despite this incident, Indians and French continued to exchange courtesies. Visiting chiefs brought bundles of furs to present to Poutrincourt. He 'did not take them to his own use, but put them into M. de Monts' store-house, because he would not contravene his monopoly,' Poutrincourt's friend explains righteously. The French, as we have seen, did attend one moose feast, but the Indians were not able to enjoy many more since there was not enough snow that winter for good hunting. For deep snow, in which moose floundered, meant that hunters on their snowshoes could catch up quite easily with their prey. So occasionally Poutrincourt gave a dinner for them and they showed their gratitude by dancing and chanting: 'We have feasted well, and we sing your praises often.'

Their songs intrigued Lescarbot, especially those they chanted when they seemed to be communing with a supernatural power that Lescarbot took to be the devil. We have a curious picture of him going for a walk one day and then stopping outside Membertou's wigwam when he heard singing: chant and reponse followed by a general 'great exclamation ... Hé-é-é-é.' After a quick look around, he whipped out his tables and busily noted down the tune and words of this ritual chant. He was perplexed at the constant occurrence of the word 'alleluyah.' This persuaded him 'that these songs are in praise of the devil, if indeed this word means with them what it signifies in Hebrew, which is praise ye the Lord' – their lord being, of course, one of the powers of darkness.

Though an interested and sympathetic observer, Lescarbot was not in a position to appreciate the all-pervasive nature of Indian religion, or to understand that, for them, the spirits could work harm as well as good, withhold snow in the winter as well as send the fish to run upstream in spring. As far as he could judge the Micmac were 'destitute of all knowledge of God, have no worship, and perform no divine service, living in a pitiful ignorance.' (Later observers would note that they did have some form of sun-worship.) What rites they had smacked to Lescarbot of witchcraft rather than worship, since divination and exorcism to heal the sick were the chief duties of the medicine-man.

Among the Port Royal Indians, Membertou was Aoutmin (physician-priest or shaman) as well as sagamo. One begins to see why he was so feared and respected. As a badge of office he wore round his neck a triangular ornamented purse. This contained something the size of a hazel nut, his Aoutem or 'devil' Lescarbot suspiciously calls it. Spirit would probably be a closer translation.

If Lescarbot's views of Indian rites and practices strike us today as superficial, based only on externals, we should remember how long it has taken non-Indian anthropologists, linguists, and historians to reach even an approximate understanding of the Indian religion. We also have to keep in mind that, whatever his quirks as a Christian, Lescarbot was a believer – in the manner of his times. He was convinced that, unless converted, these charming, generous people, who despite their 'ignorance' had so many good qualities, were in danger of eternal damnation. So he was bound to applaud and encourage Poutrincourt's evangelizing efforts.

In his 'Adieu à la Nouvelle France,' written the following summer, Lescarbot claims that Poutrincourt 'taught our religion' to the poor savages and 'often showed them his fervent desire to see them among the flock that Christ had redeemed with his life.' He claims too that the Indians were just as desirous of instruction. Here we may be somewhat sceptical. However fervently Poutrincourt pointed at a crucifix, uttering his few words of Micmac, he can hardly have conveyed much of the Christian message to his listeners. They, in turn, might well have been curious. Was it possible that this figure on the cross, this Jesus manitou, could show them where to find food, ward off accidents, help them recover from an illness? Any such curiosity or speculation Poutrincourt and Lescarbot immediately took as readiness to accept Christianity.

But not only the Indians stood in need of spiritual edification. Since the French had no priest with them, Poutrincourt asked Lescarbot, the scholar of the group, to lead them in their devotions. So besides a pagan masque, Lescarbot's little study witnessed the preparation of regular Sunday sermons. Lescarbot was pleased that he had brought with him his Bible and other books. A few years before he had translated into French St Charles Borromeo's *Guide for Parish Priests and Instructions for Pastors*. From this he might have culled some useful hints.

These sermons were not an unmitigated success. Some listeners complimented Lescarbot, saying that 'never had they heard such a good exposition of Divine things.' This seems likely, as Lescarbot would have made a lively preacher. They added that 'previously they had not known a single principle of the Christian doctrine.' This, given the times, was also likely. But his outspoken criticism of their unchristian conduct obviously irritated others. One can almost hear them murmur, 'Who does he take himself for anyway?' But 'in the end,' says Lescarbot, buoyant as ever, 'we were all of us good friends together.'

All possible precautions were taken to keep the colonists in physical as well as spiritual health. Besides being active, they were careful to wear 'wooden pantoffles' (galoshes with wooden soles and leather uppers) to keep their feet dry. They were favoured by an exceptionally mild winter. Snow did not fall until the end of December. In mid-January they could still go out without heavy cloaks, picnicking and singing in the sunshine. February and March were colder and more miserable. Though Champlain thought it rained a lot, Lescarbot found the winter less wet and foggy than in France.

But, in spite of all precautions, the sieur de Boullay had an almost constant fever, which he controlled by taking good care of himself.

Others fell victim to the scurvy. According to Lescarbot, four among the more depressed of the men died. Their bedding, he observed, was particularly bad. But about ten of the sick recovered, sipping chicken-broth or wine through a spout. When green shoots showed in the woods, Lescarbot went out to pick them and gave them to the sufferers.

The livestock the settlers had brought with them throve. Their one sheep stayed in the courtyard all winter. It was shorn twice and the wool taken back to France for an assessment of its worth. Some of their pigeons fell prey to swooping eagles. Still, hens and pigeons increased and multiplied, as did the pigs that roamed freely out of doors all through the winter months. But the French had, quite unintentionally, brought another fast-breeding creature over with them: rats. The Indians found them in their wigwams, greedily sucking at their fish oils. These destructive rodents were quite new to them and indeed the whole country. Not everything French was greeted with delight.

There was, in Lescarbot's view, another and more serious hindrance to perfect health and happiness – the absence of European women. Unlike many other Indian tribes, the Micmacs, though polygamous, were not promiscuous. Their women were noted for their 'modesty.' Advances on the part of any licentious Frenchmen were, at that time anyway, definitely discouraged. Nor would the French leaders have been happy to see their Christian men seducing pagan girls. Lescarbot's pleasant solution for sexual frustration was that everyone should have 'the honest company of his lawful wife; for, without that, the cheer is never perfect: one's mind is always upon that which one loves and desireth.'

This was a theme he was to return to later in his verse, where he declared that Port Royal provided men with almost all they might wish for. Nothing was lacking

> Sinon d'avoir près soi un chacun sa mignonne
> En la sorte que Dieu et l'Eglise l'ordonne
>
> (Save only at man's side his dearest love,
> Their union blessed by Church and God above).

But, all things considered, the French had proved to themselves that they could weather an Acadian winter. They had survived, they had amused themselves, and they now enjoyed unprecedented good relations with the native peoples. The old myth that New France was uninhabitable was wearing thin. At last it looked as though a French colony in the New World was really possible.

CHAPTER EIGHT

Farewell to New France

OPES ROSE EVEN HIGHER as spring advanced. Even so, it performed the usual one-step-forward-two-steps-back routine that Maritimers today have come to expect. By early April those who had cleared plots for gardens in the fall were out preparing them for planting in May. Snow fell that month but melted quickly. Just as there had been friendly rivalry in winter as to who could provide the best meal, so now the men vied with one another as to who could grow the finest crops. Poutrincourt's son, Charles, showed a taste for the exotic and planted orange and lemon seeds which grew to plants a foot high.

Lescarbot was a particularly keen competitor. Home in France he was to look back nostalgically on those idyllic days:

I can say with truth that I have never done so much bodily work through the pleasure which I took in digging and tilling my gardens, fencing them in against the gluttony of the swine, making terraces, preparing straight alleys, building storehouses, sowing wheat, rye, barley, oats, beans, peas, garden plants, and watering them, so great a desire had I to know the soil by personal experience. So much so that the summer days were too short for me, and very often in the spring I was still at work in the moonlight.

Hébert, the apothecary, was as interested in cultivating crops as in growing the medicinal herbs he needed for his trade. Of all the French at Port Royal in those early years he is the only one whose name, though somewhat deformed, lingers on in the area. Champlain had named the large river on the south of the port the St Antoine. Lescarbot, on his rather fanciful map, labelled it the Hébert, and Bear River it has become today, while Lescarbot's Isle Claudiane opposite is now Bear Island. So a French apothecary yields to an indigenous animal called by its English name.

Birds started arriving from the south. Once more Champlain could spend his leisure hours strolling down to his summer house, watching them and listening to their trills and warbles. Lescarbot was fascinated by the whir of the gem-like hummingbird that he heard on his morning walks. In his 'Farewell to New France' he devoted a long passage to 'Niridau,' as the Indians called this delicate, nectar-sipping creature. Why some of his companions should train their muskets upon these exquisite little birds was quite beyond him.

If eyes and ears vibrated to richer sights and sounds, so did noses to richer smells. Lescarbot was satisfied with his soil as it was, but others fertilized theirs with pig dung, kitchen refuse, and shells of lobster, clam, and mussel – a pungent rottenness that worked wonders. The fall sowing had indicated that the soil was good, but no one had expected crops to flourish quite as well as they did. Untaxed as yet by tillage, the earth was rich in nutrients. Soon the French had an abundance of the fresh herbs and vegetables that over the winter they had come to crave, despite the succulence of the mainly meat dishes served by the Order of Good Cheer.

The fields cultivated at the mouth of the Equille (the Dauphin on Lescarbot's map) promised a fine crop of wheat. Grinding all this on the hand-mill would be a laborious task. So Poutrincourt decided, as de Monts had done before at Ste Croix, to build a water-mill. The site he chose was on Allen's River, probably near the spot where a hydrogenerator now stands to mark the place where grist mills have turned and ground grain for over three centuries. The damming of the river brought another benefit. Alewives swimming upstream at high tide found themselves trapped. They were so numerous that Poutrincourt had two casks of these salted, also one of 'sardines' (smelts?) to take back to France. Somehow he even obtained a dozen eggs of the Canada goose ('outarde' as the French called them) and raised the young from the shell.

Here then was proof of the potential of Port Royal to confound the critics. Poutrincourt's dreams might yet be realized. This was a fruitful spot on which to establish himself and his line. The land needed only a little care and cultivation to produce crops as good as, if not better than any in France. They had fish in summer and game in winter. His son had readily adapted to the tougher life and was getting to know the Micmac language. He felt that he had the love and respect of Membertou and his people. And the Indians were not, he persuaded himself, unaffected by the rituals of the Christian faith. He was sure that they could be taught to farm and thus protect themselves against the hunger of the harsh winter months. So there was no need to go exploring farther south. To judge by Poutrincourt's energy and enterprise, that spring he was in high spirits.

But however hopeful he might feel, knowing that the waters teemed with fish and the fields were green with shoots, he had to be realistic too. The workmen were engaged for one year only. Another ship should be arriving any day from France with de Monts, new colonists and supplies for the following winter. But, as he well knew, accidents happened. If no ship came, they would all have to leave for Canso to find fishing vessels to take them home.

As early as April Poutrincourt had Champdoré at work fitting out two long-boats. But when it came to caulking these ships, they discovered that they had not brought any pitch with them. With some help Poutrincourt gathered a good quantity of spruce gum. This he melted over an open-air furnace, distilling it in a kind of retort fashioned by placing kettles one inside the other. Lescarbot claims that the Indians were most impressed by this fresh example of 'Norman' know-how. (Because of the predominance of Norman ships and crews, they called all the French Normans.) One suspects that the person who was really impressed was Lescarbot himself. It must have been about this time that, seated on the grass in conventional poetic pose and listening to burbling brooks, he penned an ode to Poutrincourt. Among his friend's talents as soldier, colonizer, planter, mathematician, and musician, he makes particular mention of his amazing knowledge of all practical skills. Lescarbot was a loyal friend.

In May, groups of Indians started to arrive at the entrance to the port. This was in response to the call to arms that Membertou had sent out during the winter. The hard season over, they assembled to prepare for war against the Almouchiquois in order to avenge Panounias. Membertou was anxious to show his allies what good relations he enjoyed with the French. He requested Poutrincourt to give him corn, beans, and wine so he could entertain his visitors in the style they expected from him as the Normans' special friend.

Membertou needed to be in good voice, for custom demanded that he deliver lengthy orations to the mustering Indians who, when in agreement, would 'make an exclamation, saying *Hau*, in a long-drawn-out voice.' Though not admitted to councils, the women were called upon to act as warriors in a curious mock battle. The men entrenched themselves in a kind of fort which the women encircled. The besieged men then tried to escape, while the women were expected to 'drive them back, arrest them, do their best to capture them … beat them, strip them.' If the men managed to slip away, this was interpreted as a bad sign. By a trick of inverse logic, the women's triumph meant ultimate victory for the men.

No doubt the French were highly amused by the spectacle of the women turned Amazons. They obviously enjoyed teasing them – the only form flirtation could take – for when asked about the women in France, they solemnly described them as bearded.

So the Indians prepared for war and the French fished, gardened, ground wheat, made bricks, and even started building in preparation for the newcomers. But when would they arrive? Would they come at all? With all the spring activity went a certain anxiety. Eyes were fixed upon the port. Often they would make out a speck, a sign of movement on the waters, but then this would turn out to be just another Indian canoe. In spite of all the excitement of the new season, it seemed a weary wait.

But at last on the 24th May, Ascension Thursday, news came. Morning devotions and breakfast were just over when Membertou came hurrying up to say that a sailing ship had entered the port. But it was not de Monts in a ship bearing the royal ensign, just a small ship captained by Chevalier, a Breton. He had letters from de Monts. These Poutrincourt read out to the assembled company.

The news was devastating. They were all to return to France. The *Jonas* was at Canso, her orders being to remain there fishing for cod. Only if it was absolutely necessary should Poutrincourt send for her to come to Port Royal. Strict economy had to be practised as the King's Council had cancelled the monopoly and de Monts' company was dissolved.

It was a triumph for the free traders, a blow for the colonizers. But, as we have seen, there had been fierce opposition to the monopoly from the first. Sailors and merchants of the seaports had continued to protest to the King about interference with their traditional rights. Regional parliaments made difficulties about registering the King's decree on the fur trade. Hatters and furriers complained to Sully about rising prices and a falling off in demand for furs, which they blamed on the monopoly. Later Champlain was to hear hints of a dark plot: bribery, corruption at court, 'a certain person' receiving 'a certain sum ... without his said Majesty knowing anything about it.'

And there were rifts within the company itself. The partners had not worked well together. Some shareholders, although still members of the company, had attempted a little trading on the side for personal benefit. There was even a suspicion that de Monts himself was implicated in something of the sort.

Not all of this could be known then to the people at Port Royal. At first all they could register was that they had to pack up and leave. The hired workmen would not have been much affected by the news. Their wages and their passage home were assured. But those concerned with the cause of colonization felt bitterly disappointed. Had the last three years been nothing but a waste of time, effort, men, and money? Why should the French give up just when things were at their most hopeful? Since the Ste Croix disaster they had had two fairly good years at Port Royal. The last winter was even something of a triumph. They had a fort, the soil was good, crops flourished. With sensible farm management they might soon become self-sufficient. The neighbouring Indians were friendly. But what could be done? For de Monts' company simply could not afford to carry on without the monopoly. Again and again over the years would-be colonizers were to feel hampered by the hostility or indifference of the merchants and the lack of government support.

For Champlain it was a major set-back. He had been with de Monts' enterprise from the beginning and now felt committed to the New World. As for Poutrincourt, he saw his dream menaced. Yet it had all seemed so close: the glory of founding a fief in New France, watching it flourish, adding lustre to the family name. With his usual reckless determination he declared to Lescarbot 'that though he were to come alone with his family, he would not abandon the venture.' During the course of that day he turned the matter over in his mind. Perhaps he could persuade some of the men to stay on? He sounded them out and offered a cask of wine each and enough corn for a year to the eight men who were willing to be rehired. But, says Lescarbot, 'they demanded such high wages that he could not come to terms with them.' Dreams and reckless determination were not enough. Poutrincourt would need funds.

The day brought another – though minor – disappointment. When Poutrincourt asked for the provisions the company must have sent out, Chevalier had to explain that there was nothing left. He had a list of what they should have received, and gourmet Lescarbot noted or remembered every item of it from livestock to sugar loaves. But all this had disappeared down 'Gutter Lane' as Erondelle, Lescarbot's seventeenth-century translator, expressively put it: that is, down the throats of Chevalier and his men. Lescarbot was not impressed by Chevalier's embarrassed excuse that the ship's crew had given up the Port Royal settlers as dead. Altogether he formed a poor opinion of the captain and his men. And the better he got to know them, the lower it sank. Nevertheless Poutrincourt and his people welcomed the new-comers by sharing their wine and their plenty with them.

But Chevalier did not feel easy at Port Royal and wanted to return to Canso. Poutrincourt was mistrustful. Someone had started a rumour that Chevalier was going to sail off and leave them behind. Poutrincourt put a crew on the Breton captain's ship, thus preventing him from making off. Still, it was not quite a forcible detention, for he promised Chevalier a chance to barter for furs. Young Biencourt probably noted with approval his father's imperious exercise of authority, which he was later to emulate – though in quite different circumstances.

On this occasion, however, such high-handedness may not have been unjustified. There was no real hurry. It was still early in the summer. If any profits were to be made, the *Jonas* would have to remain fishing off Canso a few weeks longer. Also, Poutrincourt was anxious to wait until the grain ripened in order to grind flour for the journey home and collect more samples of Port Royal's bounty.

Early in June Membertou and his allies set out for Saco in their canoes. They would be joined on their way by others. For Indians and Europeans alike this was the time for voyages. Champlain and Poutrincourt sailed north-east to have one more look at the copper mines of the Minas Basin. And with Champdoré in command,

Lescarbot, Le Fèvre of Rethel, and Chevalier went west first to the Saint John River and then to Ste Croix Island.

If Poutrincourt wished to take home evidence of rich copper mines, he was disappointed. Only with great difficulty was he able to extract a few pieces from the trap rocks. But the explorers sailed to the head of the Bay of Fundy, noted some limestone, caught seagulls, and discovered, probably at Parrsboro, a very old moss-covered cross. Who were the Christians, they wondered, who had been there before them? And when? Poutrincourt, in adventurous mood, insisted on climbing up a steep, high cliff, probably Cape Split. The thick moss at the top made a precarious foothold. Poutrincourt slithered upon some stones and nearly fell to his death. He found the way down even more hazardous than the way up. The sailors had to throw him a hawser. With the help of this the long-legged nobleman lowered himself to the pebbly beach below. In commemoration of this exploit, the place was called Cape Poutrincourt (though, on Champlain's map, as Ganong remarks, the name seems to apply to Blomidon). When Champlain came to recount the incident, he did so in a deadpan manner. Did such a feat strike him as exhibitionist bravado?

Lescarbot, as usual, made the most of the experiences offered him. Crossing the Bay of Fundy, the little group arrived at Secoudun's encampment on the Saint John River. Quite a number of Indians were assembled there to join Membertou in his advance upon Saco. As their purpose was not barter, they did not have many furs with them. Chevalier, determined to make some profit, haggled for an hour 'for their old lousy skins.' Lescarbot felt ashamed and contemptuous. For this meanness, he wrote, Chevalier earned from their hosts the name 'Mercateria ... signifying a cheese-parer.'

During the few days they we there, Lescarbot was most edified to observe the customs Secoudun had adopted from the French. He knelt to pray, made the sign of the cross, wore one, and had one erected outside his cabin. Here was one Indian, Lescarbot was convinced, who was 'Christian in mind.' But not all the Indians they met were quite so well intentioned. After being treated to a military display of eighty naked warriors who advanced yelling and dancing, the French had a brief encounter with a medicine-man. Within two years' time, he ominously predicted, either the Indians would kill off all the Normans or be killed by them. Lescarbot and his company took this quite lightly, though the incident does show that Indian good will to the French was not as wholehearted as they later liked to believe.

Leaving the Saint John, they found the wind against them, so anchored off a small island for a couple of days. Champdoré and Lescarbot, also in search of mines, explored its rocks with hammer and chisel, and actually managed to extract some iron. As the winds remained contrary, they took three days to reach Ste Croix. A number of Indian canoes, mustering for the attack on the Almouchiquois, were on the waters. At night, with some reason to feel mistrustful, the French kept careful watch. But all they heard in the summer darkness were the long, mournful cries of seals.

Lescarbot was much moved by the abandoned site of Ste Croix. He went to pray at the graves of the men buried in a little cemetery and composed a sincere but unoriginal ode to de Monts. Death ends all is the tenor of his verse, but noble deeds rescue the valiant from oblivion. Some of the buildings where so many men had suffered and died were still intact, though one side of the stoutly built storehouse had a gap in it. Wandering around among these desolate ruins, they found some drinkable Spanish wine. Cabbages, sorrel, and lettuce still growing in the weed-choked gardens 'went to fill the pot.' But Lescarbot's elegiac mood was jarred by the noisy destructiveness of the men, for 'the courtyard was full of unbroken casks which some undisciplined sailors burnt for their pleasure, a sight which filled me with disgust, and confirmed my previous opinion that, from a human point of view at least, the savages were more humane and honourable than many of those who bear the names of Christians.' He observed that, over the last few years, the Indians had left everything just as it was.

On their way home they fell in with Ouagimou, by now an old friend. He too was on his way to Saco but went with them part of the way in their boat before putting back in his canoe. By daybreak on a fine summer morning Lescarbot and his group were back in Port Royal and dropped anchor opposite the sleeping Habitation. More alert than their masters, the dogs barked and woke one man. Trumpeters on the boat sounded their return and the loud report of musket shots roused the others. Lescarbot, who had found no reason to reproach Champdoré for poor seamanship, rewarded him with a sonnet. If Champlain saw it, he quietly kept his counsel.

He and Poutrincourt had returned from their journey just the day before. The iron that Lescarbot and Champdoré had pried from the rocks was melted down in the forge. From one of the bars Poutrincourt got François Guittard to fashion a keen-bladed knife. Lescarbot went to visit his beloved garden and found that moles and field-mice had been to work on his little plot of Indian corn and had quite spoiled it.

In mid-July, Ralluau, de Monts' secretary, who had been at Canso with the *Jonas*, arrived in a long-boat with three others. It was just about a year since he had made a similar journey along the coast where he had met Gravé with news of the arrival of Poutrincourt, men, and provisions. Now his message was more sombre. The monopoly was definitely cancelled, so those at Port Royal should be making arrangements for joining the *Jonas*.

On the 30th July Lescarbot took a last look at gardens, fort, Biencourt Island opposite, of which he was particularly fond, and the streams that glistened down the flanks of the hills surrounding the lovely port. While waiting to embark on one of the two long-boats that were to leave for Canso that day, he started his 'Adieu à la Nouvelle France' with its detailed catalogue of the flora, fauna, and delights of Port Royal. But winds were favourable; it was time to leave. He bade a temporary farewell to Poutrincourt, Champlain, and some others who were to remain behind for another few days. One wonders whether Lescarbot was intent on gazing or writing as Champdoré guided the boat safely, this time, through the Gut.

For a week they were held up by fog. Then a swift current took them to La Have. There they spent two days eating red gooseberries and watching cod 'nibbling at the hooks.' Some Indians were there, so those anxious to take furs back home with them were able to trade. But Chevalier's men were not content to barter and disgraced themselves by an ugly act of greed. An Indian unwisely showed them the place – probably an island – where his people lay buried. The sailors took advantage of this information to rifle the graves for beaver pelts. The site of their burial grounds was one of the Indians' most jealously guarded secrets. French sailors might escape with their loot, but an Indian who had betrayed such a secret could expect no mercy from his tribe. Later the French heard that the Indians had killed the man whose blabbing had resulted in such desecration.

At La Have the Indians with whom they bartered may well have been the same ones who had gone on board an English ship just a few days before. For in May that year George Popham and Raleigh Gilbert, son of Sir Humphrey, sponsored by the Plymouth Company, had left England in two ships to found a colony somewhere off the coast of Maine. On the 31st July Gilbert's ship was in the La Have area. The Englishmen learned from the Indians who came on board that their chief was 'Messamott,' obviously Messamouet, now on his way down to Saco. But the Indians do not seem to have told the French party about the English ship. How indignant Lescarbot would have been if he had learnt of the projected English settlement, and how many more reproaches he would have heaped upon the defaulting French!

Before reaching Canso, they put in at a little port in Tor Bay where they met Captain Savalette of St-Jean de Luz, one of the real old-timers. This was, he said, his forty-second voyage to these fishing grounds – so he had been crossing the Atlantic since 1565. Business prospered. His ship, an eighty-tonner, took back a hundred thousand dried fish annually. He employed sixteen men who caught, every day, 'a good fifty crowns' worth of cod,' and every voyage brought him ten thousand livres. He was glad to see other Frenchmen, for he wanted to enlist their help against the local Indians, who persisted in helping themselves to his best fish. Europeans usually found it difficult to adjust to Indian notions of liberality and to the idea that more was expected from them because they had more. But Lescarbot was charmed with Savalette's courteous welcome of his French visitors, and on his map marked the harbour as Port Savalette. To his disgust, some of Chevalier's men again 'behaved worse than savages,' treating the old Basque captain with all the arrogance of soldiers encountering a peasant.

Back at Port Royal, Poutrincourt was busy choosing samples of grain to take back to France. Surely this would convince the King that settlement was worth while! He thoughtfully selected some wheat and rye from Lescarbot's gardens to present to his friend at Canso. Ten years later Lescarbot still had them among his souvenirs. And Poutrincourt had more wheat ground so they should not lack for flour on the journey home.

Just as they were on the point of leaving, a flotilla of canoes came through the Gut. Membertou and his warriors were back, waving their enemies' scalps. They had waged war at Saco and had won. The French decided to put off their departure until the next day. Now they settled down to listen to a long account of the fighting. On the basis of this account, received second-hand, Lescarbot wrote his 488-line epic on the defeat of the Almouchiquois. Carried away by the heroic mode, he no doubt allowed himself all sorts of poetic flourishes. Nevertheless, we do learn something of the fate of those chiefs whom de Monts, Champlain, and Poutrincourt had met in the course of their explorations.

At Saco Membertou had taken the Almouchiquois unaware by first pretending that he had come to barter with them. Among the merchandise offered was a trumpet. Membertou blew on this – a prearranged signal for his hidden allies to fall upon the Almouchiquois: 'Et trompant les trompeurs trompeusement il trompe,' wrote Lescarbot, savouring his triumphant and untranslatable pun. ('Tromper' means 'to deceive' and 'to trumpet.' So, literally 'And deceiving the deceivers deceitfully he trumpets ...')

In the ensuing fighting, Panounias' brother, Secoudun, and Oua-gimou were wounded along with some others. But, at a critical point in the battle, French muskets wrought havoc upon the Almouchiquois whose bone-tipped arrows had already proved less effective than the steel-tipped ones of Membertou and his allies. (From this it is clear that the French had trusted their Indian friends enough to supply them with firearms. Secoudun even had two muskets.)

Among those killed were handsome Onemechin, the chief at Saco who had felt so hampered by European clothes, and the impressive, dignified Marchin. Though several of Membertou's warriors were wounded, none died. Lescarbot rattles off names with great confidence as though he knew a number of the Indian warriors personally, or at least knew of them. And though a catalogue of sonorous names is, of course, in the epic tradition, it does seem as if Lescarbot is alluding to real people and not just using names. There is Etmeminaoet, for example, whose 'gallantry can satisfy the amorous desires of six wives.' A Bituani is also mentioned. Was it the same who had distinguished himself as gourmet and lover that first summer at Ste Croix?

In the full flush of victory Membertou was sorry to see his French allies go. The parting, according to Lescarbot, was tearful and affecting. Poutrincourt gave Membertou ten barrels of flour, offered him the use of the Habitation, and promised that the following year French settlers would return to stay.

On the 11th August Poutrincourt, Champlain, and seven men left in a small long-boat laden with baggage and provisions. In the three years he had been there, Champlain's voyages had taken him west and south so he had not had the chance to survey the area from La Have eastwards to Canso. Now came the opportunity to make notes and observations of this coastline so he could complete his general map. Among the places he took careful note of were Sambro (Sesambre it was known as then, named by the Malouins after the island Cézembre off St Malo), St Margaret's Bay (it was only the river then that was called Ste Marguerite), and Halifax harbour, which he called Baye saine (Healthy Harbour). Further on came Musquodoboit, or perhaps it was Jeddore, which he named after St Helen, and St Mary's River, as yet unnamed, with Wedge Island at its mouth (Isle Verte or Green Island to Champlain). Champlain too was impressed by kindly Captain Sava-lette – still grumbling about the Indians – whom they put in to visit.

On the 27th August they arrived at Canso. Champdoré and Lescarbot rowed out to meet them. By this time the whole homebound company had assembled. But for a week they lingered on, enjoying the many wild raspberries that they found on the islands. Champlain continued to make notes on the region and inquired about Cape Breton so he could give a satisfactory report of it. He mentions two harbours: Port Aux Anglais, later to be Louisbourg, where the French would erect an impressive fortress, and Ingonish, where a hundred years earlier some Portuguese had spent a wretched winter as would-be settlers. Champlain was unenthusiastic about the land and the scenery, judging the winters to be long and cold. By this time he probably knew that he would not be returning to these parts again. But he hoped to be back in the New World, dreamt almost obsessively of exploring the river that must flow across the continent and so lead to China. Lescarbot paid tribute to Champlain's dreams and ambitions in a sonnet written while the men stocked the ship with firewood and fresh water.

The *Jonas* sailed from Canso on the 3rd September with a cargo of a hundred thousand cod, green and dried. It was, for those times, a short and uneventful voyage, even though it must have presented some interest to an Indian who journeyed with them. Somewhere across the Atlantic Poutrincourt lost an eagle that he had brought on a leash from Port Royal and had been trying to train. Five of his Canada geese died. Lescarbot found the rations most disappointing. But he consoled himself with his Muse, worked on his 'Adieu à la Nouvelle France,' his epic on the war against the Almouchiquois, and a humorous 'Tabagie Marine' ('Feast at Sea'). In the last he speaks regretfully of the good food and wine they enjoyed at Port Royal and gets in another dig at Chevalier and his greedy men. Each composition ends with the same refrain:

> Cherchant dessus Neptune un repos sans repos
> J'ai façonné ces vers au branle de ses flots.

> (Seeking on Neptune's waves a restless rest
> I penned these lines while tossed upon his breast.)

He was to pen many more lines in prose but this was his last long sea voyage.

On the 28th September they anchored for a couple of days in the harbour of Roscoff in Lower Brittany. Here they were amused at the amazement of their Indian, who exclaimed at the profusion of 'buildings, spires and windmills.' But what astonished him most were the wide skirts, farthingales, and headdresses of the – unbearded – women.

The *Jonas* unloaded at St Malo. The former companions of the Order of Good Cheer made their farewells and went their separate ways. Lescarbot, along with Poutrincourt and young Charles, visited the famous and formidable Abbey of Mont Saint-Michel, a tourist attraction even then. But Lescarbot had doubts about the usefulness of such religious establishments and wished that 'the machines of some Archimedes might transport them to New France, there to be better employed in the service of God and of the King.'

Arriving in Paris, Poutrincourt had an interview with the King. He presented him with the surviving Canada geese, his samples of corn, wheat, rye, barley, and oats, and showed him the knife made from New World iron. So there was something from each category: animal, vegetable, and mineral. No doubt he spoke of Membertou's interest in the French monarch and Indian curiosity about the Christian faith. Henri praised Poutrincourt's efforts, encouraged his ambition to colonize New France, promised letters to confirm de Monts' concession to him of the seigneury of Port Royal ... but breathed no word of financial aid.

If the King then mentally reviewed the Charter he had signed in November 1603, he might have noted that de Monts, his Lieutenant-General, along with his officers had carried out the terms of his mandate as faithfully as possible. Though there had been no conversions, some Indians had at least become aware of Christianity. The French leaders had formed alliances with chiefs who expressed good will to the King of France, a desire for trade, and an eagerness to see the French settle in their land. Some looked to the French as arbiters in their disputes among themselves. One grant of land had been made and cultivation begun. They had doggedly searched for mines, although nothing spectacular had been discovered. (So Sully could look smug!) And finally Champlain had carefully charted the coasts and rivers that the French had explored. Something – the King would have to admit – had been achieved for the maintenance of the French crown in its 'ancient dignity, greatness and splendour.'

And yet, there were now English settlers in Virginia and in Maine, while for the first time in three years no Frenchmen would be watching the fleur-de-lis brave the snow and storms of the New World winter.

PART II

THE MISERIES OF THESE PARTS

CHAPTER NINE

Westward Once More

THOUGH HIS COMPANY HAD BEEN DISSOLVED and his monopoly of the fur trade withdrawn, de Monts still bore the title
of Lieutenant-Governor of New France. It was an honour
that had been dearly bought. The past three years had
brought in some profits to the company. But it had sustained many
more losses. De Monts himself was out of pocket by ten thousand
livres. He had every reason to feel discouraged. But Champlain,
returning to France in the fall of 1607, put new heart in him. He went
immediately to visit his old leader and reported on all that had
happened during the two years since de Monts had sailed from Port
Royal with his collection of curios. He unfolded his maps and charts.
These very documents were concrete proof that something *had* been
achieved, that previously unknown territory had been discovered and
charted. The soil had proved fertile, and peaceful coexistence with the
native people seemed possible. The last winter, with the Order of Good
Cheer, the singing and picnicking, had been a fairly happy one.
Comparatively few men had died of scurvy. In just two short years,
what a contrast this was to the horrendous winter they had both
experienced at Ste Croix! There was much that might still be
accomplished in New France.

Yet Champlain himself had lost interest in Acadia, principally
because it had become clear that further exploration of its coasts and
rivers would not lead to China and the fabulous East. Then too, Port
Royal was Poutrincourt's fief. And though he and Poutrincourt had
shared adventures and amusements, they had never become close.
Indeed, Champlain's later references to Poutrincourt and Lescarbot

become quite acidulous. In the several discussions that Champlain had with de Monts he persuaded him that they should turn their attention to 'Canada,' the name then given exclusively to the St Lawrence region. This would be a much better starting-off point for exploration westward. Also, from de Monts' point of view, business should prove more profitable. There they would find many more Indians to trade with: all those tribes who stretched far into the interior and who were already sending furs to the St Lawrence along established trade routes. De Monts had been out seven years before and had seen the trading. And this meant many more possible converts to Christianity as well. Quebec, where the river narrowed, would be a good place at which to build a new settlement that would be both fort and trading station.

De Monts' enthusiasm rose again. Together he and Champlain went to see the King. As we have seen, Henri had already learnt something of French achievements in New France from Poutrincourt. He was quite aware that it was to his advantage to encourage French settlement in the New World. But in spite of news of English in Virginia he was not prepared to outface Sully, the Council, and the free traders on the question of a long-term monopoly. However, to give de Monts a start, he promised to grant him the monopoly of the fur trade for one year only. His decree giving de Monts these exclusive rights was published in January 1608.

With this much gained, de Monts pulled all his resources together and organized a new expedition. He appointed Champlain as his lieutenant and charged him with building a fort at Quebec. Champlain sailed in April. On the 3rd July that year he founded Quebec, and there, with one brief interruption between 1629 and 1632, the French flag flew for approximately a century and a half until Wolfe defeated Montcalm on the Plains of Abraham in the fall of 1759. From 1608 on Champlain's struggles and explorations, his defeats and victories are all part of another story that only rarely touches on the history of Acadian settlements.

But though his attention was now concentrated on Quebec, and the St Lawrence, de Monts did not altogether neglect Acadia in the summer of 1608. To take full advantage of his monopoly he sent Champdoré along with his secretary, Ralluau, to trade with their old friends on the Acadian coast. When they put in at Port Royal, Membertou joyfully greeted them French fashion with musket-shots and bonfires. He and his family crowded round the traders and asked after all their old friends. Champdoré and Ralluau walked round the gardens, admired the crops that Poutrincourt had sown before leaving and those that had flourished on reseeding themselves. Membertou had collected several barrels of grain, reserving one for the French whom he had been expecting. The buildings were in good repair, proof that Membertou had been a faithful caretaker. But this time the French had not come to stay.

Crossing the Bay of Fundy, they went fifty leagues up the Saint John River and so were the first Europeans to explore this splendid waterway.

From there they went down to Saco where they met the new Almouchiquois chief, Asticou, who had taken over from Onemechin when the latter had died in Membertou's war. Champdoré promised him French protection and persuaded him to agree to a peace with his northern neighbours. So the stubborn pilot could congratulate himself on pursuing de Monts' policy of pacification in reconciling Almouchiquois and Etchemins.

There is no indication that this little band of Frenchmen heard any rumours relating to the English colony that Popham and Raleigh Gilbert had established at the mouth of the Kennebec in the fall of 1607. There the new settlers had built a good solid fort with chapel, storehouse, and other buildings, all protected by twelve cannon. But President Popham had died in February after a winter so disastrous that those who survived abandoned the fort in the early summer of 1608 and sailed back home.

As for French colonization, what had become of Poutrincourt and his firm resolution to return and settle at Port Royal with his family? 'And God grant him the means' was Lescarbot's wish for his friend. But the means were precisely what Poutrincourt lacked. He owned two properties – Guibermesnil in Picardy and Marcilly-sur-Seine in Champagne – and was to inherit another at St Just, also in Champagne, from his mother, Jeanne de Salazar. But he was, it seems, involved in costly lawsuits and had no ready capital. And without capital how could he fit out a ship, engage a crew and workmen, purchase all the food and supplies needed? He had not even been able to hire the five workmen who, the previous year, had declared themselves willing to stay on with him at Port Royal. Why in these circumstances did he continue with what to many must have seemed a foolhardy enterprise? Only by looking a little deeper into Poutrincourt's background and character can we try to answer this question and so understand the course of subsequent events.

Men's motives are necessarily mixed. Poutrincourt's ostensible reason for settling at Port Royal was 'to establish the name of Christ and of France' in the New World. But he was not himself without a thirst for glory. Indeed, in all one reads about Poutrincourt one senses that he was a man of some ability driven by restless, even reckless, ambition to achieve distinction. This, of course, was part of his heritage and his times – in fact it is one of the constants in human nature. But one guesses that Poutrincourt's ambition was accentuated by his immediate family history.

He was the youngest of four brothers, two of whom had been killed in battle. The third brother, Jacques, then became principal heir to the family property and titles, among them the domain and name of Poutrincourt. (Of these, the ruined keep of Poutrincourt near Cayeux in Picardy, now a crumbling ancient monument of silex and sandstone surrounded by pastures and cattle, is all that remains of the castles, manors, and houses once held by the Biencourt family.) The Biencourt parents, Florimond and Jeanne de Salazar, were extremely careful, when drawing up their will, to play down the right of primogeniture so that they could distribute their possessions as fairly as possible among their sons and daughters. Jean inherited some share in the secondary domain of Poutrincourt – the main family estate being at Saint Maulvis. So he, as well as Jacques, was known to his contemporaries as the sieur de Poutrincourt – 'the younger' being sometimes added. It is most probable that Jean, like many younger brothers, was anxious not to be outdistanced by his older brother. For Jacques had had something of a position at the Valois Court, and was one of the gentlemen who had accompanied Henri III (then Duke of Anjou) to Poland when he became king of that country in 1573.

If Jacques had achieved some distinction, their father had been even more illustrious. Though Jean was only about ten when his father died in 1567, he must have heard much about his renown. For with Florimond de Biencourt, the family fortunes had reached their peak. He became a protégé of the ambitious Guise family, whose star rose at the French court in the mid-sixteenth century and even threatened to eclipse the monarchy itself. As a Guise favourite, Florimond had found himself on one occasion cutting a figure as ambassador for France at the sumptuous court of Charles v, the Holy Roman Emperor. And it was he whom François de Guise sent in 1549 to another famous Renaissance court, that of Ferrara. There his task was to act as François' proxy on the occasion of his marriage to Anne d'Este, daughter of the powerful Duke and granddaughter, through her mother, of a French king, Louis xii. Florimond obviously was not unwilling to cultivate royal connections. As had been mentioned, his daughter, Jeanne, an older sister of our Poutrincourt, was appointed as attendant to the young Mary Queen of Scots, herself a niece of the Guise brothers. But Jeanne did not bring her family further prominence for she died at court at the tender age of eleven.

At home as well as abroad Florimond's affairs prospered. He made substantial additions to his own property and that of his wife – the Salazars were a family of considerable note. Naturally the division of the property at his death meant that none of his children could be as well off as he had been. Further, the wars of religion made heavy inroads on their inheritance and on Jacques' estate in particular. In 1589 this elder Poutrincourt was obliged to sell cart-horses, a cart, and farm equipment to pay off some of his debts. When he died in 1603 these debts were found to be so extensive that his son, Philippe, made a formal application to the King to delay being recognized as heir until an inventory could be drawn up.

At this time Jean, despite lawsuits, was not in quite such straits, though he too had been affected by the wars. Still, he must have been very conscious of the difference between his father's position and his own. His mother was still alive at this time and on the occasion of family weddings and gatherings might be regarded as a witness of former splendours. In various legal documents Florimond is referred to as 'noble et puissant seigneur' (noble and powerful lord). His sons receive the simpler, in fact quite ordinary, appellation 'noble seigneur.' One wonders if, among Jean's dreams, lurked that of restoring the 'puissant.' By his wife, Claude Pajot, who was of respectable Parisian bourgeois stock, he had several children, among them two sons, Charles and Jacques. It is highly possible that he wanted to distinguish himself in their eyes as his father had done in his. To establish these sons in estates in New France would be a novel and striking way of restoring lustre to the family name.

All this still does not necessarily mean that Poutrincourt cynically undertook to settle Port Royal from purely personal motives. He certainly thought himself to be less self-interested than the merchants who refused to have anything whatsoever to do with colonization and were interested only in profits. His glory would, after all, be France's glory too. The main drawback was that he himself had no capital to invest. But since he regarded himself as having a civilizing and Christianizing mission in the New World, he felt it was up to civilization and Christianity to support him in his endeavours. His sponsors could offer money. He himself could contribute enthusiasm, energy, and experience. But civilization and Christianity are vague sponsors. He would need to turn to particular patrons to finance his good works.

First of course there was the King. Poutrincourt knew that Henri realized that any achievement of his in the New World would be in the King's own interests. But it was not Henri's policy, as we have seen, to subsidize colonies. And Poutrincourt must have pondered the fact that no royal funds had been forthcoming for de Monts, who was closer to the King than he was – and the Lieutenant-Governor too. But then again, de Monts was a Protestant. This had caused some critics of his monopoly to question the seriousness of the King's evangelizing intentions. After three years, they scoffed, where were the converts? As a Catholic, Poutrincourt could hope to be regarded as a genuine Christianizing colonist. Might not that loosen the royal purse-strings?

So, during the course of 1608, Poutrincourt made various efforts to consolidate his position in the eyes of the King and to promote his plans for Port Royal. Early in February de Monts ceded the Habitation to him. Then in March Henri officially confirmed the grant of Port Royal that de Monts had made Poutrincourt in August 1604. On this occasion the new seigneur possibly had another interview with the King, spoke to him about his plans for converting the Indians, and hinted that financial assistance to further this pious aim would be welcome. But like Queen Elizabeth, whom he had much admired, Henri was a great believer in encouraging private enterprise among his subjects. Blithely and wilily ignoring the fact that Poutrincourt had to sail and settle before the work of conversion could begin, Henri promised a sum of two thousand livres a year – to go directly to two Jesuit missionaries. This was not what Poutrincourt had hoped for at all. But the King obviously wished to underscore his conversion-not-conquest policy towards the New World by subsidizing missionaries rather than colonists. So what was a disappointment to Poutrincourt came as a trumpet call to French Jesuits.

And indeed, even since 1604 the Jesuits, then engaged in mission work almost all over the world as then known to Europeans – in China, Japan, Brazil, Paraguay – had been particularly anxious to extend their labours to New France. Now, at last, in a letter dated 5th March, Henri's confessor, the Jesuit priest Father Coton, was able to report the King's promise of a subsidy to his General at Rome, the famous Aquaviva. A number of French Jesuits waited to hear whether their superiors had listened to their requests and had chosen them for the mission field. About May 1608 it was rumoured that Poutrincourt's expedition would be shortly on its way. But in August General Aquaviva in Rome heard from Father Coton in Paris that Poutrincourt had met with obstacles – the major hindrance we must assume being a still-empty purse. Information regarding Poutrincourt's activities at this time is lacking. We may note that it was this August – a healthy ten months after his return – that his seventh child, a daughter, was born. Still, it is unlikely that it was this happy event that held up his plans for settling at Port Royal.

Despite the delay, the King's promise continued to be discussed in the Jesuit houses in France. One of the volunteers for New France was Father Pierre Biard, then teaching theology at Lyons. There it was thought that, instantly obedient to the King's will, Poutrincourt must surely be on the point of sailing. In the fall of 1608 Father Biard was dispatched to Bordeaux, only to discover that no one had heard anything about a new expedition to Canada, though 'of the former wreck and ruin ... each one philosophized in his own fashion.' In the meantime, to Father Biard's disappointment and annoyance, there was 'no preparation, no reports or tidings.' After this, another two years were to elapse before Father Biard would be called upon again.

That same fall Champdoré was back in France. The good report he gave Poutrincourt and Lescarbot of the state of the Habitation and Membertou's faithful friendship brought Port Royal vividly and encouragingly before their minds. In the course of that year Lescarbot had been hard at work on his *History of New France*, which was to come out early in 1609. His fluent pen, put to the service of his friend, praised his purpose, lyrically insisted on the beauty and promise of the land, and pointed to the glorious opportunities for saving savage souls. Readers were left in no doubt whatsoever that they too might contribute to furthering so worthy an enterprise. The book sold well over the course of the next few years. In fact, it was reissued with changes in 1611 and with additions in 1618. But it failed to bring sponsors flocking purse in hand to Poutrincourt.

In October 1608 Lescarbot also drafted a letter to the Pope, Paul v, on his friend's behalf. This, couched in magniloquent Latin and studded with Biblical quotations, was dispatched to Rome along with missives from the King. It was not ostensibly a begging letter – Poutrincourt proclaims himself as willing 'to expend [his] every resource.' However, he did not have very many of the financial sort. Did he secretly entertain visions of papal largesse? Or did he merely hope that the Pope's august approval would lend credibility to his endeavours and encourage others to disburse?

In any case the search for suitable backers continued. About this time Poutrincourt may already have been in touch with Eric of Lorraine, Prince of the Holy Roman Empire and Bishop of Verdun. Not very much is known about the episode, though it is probable that Poutrincourt used his connections to obtain an interview with this prelate. One can only imagine the enthusiasm of the tall fifty-year-old nobleman as he endeavoured to catch the imagination of the rich, powerful old bishop. Did the latter, seated in a great chair, listen wearily or attentively to descriptions of vast, forested coasts, waters teeming with fish? The soil, he would have been assured, was far from barren. Once cultivated, it had brought forth magnificent grain. And the souls of the native inhabitants were like the soil, untilled but ready to receive the word of God. Of course, nothing could be done without money and if His Grace wished ...

Poutrincourt received a document signed by both the Bishop and his secretary. This he interpreted as authorizing him to draw on the Bishop's credit for goods worth fourteen thousand livres. Here at last was the support he needed. On the strength of this note he bought a small ship of about sixty tons auspiciously named the *Grâce-de-Dieu*, arranged for it to be fitted out, and hired a crew. Some time in 1609 all was ready. Many of the transactions Poutrincourt entrusted to a Parisian businessman, Fortunat du Gué, who sent the Bishop a bill for

four thousand livres. But it seemed His Grace had not really wished. ...
He refused to pay, claimed that Poutrincourt had presumed too far and
had quite misinterpreted the tenor of his note. It was a severe set-back.
There was nothing Poutrincourt could do but engage in yet another lawsuit, this time against the Bishop. Fortunat du Gué recouped his losses
by selling the cargo, but Poutrincourt still owed him a thousand livres.

So another summer would go by at Port Royal. The occasional trader
might put in, but Membertou would look in vain for the friends who
had promised to return. Taking stock of the period of two years since he
had returned to France, Poutrincourt had to face the bitter fact that
nothing had been accomplished. He was no nearer his domain of Port
Royal, and had become embroiled only deeper in litigation and debt.
Did the voice of prudence, or that of his wife, advise him that it was
now time to stop?

In October 1609 Champlain, his former companion of the Order of
Good Cheer, was back in France. He had survived his first winter at
Quebec, though more than half of his men had died and he too had
come down with scurvy – for the first time. In the summer he had been
on the warpath and had fought alongside the Hurons and Algonquins
in the historic battle against the Iroquois on the shores of the newly
named Lake Champlain. At Fontainebleau Champlain saw both the
King and de Monts. The King declined to renew de Monts' monopoly
which had expired some months before. Still, profits from furs had
been good that year. So de Monts and his partners decided to continue
with their enterprise and support the Habitation at Quebec for at least
another winter.

But Champlain had not forgotten that the principal reason for the
French presence in New France was supposed to be the conversion of
the Indians. He had probably learnt of the King's promise to grant an
annual subsidy of two thousand livres to two Jesuit missionaries. And
he had heard of a potential and powerful patroness at court. For in the
summer of 1609 one of the Jesuit volunteers for foreign missions had
arrived at court to assist Father Coton. This was Enemond Massé, a
native of Lyons who had become confessor to Antoinette de Pons,
Madame de Guercheville, wife of the Governor of Paris and chief
lady-in-waiting to the Queen.

This lady was to play a distant but decisive role in the story of Port
Royal. So some brief mention should be made of her here. In a court

Madame de Guercheville

titillated by tales of the King's gallantries she stood out as a model of virtue and piety. When Marie de Médicis had arrived to become Queen of France, it was reported that the King had presented Madame de Guercheville to his new wife saying, 'Madam, I give you a lady-of-honour who is a true lady of honour.' The King had reason to know. While out hunting some years before, he had sent to her château nearby to ask for shelter for the night. For some time Madame de Guercheville, then a young widow, had suspected that the royal intentions regarding herself were less than honourable. Responding with both wit and propriety, she accorded the King an elaborate welcome and then withdrew to spend the night at a neighbour's château. Dismayed on seeing her depart, Henri exclaimed: 'What! Am I driving you from your house?' Madame de Guercheville's reply showed she was in admirable command of the situation. 'Sire,' she answered, 'where a King is, he should be the sole master: but, for my part, I like to preserve some little authority wherever I may be.' To his credit Henri took this well. He always respected a spirited adversary. Madame de Guercheville continued to take good care of her reputation. Married for a second time to M. de Liancourt, the Governor of Paris, she refused to take his name and become known as Madame de Liancourt. For the very similar 'Madame de Liencourt' was a title belonging to Gabrielle d'Estrées, one of the King's best-loved and most famous mistresses, with whom the prudent Antoinette de Pons did not care to be confused.

Father Massé, Madame de Guercheville's new confessor, would have appreciated such scruples. He was later to admit that he himself had been mercifully preserved from experiencing any of the temptations of the flesh. Now destined for the mission fields, he succeeded in arousing the interest of his penitent in the spiritual plight of the hordes of heathens who inhabited New France. She was, the rumour ran, prepared to make a generous contribution to support the Jesuits abroad.

This was an opportunity Champlain could not pass over. He went to see Father Coton several times and suggested that Madame de Guercheville take over Quebec for the sum of thirty-six hundred livres – but without success. Writing in 1632, Champlain was still somewhat bitter after almost a quarter of a century. For Father Coton 'would have liked the arrangement made on lower terms or by other means, which could not have been to the advantage of the Sieur de Monts, and this was the reason why nothing was done, in spite of all I could urge upon this father, along with the advantages it might possess in the conversion of the heathen, as well as for ... commerce and trade. ...'

Father Coton was no doubt reluctant to suggest to Madame de Guercheville that she aid the efforts of the Huguenot de Monts – though he himself *had* admitted in 1607 that de Monts was one of those 'heretics ... not too far removed from the Kingdom of heaven.' Nonetheless, even Father Coton could not feel happy about sending his priests off to participate in an enterprise directed by a Huguenot, however good a Catholic his lieutenant Champlain might be. Further, he was still counting on Poutrincourt's establishing himself in Acadia. And Poutrincourt was a 'known Catholic,' a member of the provincial Catholic nobility like Coton himself. The Jesuit felt surer about entrusting his missionaries to the care of someone of his own background and religion rather than to de Monts, honourable gentleman though he was. So it was in vain that Champlain pointed out the advantages that the St Lawrence area had over Acadia: the more easily protected terrain, the larger number of Indians. Father Coton was not interested. Events later were to show that he had every reason to regret this bias.

There was nothing underhand in Champlain's attempt to win the Jesuits to Quebec away from Acadia. And in fact Father Coton was mistaken. The 'known Catholic' Poutrincourt was not at all eager to avail himself of Jesuit services. To understand why involves examining some of the prejudices against the Jesuits that, whether justified or not, were then current. Only in this way will we be able to understand subsequent developments at Port Royal.

In the course of the sixteenth century, mighty Spain had made the cause of Catholicism the cause of Spain. Since it was a Spaniard, St Ignatius of Loyola, who had founded the Society of Jesus in 1534, Jesuits were commonly suspected of being more loyal to Spain than to their own countries and of favouring Spanish domination of Europe. But this, their enemies insisted, was only part of their ultimate ambition. They might be pro-Spain and also proclaim themselves the devoted servants of the Pope. What the Society really wanted was nothing less than mastery on its own behalf of the entire world.

According to their ill-wishers, to effect this they insinuated themselves everywhere, but principally into the good graces of monarchs and rulers. They studied their foibles, made themselves agreeable and useful and then indispensable. Having caught the consciences of kings, they could then dictate policy – policy of course always favourable to themselves and their cause. They persuaded the wealthy and influential to send their more able sons to their colleges. There the priests could train the men of the future, the potential royal advisers and administrators, in *their* ways, become their confessors and through them direct events. A monarch who opposed them or was not approved of by them could not be safe. Elizabeth of England herself had been threatened. And did not the writings of the Spanish Jesuit Mariana, published in 1598, condone regicide?

It was on the count of favouring regicide that the Jesuits had become suspect in France. For in 1594 a youth named Chastel had attempted to stab the King. He was condemned to die a traitor's death. Investigations showed that he had spent some time in a Jesuit college. Two of his former teachers were arrested, and inflammatory anti-Henri pamphlets dating back to early League days were found in the possession of one of them, a Father Guignard. He was hanged and the Jesuits expelled from France. Chastel's house was razed to the ground and a pyramid erected on the place where it had stood. On its base passers-by could read vehement denunciations of the Jesuits.

But in working for the greater glory of God, the Jesuits were nothing if not resourceful. Their ablest diplomats set about negotiating a reconciliation between the Pope and Henri IV. In 1603 as reward for these efforts Henri allowed the Jesuits to return to France, but only on condition that they took a solemn oath never to attempt anything against the King or the peace of the realm. And he stipulated that one Jesuit was to remain at court as security to guarantee the good conduct of the others. Also they would be allowed to teach in their colleges but not publicly. Father General Aquaviva found these conditions humiliating, but the Jesuits returned. Father Coton was placed at court where his discreet, well-bred manner so charmed the King that he asked him to become his spiritual director. At Father Coton's request, the Chastel pyramid was pulled down and at high noon too rather than at dead of night as Protestant Sully advised. Later Henri promised the Jesuits that on his death they could have his heart to place in their college of La Flèche, a property of his own that he had given them. But matters of state the King definitely considered to be his own affair. In the interests of France he was quite prepared to ally himself with the Protestant powers of Europe against the Catholic Hapsburgs of Spain and Germany, whatever Father Coton might say.

Though the King had become reconciled to the Jesuits, a number of his subjects had not. The Sorbonne and the Parlement, Sully and the Protestants were all suspicious and hostile. They insisted on seeing every Jesuit as an ambitious intriguer, travelling the world in disguise and under many aliases, using his smooth, clever tongue to flatter, persuade, control – all in the name of religion. This attitude comes over especially clearly in the journals of Pierre de l'Estoile, the fascinating chronicler of those times, who made many references to the Jesuits, none of them complimentary: 'Their long cloak of devotion is only a cover for sedition' is one of the mildest. 'Pères Jésuites' he deforms to 'vipères Jésuites.' And l'Estoile was a keen though morose observer of the public scene, an avid collector of books, pamphlets, pasquinades, a gleaner of gossip and graffiti. So while his anecdotes and comments are outrageously prejudiced, they nevertheless convey a certain current in public opinion.

L'Estoile's obsession with this question led him to make a special collection of 'Jesuitries': books and pamphlets written by both pro- and anti-Jesuit factions and hectic with polemical exchanges between them. Here it is significant that one of the controversies that raged concerned Jesuit foreign missions. Malevolent accusations portrayed the priests as greedy for gain and engaged in trade under cover of converting the heathen. Of course, it might be noted that missionary work anywhere was impossible without financial aid and that the Jesuits, especially in Mexico and South America, often found themselves protecting the Indians against European exploiters. And with regard to his 'Jesuitries,' l'Estoile himself often complained that he found the invective on both sides so much windy rhetoric, quite lacking in dialectical skill or literary merit. He labelled these works 'fadèzes' ('fadaises,' twaddle), one of his favourite words. (He also used it to describe Lescarbot's grand 'epic' on Membertou's war!).

But all this twaddle was not considered innocuous by the authorities. Books and pamphlets produced by both factions were seized and banned, printers and pamphleteers imprisoned and punished. In his journal for the year 1609 l'Estoile dwelt at some length on the case of his friend, Antoine Fuzy, the curé of a church in Paris. It appears that Fuzy had refused to lend his pulpit to the Jesuits and said that he would rather lose his living than allow a Jesuit to preach in his church. In November Fuzy found himself in court charged with various crimes. Another charge was that he had written an anti-Jesuit book, *Mastigophoros*, which had been banned. Fuzy refuted all these accusations and claimed that the Jesuits had tried to frame him. Lescarbot too was implicated. In a note to his account of this affair, l'Estoile added, 'An advocate friend of mine, named Lescarbot, in trouble and in prison, because of the *Mastigophoros* of Fuzy ...' On reading the banned book, l'Estoile found it such fustian stuff that he hoped that no friend of his had had anything to do with it. Still, it is interesting to see Lescarbot already associated with anti-Jesuit pamphleteering.

Such circumstances do not make for plain, open dealing. Back in France, Champlain was so far removed from this climate of heated suspicion and slander, libel, and polemics that he actively sought out Jesuit support for his labours in the new world. Poutrincourt, friendly with Lescarbot and imbued with all the current prejudices against the fathers, kept away. Meanwhile, the optimistic Father Coton went on happily assuming that once Poutrincourt made a move, for the Jesuits too it would be 'westward ho!'

CHAPTER TEN

First Converts

A FEW ADVENTUROUS FRENCH SPIRITS might direct themselves westwards, but in late 1609 France was uneasily looking east. Earlier that year the Duke of Cleves-Julich-Berg had died, and the Holy Roman Emperor, a Hapsburg, had occupied the former Duke's lands until it was decided who should succeed him – a Catholic or a Protestant. The Protestant princes of the Reich were alarmed, for these duchies on the Rhine frontier of the Netherlands occupied an important strategic position. Henri, who had no love for the Hapsburgs, declared himself on the side of the Protestant princes against the Spanish-dominated Catholic forces – though his object was not to combat Catholicism but to weaken Spain. (This was, of course, the same policy which Cardinal Richelieu, that great promoter of the French monarchy, would later pursue for Henri's son, Louis XIII.) At the Arsenal, Sully began stockpiling arms and vast sums of money. Preparations were made for war, troops mobilized and provisions stored. Still, a number of Henri's Catholic subjects were unhappy that their King should back the Protestant side, for they themselves emphatically preferred Hapsburgs to the disciples of Luther and Calvin.

Henri himself was in a tetchy mood when his thoughts went eastwards – but for personal rather than political reasons. His latest love had eluded him. Wild with desire for the lovely young Charlotte de Montmorency, he had married her off to his relative and first prince of the blood, the Prince de Condé. In this way he hoped to keep her within easy reach of his royal attentions. But she had disobeyed his orders to return to court, riding off instead with her husband to Brussels. Here they were protected by the Spanish Imperialist forces who delighted in the discomfiture of the ageing lecher.

Some time towards the end of November, Poutrincourt found himself in Paris. His mood was not hopeful. He had done his best to obtain funds, but no one seemed really interested in his enterprise. Though his mother had died recently and left him the manor of St Just in Champagne, he still did not have the means to engage in a costly colonial venture.

At some moment while Poutrincourt was at court, the King's eye lighted on him. Amazed and angry, he wanted to know what Poutrincourt was still doing in France when he was supposed to be out in the New World, establishing a French colony and converting the Indians. Henri's quick temper and round oaths were a byword in the land. Poutrincourt was shaken. He could feel nothing but utter humiliation.

His mind might have flashed back to another meeting with Henri, nineteen years earlier in 1590. While fighting for the League against the yet unconverted monarch, he had held Beaumont-sur-Oise so valiantly against the King that the Gascon had tried to win him over to his own cause. Loyal to his party, Poutrincourt had resisted both the honour and the promise of a reward. Finally he had had to surrender Beaumont to Henri's superior forces. Nevertheless, the King had been generous in his praise of this tough opponent. He declared Poutrincourt to be 'one of the most honourable and valiant men in his kingdom.'

And now this same King, grizzled beard bristling, was speaking to him as though he were a laggard flagging in the field of battle. In the gentleman's code of the times all honour stemmed from the King. Unless Poutrincourt proved himself immediately in his sovereign's eyes, he could consider that he had lost his honour, that precious essence of a nobleman. It was a turning-point in his life. Mustering all his dignity, he answered that 'since his Majesty had this affair so much at heart, he would take leave of him at once, to go directly and look after the equipment for his voyage.' It was a proud answer, but not one that made him any less penurious. Poutrincourt's attempt to salvage his honour was to lead him into strange ways.

The news of this interview and Poutrincourt's declaration soon reached Father Coton. For five years he had been trying to send 'Our Men' into New France. He was keenly aware of their eagerness to go and of Father Biard's disappointment at Bordeaux. Now, at last, the right opportunity had presented itself. He went to see Poutrincourt and offered him the company of Jesuit missionaries. It was not an offer that Poutrincourt was happy to accept. He hedged, pointed out that in such enterprises conditions were often rough. The kitchen, he claimed, was not yet built. (This from a distinguished member of the Order of Good Cheer!) The Jesuits, he insisted, as learned scholars, men concerned with matters of the mind, would not want to put up with physical hardship and drudgery. Father Coton riposted that Jesuits asked only to offer their bodies to save souls. Poutrincourt stubbornly maintained that now was a bad time for them to come. Let them wait until his son returned from Port Royal when settlement would be under way. Then, if the King wanted to send out Jesuits ... It was grudging encouragement, but Father Coton remained hopeful.

Poutrincourt had a busy winter. He made arrangements for his ship, the *Grâce-de-Dieu*, to be got ready and outfitted, signed on crew and artisans, tried to interest relatives, friends, and acquaintances in the expedition. Towards the end of January he signed a document giving his wife power of attorney so she could administer family affairs in his absence. In early February he was at his seigneury of St Just – a fine domain, says Lescarbot, where the Seine and the Aube meet. Here Poutrincourt loaded a ship that was to sail down the Seine, still flooded by winter rains, and then along the Norman coast to Dieppe. It is not clear just how Poutrincourt had managed to find the necessary funds. Perhaps he had been able to squeeze something out of his new inheritance to take to Port Royal: wheat from his mill, wine, old furnishings that Madame de Poutrincourt was prepared to discard.

On the 15th February Poutrincourt was in Paris – it is even possible that he moored his ship here for a day or two – to sign another document. This gave his lawyer, Nicolas Desnoyers, who was also his creditor, power of attorney regarding his business affairs. Desnoyers was also to continue with proceedings against Eric of Lorraine, the Bishop of Verdun, and others who owed his client money.

The prospective voyagers, 'many worthy gentlemen and artisans' according to Lescarbot, assembled at Dieppe. With Poutrincourt was his son Charles, then about eighteen or nineteen. From Paris came a sieur de Jouy, related to the furrier Louis de Jouy and so particularly interested in looking into the possibilities of the fur trade. Also with an eye open for business opportunities was sieur Bertrand, who, though a moderate man, suffered from frequent attacks of gout. Then there was another gentleman, Belot 'called Montfort.' Someone who had already heard much about New France was Réne Maheut, nephew of Louis Hébert, the apothecary, and so, like Hébert, related to Poutrincourt through marriage. Also, like Hébert, he was later to settle and die in Quebec. It is uncertain whether Hébert himself was of this party for we do not hear of him as being in Acadia until the next year (1611). The same goes for another and younger relative, Valentin Pajot, son of a notary. And Charles La Tour too went out again either this year or the next, but this time without his father, Claude. Someone who was definitely on this voyage was Thomas Robin de Coulognes, a young man of good family. His father was a fairly important functionary in the household of the King's ex-wife, the ugly, witty, extravagant Marguerite de Valois, or the Reine Margot as she was popularly known. (Henri and Marguerite were related, so in 1599 the Pope had annulled the marriage without demur.) About the crew and artisans, some fifteen or twenty in number, we know very little. Later incidents suggest they were not likely to prove solid New World citizens.

As Poutrincourt could hardly launch an evangelical crusade without a priest, he had enlisted the services of one Jessé Fleché, a secular priest from Langres. Lescarbot, who never met him, describes him as 'a man of good life and good learning.' He held his commission not from any French bishop, as was usual for French priests, but from the Papal Nuncio in Paris, Robert Ubaldini. From this prelate he had permission 'to hear the confessions of all persons ... to consecrate and bless ... vestments' and also, obviously, to baptize. One has the feeling that Father Coton would not have been impressed.

Before leaving, Poutrincourt, who knew that his supplies would not last long, was in touch with two Huguenot merchants or ship outfitters of Dieppe, Dujardin and Duquesne. It is not clear exactly what arrangements Poutrincourt made with these merchants for reprovisioning the *Grâce de Dieu* when she returned from Port Royal. Only some time later would he realize how desparately short he was of provisions, for his overseer, charged with loading the wheat, had sold some of it, and pocketed the profits.

About the 25th February the ship sailed out of the well-protected port of Dieppe, dominated by its fortress on the hill. The voyage proved long and difficult as the ship was beset by raging tempests and wearisome calms. During the calms some members of the crew found time to dream up plans for easy riches. They plotted to seize the ship, pillage the 'savages,' turn pirate upon the high seas, become highwaymen on the road to Paris, then finally retire to enjoy their ill-gotten gains in peace. Poutrincourt got wind of this highly unrealistic conspiracy but pardoned the culprits. Of course, he did not have a large crew, so perhaps his clemency was thrust upon him.

About two and a half months after leaving Dieppe, on the 11th May, they found themselves on the Grand Banks. Fortified by fresh fish caught there, they sailed on to Port Mouton. Port Royal was not far, but on rounding Cape Sable they got lost in the fog and were blown off course towards the Penobscot River. So on the 20th May, Ascension Thursday, they left the ship to hear Father Fleché say Mass on an island somewhere off Mount Desert Island – but no map or chart records the place and the name. From there they went up the Ste Croix river to visit the old island settlement and say the prayers for the dead over the graves of those buried there. By this time Ste Croix had become something of a place of pilgrimage.

Towards the end of May they were still in Passamaquoddy Bay. There an Indian chief recognized Poutrincourt and came to see him. He had a complaint to lodge against one of Poutrincourt's fellow countrymen. A Frenchman, while trading in those parts, had made off with a young Indian woman already married or at least promised in marriage to one of their group. The culprit, Poutrincourt soon discovered, was his old companion Robert Gravé, the handsome son of François, whose injured hand he had had treated with Port Royal clay. (The New World had obviously continued to exercise its charms on young Gravé, now commander of his own trading vessel.) As this rape might well cause ill feelings between French and Indians, Poutrincourt took it upon himself to deal with the affair.

On the 2nd June he commissioned Robin de Coulognes to institute proceedings. On the 3rd Robin managed to arrest Gravé. On the 4th Poutrincourt heard witnesses and interrogated the erring Frenchman. The latter spiritedly declared that he would recognize Poutrincourt only as a gentleman, not as his judge, since he had no real judicial authority over him. This was quite true. Nevertheless, on the 5th the 'court' decided to refer Gravé and his case to the King's council. But in the meantime he was kept prisoner on his own ship while an inventory was made of his goods. On the 15th on the pretence of going hunting –

survcillance can hardly have been strict – he escaped and went to live with the Indians on the Saint John River. They obviously took a more lenient view of his offence. At the same time, an officer on Gravé's ship drew up a report of the proceedings, and Gravé's ship and crew went free. This episode marks the beginning of much bad blood between young Gravé and the Biencourts, the trader-adventurer and the would-be colonists.

The *Grâce-de-Dieu* reached Port Royal towards mid-summer, on the 17th June. It was almost three years since Poutrincourt had been there busily harvesting the grain so he could take back the first fruits from New France to Old. The Habitation was still standing. Not a stick of furniture had disappeared. However, the gales and blizzards of the last winters had blown off and caved in the roofs. The mill, too, on the river opposite, had taken a beating. In the overgrown gardens some vegetables struggled through the weeds.

On this occasion no Membertou came rushing to the shore to greet them. So someone, probably young Biencourt, went off to look for him along the shores of St Mary's Bay where the Indians often made summer encampments. And within a few days a small band of Indians arrived at the Habitation. The two captains, tall Membertou and the taller Poutrincourt, embraced like long-lost brothers. The other Indians crowded round. Where were their other friends: Champlain, Champdoré, Lescarbot, Gravé? In the buzz of explanations, Membertou heard that Lescarbot had written about him and his war in a book and that his fame as a warrior had now spread to France.

Membertou and his family met the new arrivals. Chief among them was Jessé Fleché – a very special man, the Indians were told. This time, Poutrincourt assured Membertou, the French had come to stay. And did Membertou remember how Christians put their trust in one God by making the sign of the cross; how by this sign they were saved from the torments of the devil both during their life and after death? For on dying, good Christians went to heaven, a beautiful place where they were happy forever. Charles de Biencourt interpreted. He had been young and adaptable enough on his first visit three years before to be more proficient in the Micmac language than the others. It was then put to Membertou that he and his family should renounce the devil and accept the Christian God and the loving Jesus whom they could see on the crucifix. Jessé Fleché would make the sign of the cross with some water on their foreheads, and give them a French name. They would then be Christians like the French. After this ceremony Poutrincourt would hold a tabagie for them to celebrate their deliverance from the devil. Membertou listened and decided that he and his group would all become Christians.

The great day was set for the 24th June, appropriately enough the Feast of St John the Baptist and Poutrincourt's own feast day. Jessé Fleché, robed in vestments which marked him off from the other Frenchmen, heard a general confession from Membertou. The old chief repented of all the sins of his past life, and particularly the dealings he, as Aoutmoin, had had with the devil. And he replaced the triangular sorcerer's bag he wore around his neck with a cross.

French and Indians then gathered together for the main ceremony, the Indians dressed in their finest clothes and ornaments, their faces freshly painted. Poutrincourt stood by Membertou and promised on his behalf to renounce the devil and all his works and pomps. The 'patriarch,' as Fleché came to be called, poured the holy water over him and baptized him Henri 'in nomine Patris et Filii et Spiritus Sancti. Amen.' And so Membertou became the first Indian to receive the sacrament of baptism on the shores of New France. As sagamo he was named after the King, who was considered to be his real godfather while Poutrincourt was only his sponsor by proxy.. For this gentleman had no means of knowing that in May an assassin's knife had ended Henri's eventful life and that now all France was mourning his death.

Then came the turn of the other twenty Indians, all members of Membertou's family. His wife was baptized Marie after the Queen, his daughter Marguerite after Henri's first wife, both Queens of course being regarded as the real godmothers. Another instant convert was Membertou's oldest son. Three years before some of the French used to tease him by calling him Judas, a name he knew meant something dishonourable. On this occasion he was graced with the name of Henri's eldest son, Louis, Charles de Biencourt acting as godfather. Louis had two wives. The Patriarch made no demur about admitting them both to the Christian fold, also Louis' young son aged five and his six daughters, children presumably by both wives.

The ceremony continued. Poutrincourt himself was sponsor by proxy for most of these new Christians, though some of the other Frenchmen there also stepped forward to perform this office. Another of Membertou's sons was called Paul after the Pope, while a cousin of

Membertou's received the name of his Nuncio in Paris, Robert. Then there was another of Membertou's cousins, his wife and two daughters, and last of all a niece, probably a widow. Two of Louis' daughters were named after royal children. But a number of the group were accorded members of Poutrincourt's own family as godparents. Robin de Coulognes was sponsor for a girl named Catherine after his mother, and René Maheut was sponsor for another named Charlotte after his.

So the holy water flowed as the Latin phrases and French names resounded. What did Messire Jessé Fleché think as he 'accomplished this masterpiece of Christian piety,' to use Lescarbot's hyperbolic phrase? Did he consider the Indians such children that to confer baptism on them was like conferring infant baptism? Did he pray that the grace received would gradually work on their souls, so bringing them close to Christian ways? Or did he just not ask any questions at all?

As for Poutrincourt, he had the proceedings carefully noted down: the names of the neophytes, their sponsors by proxy, the godparents for whom they were named. Here at last was some proof of his zeal, an earnest of his evangelizing endeavours. The King had wanted results. Now he had them. And with results surely some recognition, encouragement, remuneration would follow? Might not the King now grant him the monopoly of the fur trade in this region?

The new Christians arose from their knees. The French sang the *Te Deum* with great gusto. Cannon shots were fired. For a full quarter of an hour echoes boomed off the surrounding hills. Though food supplies were diminished by the long journey, there was a feast and, no doubt, some wine for Membertou. The latter had thrown himself into the day's ceremonies 'with as much enthusiasm, fervor and zeal for Religion as would have been evinced by a person who had been instructed in it for three or four years.' This, at any rate, was the impression he made upon sieur Bertrand. With all the enthusiasm of the recent convert – or was it the wine? – Membertou promised that he would have other Indians baptized too. If they resisted, it would be war! Poutrincourt did what he could to temper but not extinguish this excessive zeal.

On the day of the baptisms Poutrincourt wrote an affectionate letter to Lescarbot to share the good news with him. He regretted that Lescarbot was not at Port Royal so he could enjoy his 'pleasant company'; remembered how he had 'laboured so well at the cultivation of [his] garden'; wished he were there to assist in the conversions and 'aid me to labour in the garden of God.' This letter young Biencourt was to take to France when he sailed two weeks later with news of the conversions. Poutrincourt himself was to remain behind to direct the Habitation.

During those pleasant summer days the French settled into the fort. The men began to till the soil and to plant seeds and trees – perhaps the first fruit trees in a region that was to become famous for its apples. The blacksmith's anvil rang out in the forge. Saws grated through wood. Some roofs, though not all, were replaced and the mill repaired. Fetching water from a stream outside the enclosure of the fort had always been a nuisance. Poutrincourt had a well dug in the centre of the courtyard. Bricks made of Port Royal clay lined the foundations. Jessé Fleché took over Lescarbot's room – also his beloved garden, where, Lescarbot proudly reports, 'he found, at his arrival, a great many radishes, parsnips, carrots, turnips, peas, beans, and all kinds of good and productive culinary herbs.'

A few days after the conversions, Bertrand wrote a letter to his brother in which he showed considerable enthusiasm for Port Royal:

As to the country, I have never seen anything so beautiful, better, or more fertile; and I can say to you, truly and honestly, that if I had three or four labourers with me now, and the means of supporting them for one year, and some wheat to sow in the ground tilled by their labour alone, I should expect to have a yearly trade in Beaver and other Skins amounting to seven or eight thousand livres, with the surplus which would remain to me after their support ... I assure you it is delightful to engage in trade over here and to make such handsome profits. If you wish to take a hand in it, let me know your intentions by the bearer, who desires to return and traffic here in pursuance of what he has seen.

The bearer he refers to was probably Thomas Robin de Coulognes.

The news that the French were back sped along the coast. Indians came to visit and trade. We can imagine the sieur de Jouy closely examining the pelts, deciding what advice to send his furrier relatives in Paris about a possible business association with Poutrincourt. As for the Indians, they were curious about the ceremony at which their fellow tribesmen had become Christians like the French.

An unpleasant rumour reached the habitation. Robert Gravé, now living with the Indians on the Saint John, was doing his best to make trouble between Secoudun, the chief there, and Poutrincourt. All these baptisms, Gravé allegedly told Secoudun, were nonsense, a mere ploy. Poutrincourt was just out to get the Etchemin chief's furs and would kill him if he got a chance. The Biencourt-Gravé feud was now well under way.

On the 8th July Biencourt sailed out of Port Royal with some pelts as well as the precious list of new Christians. With him went Robin de Coulognes, who had been only a summer visitor. Poutrincourt urged his son to return within four months, that is before the onset of winter. Provisions were meagre. He had twenty-three people at the Habitation to feed and hoped also to entertain Membertou, his family, and friends in the manner to which they had all grown accustomed.

Before departure Biencourt also placed in his chest a letter from his father to the King. In this Poutrincourt requested the King to grant to the seigneurs of Port Royal sole rights to the fur trade in Acadia. This would enable them to continue with the work of colonization and conversion which was now so well under way. He also requested that his son be appointed Vice-Admiral for the region so that he might have the authority to enforce such a monopoly. Was it Gravé's proximity, one wonders, that made this request more urgent?

The *Grâce-de-Dieu* did not leave Port Royal unescorted. Poutrincourt decided to accompany his son in a long-boat as far as Cape La Have. On the way there they stopped at one of the islands between Yarmouth and Cape Sable Island. Here they met some Indians they knew who had set up camp to fish. In the greetings and exchange of news Membertou's name came up and the story of his baptism. Poutrincourt lost no opportunity to proselytize, asked them if they would not like to be baptized too. If Membertou had made this gesture of friendship, these Micmacs must have thought, why should not they? So Poutrincourt dispatched them to Port Royal and the waters of salvation.

At Cape La Have father and son embraced. They were not to see each other for another ten months. By the end of July Biencourt and the crew of the *Grâce-de-Dieu* were on the Grand Banks fishing for cod. There they met French fishing ships from whom they had news of the King's death. But who the assassin was the sailors could not say. An English ship that Biencourt encountered a little later elaborated. Who but the Jesuits could have directed the dagger that killed a King, especially when this King was involved in a Protestant alliance of which these priests disapproved? On the 21st August when Biencourt sailed into Dieppe he expected to find France in considerable turmoil.

Meanwhile Poutrincourt went off in zealous search of more converts. At the mouth of the La Have river he inquired after a sagamo whom the French called Martin. (One cannot but wonder if this Martin were Messamouet, since it is generally Messamouet who is regarded as chief of the La Have area.) But dysentery had broken out there and Martin had moved away.

On the way back to Port Royal, Poutrincourt put in at Cape Sable. There he found Martin with about forty followers. They had come looking for him after hearing about his visit to La Have. Again one is struck by the speed with which news circulated along the coasts and through the forests. Poutrincourt invited them to go to Port Royal to learn more about Christianity and be baptized. Martin accepted the invitation. But first, he said, he and his band would go hunting on the way there so as not to arrive empty-handed.

But the Indians, making their way through the woods (today's Kejimkujik Park gives a fair idea of the terrain they must have passed through), arrived at Port Royal long before their host. For Poutrincourt went off course, was tossed about by tempests, had to put into the Ste Croix River and finally did not return to the Habitation until six weeks later, on the 22nd August.

During his absence Jessé Fleché had not been idle. Even without the services of Biencourt as interpreter, he had held baptismal services on the 14th and 15th August. Again some of the French present were sponsors by proxy for grandees and relatives at home, who went about their business and pleasures quite unaware of what things were being promised in their name on the other side of the Atlantic. So Poutrincourt arrived to find Martin and his friends already baptized and listening to liturgical music that Poutrincourt himself had composed.

He also found Martin very weak with dysentery, one of the diseases that had been plaguing the Indians ever since European sailors had first begun to frequent these shores. A short time later Martin died with 'the sacred name of JESUS upon his lips.'

Martin had asked to be buried in the Christian cemetery just outside the Habitation – or perhaps he just gave a feeble nod when asked if that is what he wished. To his friends and family this break with tradition came as a shock. As we have seen, everything to the Indians was sacred, but particularly sacred were their burial ceremonies and their burial grounds as links between the living and the dead. So Martin's 'request' to be buried in Christian ground was not something his people were prepared to countenance. They began the customary wailing about the body, got together his furs, weapons, and ornaments. He was to be buried somewhere on Cape Sable Island. Poutrincourt appeared with some of his men to say that the dead man had become a Christian and has asked for a Christian funeral. Seizing their bows and arrows, the Indians closed round the body. Poutrincourt retreated and armed twelve men with muskets. They advanced upon the group of mourn-ers, who backed off before this *force majeure*. Jessé Fleché, intoning the prayers for the dead, accompanied the body to the grave that had been dug in the Christian cemetery. The French crossed themselves and threw handfuls of earth upon their brother in Christ. The Indians were all given bread and, says Lescarbot, 'went away happy.' We cannot be so sure.

It was probably at this time that Membertou, disturbed by this incident, discussed his eventual death and burial with Poutrincourt. Would it not be possible for him to be buried among his ancestors at the entrace to Port Royal instead of in the Christian cemetery like Martin? Poutrincourt was willing to make exceptions for Membertou. He promised that the old chief should be buried with his ancestors. Then Poutrincourt would have a Christian chapel built on the burial site where prayers could be offered for the repose of Membertou's soul. It was a compromise that satisfied them both.

Life at the Habitation went on. Poutrincourt tried to regulate his little colony along Christian lines and assembled the men each day for morning devotions. Membertou took it upon himself to reproach them when they forgot to say grace before or after meals. The patriarch organized solemn processions up the hill behind the Habitation. Several times Jessé Fleché was called upon to travel four to eight leagues from the fort to baptize children, the weak, and the ill. But Poutrincourt's group of men was far from forming a happy Christian community. Not all the malcontents had returned to France with young Biencourt, and Poutrincourt was sore put to it to keep the grumblers and the rebellious in their place. Those who went to grind corn at the mill managed to hide some portion for themselves. Poutrincourt's most Christian exercise was a continual pardoning of his men for such offences. He could hardly risk a sedition.

The leaves turned colour and fell. By the end of November there was still no sign of Biencourt, no news or provisions from France. At Christmas they gave up hope of seeing the *Grâce-de-Dieu* before spring. Food now had to be severely rationed. The baptisms celebrated on 1st December were probably the occasion for a feast, but that winter there were few jollifications, no Order of Good Cheer. Wildfowl were not as plentiful as before and the French had grown wary of shellfish, thinking that eating this without bread caused dysentry. And there was no fresh bread, for the mill water had frozen and no more grain could be ground.

The men complained, and became even more difficult to handle. Lescarbot later heard that 'mutinies and conspiracies arose; ... the cook stole a part of what belonged to the others, while a certain one cried "hunger" who had plenty of bread and meat in his cell.' Occasionally the Indians brought a quarter of moose, and a brief feast interrupted the long hunger. It was perhaps on the occasion of one of these welcome visits that Poutrincourt determined to send some of the men off to live with the Indians, better able because of their mobility to go in search of game. For seven weeks those at the Habitation lived on dried peas and beans. Yet it seems, and not only on Lescarbot's evidence, that Poutrincourt still had the reputation of being open-handed to the Indians and of not being particularly greedy for furs.

One day over the winter an Indian came to the fort with an urgent message for Poutrincourt. Membertou was dying. Poutrincourt left immediately with his guide. They had four leagues of snowy landscape to pass through before arriving at a little group of birchbark wigwams. In the one Poutrincout entered, the usual fresh green branches of fir were spread on the ground. And there, among the coverings of soft pelts, lay Membertou, arrayed in his best otter robe and waiting to die. When he had fallen sick, a medicine-man had assured him that it would be better for him to resign himself to death rather than go on suffering. So, dressed in his best and deprived of food, Membertou listened to his people chant praises of his past life, his valour, his generosity – and his fortitude on dying. He faltered out suitable responses. At any moment now his dogs would be killed so they could precede him into the spirit world and be there waiting for him when he arrived. As he seemed to be a long time a-dying, his sons prepared to splash cold water onto his bared stomach to hasten him along into the next world.

Here was another Indian tradition and one of which the French had known nothing until then. Lescarbot later divined the reason for it. 'These people,' he wrote, 'being nomadic, and not being able to continue living in one place, cannot drag after them their fathers or friends, the aged or the sick.' But Membertou had been in no mood to die just then, which is why he had sent for Poutrincourt. Besides, did it not behove him to die as a Christian? Poutrincourt had him removed to the Habitation where, he told Lescarbot, 'he had a good fire prepared for him, and, placing him near it upon a good bed, had him rubbed, nursed, well cared for, and doctored; and the result was, at the end of three days, behold Membertou up and about, ready to live fifty years longer.'

Winter dragged on for the cold, hungry French. In desperation some men took to digging for *chiquebi* or ground-nut roots, tubers strung along by a fibrous root like beads on a chain, which Lescarbot recommended as being as delicious as truffles. When pressed by hunger, the Indians would go pulling up this pea-like plant, which can still be found, generally in moist areas. The cooked tubers have something of the texture of sweet potatoes, but are more delicate in flavour. After a few days of uprooting, the men found that they had been preparing for spring by clearing ground where they could plant crops.

Towards the end of March, on Palm Sunday, French and Micmacs together hunted a moose, and in mid-April the fish began running: smelts, alewives, sturgeon, salmon. The Indians brought presents of smoked herring to the Habitation. By now the worst was over and the colonists were no longer in danger of starving.

The remarkable thing was that in spite of such a restricted diet not one man had died and no one had come down with scurvy. Sieur Bertrand in fact had not suffered a single twinge of gout. Only on his return to the 'sweet land of wheatfields and vineyards' did the attacks reoccur. Nevertheless, we hear no more rhapsodies from him on the bounty of New France.

With the melting of the ice the mill had begun to function again. The men ground the wheat that remained for flour. On the 10th May they baked the last batch of bread. Poutrincourt consulted his companions. They decided to adopt the usual plan. If no help arrived within a month, they would go out along the coast to find fishing vessels to take them back to France. Poutrincourt wanted to delay departure until the 24th June, his feast day and the anniversary of the first baptismal ceremony.

On the 21st May, a Saturday, all the French were assembled at the Habitation, for next day they were to celebrate the feast of Pentecost. During the night, three hours after they had gone to bed, a cannon was heard, and a trumpet sounded. The dim shape of a ship could be seen on the water. A messenger went out in a small boat to call out inquiries. Here at last was the *Grâce-de-Dieu*. Canoes transported men from the ship to the oozy mud and stones of the shore. Poutrincourt waited on the banks to greet his son. Among the thirty-six newcomers were two men wearing long black robes and square black hats. After many negotiations, the Jesuits had arrived.

CHAPTER ELEVEN

No Rewards and a New Alliance

WHILE POUTRINCOURT HAD BEEN STRUGGLING FOR SURVIVAL at Port Royal, young Biencourt had had his own problems in France. On his return journey in the summer of 1610 his closest companion was Thomas Robin de Coulognes. This gentleman was perhaps a few years older than Biencourt, but still under twenty-five and therefore a minor. His father, as we have seen, had position and money. Robin himself had all the self-confidence – one may even say bumptiousness – of a young man with expectations. One gets this impression by reading between the lines. For, after playing a brief but important part in the following events, he slips forever from our view. But for a time he appears as the enthusiastic young patron of the Biencourts. Though there are no written contracts extant, it becomes clear that between September 1610 and January 1611 Robin publicly presented himself as a partner in the Biencourt enterprise and signed legal documents that made him jointly responsible with young Biencourt for combined debts of 1,937 livres.

How did this come about? While at sea Charles must often have talked of the potential of Port Royal – fish, furs, timber – and his father's financial difficulties in getting the venture launched. It is not improbable that Robin, warmed with wine and the generous superiority of those whom fortune favours, offered to invest his inheritance, or part of it, in Port Royal.

By the 21st August the *Grâce-de-Dieu* was back in the port of Dieppe, just six months after her departure. The cargo cannot have been substantial, just enough to pay off the crew. Biencourt immediately got in touch with Duquesne and Dujardin to ask them to see to refitting and loading the ship for the next journey – an urgent one as his father needed provisions for the winter. The hard-headed merchants naturally wanted a guarantee that they would be paid for their services. All Biencourt could offer was a possible advance loan from Parisian furriers to whom he had an introduction from the sieur de Jouy. At this point Robin may well have spoken up as someone who had visited the country and who felt so hopeful about its resources that he was prepared to invest in it himself. Duquesne and Dujardin need have no fear. The money would be found. Even so, it takes more than the enthusiasm and eloquence of a self-confident young man to persuade canny merchants into giving credit. Still, some verbal agreement seems to have been reached. Two months later work on the ship had just begun.

From Dieppe the two young men went to Paris. The capital still hummed with talk of the King's assassination. Again and again they heard the details: Henri's coach ride to the Arsenal to see Sully and make arrangements for the Cleves-Julich expedition; the heavy stalking figure of Ravaillac; the slowing of the coach as it passed down the narrow rue de la Ferronière; the quick stabs of Ravaillac's knife before any of the gentlemen in the coach could stir; the spurt of blood; the final slump of the grizzled head. And in spite of Ravaillac's claim, even under torture, that he alone was responsible, there was rumour upon rumour about who lay behind this disaster for France. Henriette d'Entragues, the King's difficult mistress, whose relatives had once plotted against Henri, the Spaniards, the Queen herself – all were blamed. Accusations and innuendoes abounded. L'Estoile reports that Father Coton, on hearing the terrible news, exclaimed, 'Who is the evil-doer who has killed so good a Prince? Was it a Huguenot?'

But the principal focus of accusing eyes was, of course, the Society of Jesus. Some people maintained that the Jesuits had nothing to gain by the death of Henri IV, who had often shown his admiration and respect for the Society. Others claimed that, as a Spanish order, they were desperate to put an end to his alliance with the Protestant princes. But whoever was to blame, it was in everyone's view a sad loss for France. For now the country was governed in the name of a nine-year-old boy by a silly foreign woman, mesmerized, it was whispered, by her sinister Italian favourites.

And Biencourt's hopes depended on the good will of this same foreign woman. The letter Poutrincourt had written to the King found its way into the plump white bejewelled hands of his widow. She, with her conventional piety, expressed a conventional pleasure on hearing of the conversions – a triumph for Christianity and for France! The news made a very minor ripple around the court – perfumed, beribboned courtiers pausing a moment to reflect on a handful of naked heathen Indians saved from hell and made their brethren in Christ. It was an edifying topic of conversation on which the pious Madame de Guercheville could dwell with Father Coton. Would some Jesuit fathers, she inquired, be going out on the next voyage to take part in these glorious labours? Father Coton was annoyed and embarrassed. He had received no letter from Poutrincourt, no request for Jesuit aid. And yet he was sure Poutrincourt had promised that his son, on his return, would be in touch with him.

Here now was an opportunity for Madame de Guercheville to exercise her influence on behalf of the Jesuits. She had some acquaintance with young Robin, since Marie de Médicis and her household were on visiting terms with Queen Marguerite, who held court in a magnificent palace just across the Seine from the Louvre. Robin had been out to New France and had been present at the baptisms. He might know something of the Biencourts' intentions as regards the Jesuits.

Robin was not displeased at the idea of cutting a figure as patron in the eyes of Madame la Marquise de Guercheville. He had, he claimed, taken on the whole responsibility for the next voyage, but 'had no especial commission for the Jesuits ... nevertheless he knew very well that sieur de Poutrincourt would feel very highly honoured to have them with him: and, as to their maintenance, he himself would take charge of that, as he was doing in regard to all the rest of the expenses.' Irritated by the airy ease of the young puppy who was taking so much upon himself, the great lady replied rather tartly that he would 'not be burdened with them ... because the King defrays their expenses.'

However, she did send Robin to see Father Baltazar, the recently appointed Father Provincial in Paris. Robin repeated to him that Poutrincourt would be only too delighted to receive the Jesuits. Father Baltazar lost no time. He immediately sent orders that Father Biard, then preaching in Poitiers, should come to Paris and prepare for departure. With him would go Father Massé, who was still at court, where, according to Father Coton, he was 'well known and loved.' Both priests were overjoyed that God had answered their prayers and, through their superiors, had designated them for a foreign mission. Within the first two weeks of September Father Coton was able to report to General Aquaviva that at last Jesuit fathers would be setting forth on a mission to Canada. Aquaviva in his reply, written a month later, expressed uneasiness about the sure financial basis for such an undertaking.

What Biencourt thought of his friend's officious behaviour and promises on his behalf is not recorded. Robin might well have been totally ignorant of the Biencourt prejudices against the Jesuits. Even on learning of them, he could have argued that no harm was done, for this alliance with the Jesuits was a sure means of bringing court favour to smile upon the expedition. If Robin was still talking about financing the expedition, there was little Biencourt could say. Yet he was certainly not relying on Robin alone.

To begin with, he had already made an application to the King's Council to obtain the monopoly of the fur trade in Acadia and had entered into negotiations with the Duc de Montmorency, Admiral of France, to have himself recognized as Vice-Admiral for Acadian waters – just as de Monts had done seven years earlier. Then there were arrangements to be made for an audience with the Queen so he could tell her in person about the Port Royal conversions.

Very soon after his arrival in Paris, Biencourt had also seen and talked to the ebullient Lescarbot. The latter was delighted to receive a letter from his friend, curious about the voyage, enthusiastic about news of Membertou and the conversions, indignant at young Gravé. Immediately he took up his quill again on his friend's behalf. By the 9th September he had obtained the privilege to print a pamphlet, *La conversion des Sauvages*, which he could present to the Queen when she received Biencourt at court.

Towards the end of September Father Biard was in Paris renewing his acquaintance with Father Massé, whom he had already known at Lyons. They soon hoped to be in touch with Biencourt and on their way to Port Royal.

On the 1st October Biencourt, accompanied by Lescarbot, was graciously received by the Queen Regent, who was still in deep mourning. She praised the efforts that the Biencourts had made to convert the Indians and encouraged them to continue in their holy endeavours. Soon, she said, they would have with them some Jesuit fathers to labour with them in the Lord's vineyard. As for Poutrincourt's request for a monopoly of the fur trade, she would do what she could, in so far as it was in the best interests of the King 'my lord and son.' She also accepted Lescarbot's little work but favoured it with no more than a cursory glance. Marie was no great reader.

Worse still, no purses of silver were delivered by a steward at a sign from the royal hand, nor was there even mention of a reward. It became clear that what money the Queen had to bestow on mission work would go directly to the Jesuit fathers themselves – a measure that suited both her conscience and her purse. To Lescarbot's dismay the Queen made no offer of food and clothing to go to those Indians who could regard themselves as royal godchildren. The only tangible honour accorded Biencourt was a letter to his father signed by the young King expressing his pleasure at the conversions and vaguely promising to remember and recognize his services. The next day, the 2nd October, the same secretary penned a similar letter signed by the Queen Regent.

This was indeed a disappointment: praise, promises, but nothing more concrete than the burden of two unwanted Jesuit priests. Lescarbot immediately wrote an extension to his pamphlet on the conversions, in which form it came to be sold. The very first paragraph of this new section betrayed his concern. There were, he wrote, already missionaries (there was in fact only one) in New France

whom nothing but their religious zeal has taken there, and who will not fail to do all that piety requires in this respect. Now, for the present, there is no need of any learned Doctors who may be more useful in combating vices and heresies at home. Besides, there is a certain class of men in whom we cannot have complete confidence, who are in the habit of censuring everything that is not in harmony with their maxims, and wish to rule wherever they are. It is enough to be watched from abroad without having these fault-finders, from whom even the greatest Kings cannot defend themselves, come near enough to record every movement of our hearts and souls.

So we can see what Lescarbot thought of the Jesuits. He clung, too, to his idyllic notion of a self-sustaining agricultural community, the necessity 'to guarantee a living before anything else, to obtain a crop of wheat, to have cattle and domestic fowls, before they could bring these people [the Indians] together.' Colonizers first, he emphasized, Jesuits later.

It was a notion he impressed strongly on young Biencourt – a pet theme of his on which he expatiated as he and Biencourt made their way along the narrow, crowded, ill-smelling streets of Paris, perhaps to talk it all over in one of the many taverns outside which hung a 'cork,' a bunch of ivy, holly, and cypress tied together. Lescarbot no doubt went on to expound a favourite maxim of the Gallicans that he incorporated a year later into his *Relation Dernière* (*Last Relation*). As he puts it, 'we must first establish the State, without which the Church cannot exist. And for this reason the first help should be given to this State, and not to what has the pretext of piety. For, when the State is founded, it will be its duty to provide for that which is spiritual.' Biencourt took all this in, as his later behaviour shows. And he was particularly susceptible to Lescarbot's talk of 'intruders' – those who followed when others had blazed the trail. For, on his friend's behalf, the lawyer was more aggrieved by the Jesuits (such is human nature) than by the great ladies who wished to support and subsidize them. Besides, both Lescarbot and Biencourt knew that Poutrincourt had put his all into the venture under pain of royal displeasure and felt that the monarch owed him some recompense.

Though the court had proved unhelpful, Biencourt did not despair of obtaining funds from sources other than Robin. There was still the question of the monopoly to be settled. On the 4th October Biencourt met seven master hatters including Louis de Jouy in a notary's study to draw up a contract. The agreement ran that the hatters were to advance twelve thousand livres to Duquesne and Dujardin (or anyone else chosen by Biencourt) for the purchase of trade goods. In return Biencourt was to deliver to the hatters all peltry from Port Royal at the price fixed. But everything depended on Poutrincourt's being granted the monopoly. For the hatters would advance the money only one month after the monopoly had been proclaimed.

Three days later, on the 7th October, Biencourt had another brief interview with the Queen. On this occasion the Queen's only aim was to commend to Poutrincourt's care the two Jesuit fathers now mentioned by name, so 'you might assist them with your protection and authority in order to promote their good and holy teachings.' This verbal recommendation was backed up by two short letters, again one signed by the young King and one by the Queen Regent. Both dealt only with the Jesuits. Biencourt might have reflected somewhat bitterly that his father was supposed to protect the Jesuits but was not accorded anything himself so he might protect the colony.

With the royal missives came a courteous letter from Father Coton. This recommended his colleagues as 'both good priests, learned and zealous.' He promised to be Poutrincourt's advocate at court, asking him to let him know through Father Massé how he could be of help. Even earlier, on the 29th September, Madame de Guercheville had written her recommendation of the Jesuit priests, 'of whom one has been my spiritual father.' This was, she added, 'a superfluous thing to do ... as I know your zeal. And yet I cannot help but to do so on account of the affection I bear them and this most praiseworthy enterprise that I see them undertake. Take care of them, I beg you, as their virtues merit. ...' This battery of injunctions to protect the Jesuits Biencourt was one day to interpret in a narrow, headstrong way quite different from their author's intentions.

At this time, it should be noted, the court was particularly anxious to support the Jesuits. After the King's assassination Father Coton had written a *Letter* refuting the accusation that the whole Jesuit order preached tyrannicide. Anti-Jesuits hostilely mustered forces to publish, in September that year, the scurrilous *Anticoton*. In this, the usual tales were told of Jesuits in the usual abusive style. Father Coton, as tutor to the young King, was a main target. For one of the principal aims of this pamphlet was to shake the Queen's faith in the Jesuits. The final effect was only to strengthen it. Nevertheless, it was widely read by those who wanted to believe in a Jesuit conspiracy to take over the world. (Indeed, when the Jesuits arrived in Quebec in 1625, fifteen years later, they were not made welcome. A copy of the *Anticoton* was going the rounds even there. Four months after their arrival everyone agreed to burn it.)

As for the monopoly that would mean so much to the Biencourts, where Henri himself had failed the Queen was unlikely to succeed. The Council, quite unmoved by news of the conversions and remembering how much trouble had arisen over de Monts' monopoly, refused to grant Poutrincourt's request. So Biencourt's contract with the hatters was annulled, and the promise of twelve thousand livres vanished like a mirage.

One can imagine young Biencourt's consternation. Still, he must have remained in touch with Robin de Coulognes, who had boasted of subsidizing the Port Royal enterprise for five years. Here our brief glimpses of Robin must be fleshed out with some guesswork. We know that his father was just on the point of purchasing the right to farm the 'gabelle,' the important salt tax, so we can surmise he was in no mood to hear of hare-brained schemes for investing good money in a risky overseas colony. As a minor, Robin *fils* could not dispose of his money as he pleased, so he was in no position to play the part of breezy young patron distributing largesse. Biencourt could only hope that Duquesne in Dieppe would be prepared to come to some agreement. In straitened circumstances, with no promise now of a substantial subsidy, he borrowed 150 livres from his father's friend, Pierre Prévôt, with whom he lodged.

Swaggerer though he was, Robin seems to have felt honour-bound to stand by his protégé and offer him some assistance. So he went with Biencourt to meet the two Jesuit fathers to make arrangements for a rendezvous at Dieppe. The 27th October was the date given, for 'by that time,' the priests understood, 'the ship would be like the bird upon the branch, only waiting to fly.' It was probably on this occasion that the Jesuits lent the two young men 737 livres interest-free. Did a certain envy stir within Biencourt at that moment as he looked at the two priests – these two intriguers for power, he was sure – on whom the court lavished money and attention while he and his father were dismissed with empty praise?

For everything at this point had gone against his interests. Only one of the several advantages he and his father had hoped for – titles, royal rewards, the monopoly, loans advanced by hatters – had been granted. The consolation prize, so to speak, was his nomination by the Duc de Montmorency as Vice-Admiral in Acadian waters. This post gave him the right to police the area but, without the monopoly, having it was like owning a scabbard without a sword. Still, it gave him something of an official position that he was to exploit to the full. If no one else would help the Biencourts set up a colony, they must help themselves.

The newly created Vice-Admiral and Robin left for Dieppe. Duquesne and Dujardin, waiting to hear news of the monopoly or of receipt of an advance from the furriers, had hardly exerted themselves on Biencourt's behalf. The *Grâce-de-Dieu* was just then undergoing repairs on dry land. Biencourt was desperate. His father was expecting him within a few weeks. It is possible that he and Robin tried to persuade the merchants into refitting and loading the ship by promising them the return cargo of fur and fish. Hard-headed businessmen though they were, the merchants were not, it seems, completely indifferent to Poutrincourt's plight. Without making any firm promises or engaging in a contract, they may have signified a reluctant willingness to come to some terms, advantageous to themselves. Then the Jesuits appeared in Dieppe.

Fathers Biard and Massé had made their farewells in Paris. The Queen had presented them with the annuity promised by Henri in 1608. But she reduced the amount from two thousand to fifteen hundred livres. Madame de Guercheville, too, had 'granted them a very fair viaticum.' Other notable ladies of the court had provided them with rich altar appurtenances and vestments.

One of these ladies was the notorious Henriette d'Entragues, the Marquise de Verneuil. From the very first month of the Queen's marriage to Henri, she had flaunted herself as the Queen's rival and was generally known as the most perverse and insolent of Henri's mistresses. But the King had enjoyed her sharp sallies even when they were directed against himself. 'Sire, you stink like carrion,' she had one day told this First Gentleman of the Land, a monarch not noted for his addiction to hygiene. After the King's assassination she humbled herself to the Queen and turned for consolation to the pleasures of the table – she became very fat – pious gestures, and prayer. Now, on the Jesuits' departure, she 'furnished them amply with sacred vessels and robes for saying Mass.' And 'thus provided for, they reached Dieppe at the time appointed.'

On learning that these Jesuits were to be passengers on the ship, the two Huguenot merchants raised an outcry. Why should they involve themselves in expenses in order to further the missionary ambitions of the hated Jesuits, the scourge of the Protestants, those Spaniards, those regicides? They certainly would have nothing to do with freighting a ship that was to take Jesuits on board. Robin and Biencourt explained that they could not refuse to take them. The Queen's orders were that these priests should accompany Biencourt to New France. The merchants offered to accept any other priests but – no Jesuits! Robin took this news to the Queen and returned with a royal letter that the governor of Dieppe read to the assembled consistory of Huguenot ministers and elders, hoping they, perhaps, could bring pressure to bear on their recalcitrant fellow Calvinists. Some of these were not themselves ill disposed to the Jesuits but felt it to be a matter for the individual conscience. It was not something on which they chose to dictate to Duquesne and Dujardin. But these latter had now taken a public stance and would not back down. The principled rebel is a not unsatisfying role to play and one of them went so far as to say he would stand by his decision even if the Queen should deprive him of his rights. 'No Jesuits,' they repeated 'unless the Queen was willing to send the whole pack of them across the sea.'

Meanwhile time was passing. Biencourt grew more and more anxious about his father at Port Royal. Could nothing be done for him? The merchants were prepared to reconsider the matter if the Jesuits were got out of the way. Duquesne and Dujardin seem to have reverted to the earlier plan that they outfit the ship in return for a heavy share of the profits. For they agreed to start loading the ship. (Father Biard later noticed that it was better fitted with fishing tackle than provisions, which might indicate that the merchants were counting on a good haul of fish to cover expenses. It is possible they even planned to establish a fishing station near Port Royal.) Even so, Biencourt and Robin had to promise that the Jesuits would not sail on the ship freighted with the merchants' money. Nevertheless, they were told, if they could find the funds to pay expenses, they could take whomsoever they pleased. Four thousand livres was the requisite sum.

About the third week in October, Fathers Biard and Massé withdrew to the Jesuit college at nearby Eu. Robin had held out hopes to them that all was not lost. If the price of the cargo could be paid, they might yet embark. From the abbot of the splendid collegiate church at Eu the priests received the loan of a precious relic, 'the left bone of the skull of out most glorious Patron, St Lawrence.' St Lawrence O'Toole, Archbishop of Dublin, dying in Normandy in 1180, could never have guessed how far this part of his mortal remains was to travel and what people it was to touch. From Eu Fathers Biard and Massé journeyed to Rouen where they received more alms for their overseas mission.

In the meantime the Queen had had news of the merchants' obstinate refusal to obey her order. She considered it beneath her dignity to plead with them. The priests could go some other time.

This might have seemed a relief to Biencourt, who had not wanted the Jesuits in the first place. But – he still owed them money. Besides, Robin was chief negotiator and Biencourt had come to rely on him. If the fathers did not leave, Robin ran the risk of looking pretty inept, for by now he had taken on the role of their 'protector' too. So he put forward another idea. If court funds could be raised to subsidize the voyage, Biencourt would be far better off financially than if he put himself deep in the debt of those two tough merchants. Besides, he may have asked Biencourt, what was wrong with Fathers Biard and Massé? Look how generous they had been about lending money!

With this Robin went off to Paris to see Madame de Guercheville. Circumstances, he had to admit, had made it impossible for him to finance the undertaking, which was now in the hands of some Huguenot merchants. And they, as she must know, were stubbornly refusing to let the Jesuits board the ship they were refitting and freighting. Would it not be possible to buy them out? The merchants' price was four thousand livres.

This interview must have taken place around the New Year, the gift-giving season. Madame de Guercheville, indignant at the 'insignificant peddlers' who dared to disobey the Queen and hinder God's work, energetically went the rounds of the court taking up a collection. Lords and ladies gave a moment's thought to ensuring their own salvation as well as that of the savages. The four thousand livres were soon found.

But Madame de Guercheville had a strong streak of prudence in her, as Father Biard later observed. Could not this money serve as an investment on behalf of the Jesuits? If they were made partners in the enterprise, half the profits from furs and fish would be theirs. In this way they could not be regarded as living at Poutrincourt's expense and would be his associates rather than his dependants. Further, the yearly profits made by the company as a whole would go to the upkeep of the colony. It was a plan that made great practical sense to Madame de Guercheville, who was anxious to see her Jesuits financially secure. It was more satisfactory, too, than taking up an annual collection on their behalf. She could not possibly have foreseen how much opprobrium this mingling of evangelical work and commerce was eventually to bring upon their heads.

So Robin returned to Dieppe with the money to pay off the merchants; and also with the obligation to draw up a contract between himself and Biencourt as partners on one hand and the Jesuits on the other. The ship by this time was freighted and ready to sail, and the crew, mostly composed of Huguenots, hired. Duquesne and Dujardin were no doubt pleased to get their money. And on the day the contract was signed they lent Biencourt and Robin twelve hundred livres.

The Jesuits had no less cause to rejoice. At last, after so many delays they were to sail. On the 20th January, the parties concerned met at the house called *The Golden Beard* in Dieppe to draw up the final contract, in which Biencourt and Robin recognized having associated themselves with the Jesuit Fathers Biard and Massé 'for half of all and each of the merchandises, victuals, instalments, and generally of the whole of the cargo' of the *Grâce-de-Dieu*. To go into all the intricacies of this contract would hold up our story. What is clear is that those who stood to gain most from it were the Biencourt family. The Jesuits lent them money interest-free, accepted to pay an unusually high price, one thousand livres, for chartering the vessel, and were to get back only a strict half of the profits. And yet through Madame de Guercheville they had provided a good deal more than half of the capital invested. If Biencourt showed no scruples about this, it was probably because, primed with Lescarbot's maxim about the State and Church, he considered it no more than his family's due. They, after all, had staked out the fields where the Jesuits were now to labour. Still, Father Biard, writing his *Relation* in 1616, might well feel bitter that, within a very short time, this contract – drawn up at Madame de Guercheville's request – was being published and cited as yet another example of Jesuit greed for gain. Later, Biencourt supporters were to rail against it. Yet, without this money furnished by friends of the Jesuits, the Biencourts might well have been in disastrous straits.

On the 26th January 1611, three months after the date set for their rendezvous at Dieppe, Fathers Biard and Massé sailed with Biencourt. By the end of the year Lescarbot would be blaming the Jesuits for this delay. If they had not aroused Huguenot antipathy, he claimed, provisions would have reached Poutrincourt much sooner. But Father Biard not unfairly doubted whether, without Jesuit aid, they would have reached him at all.

CHAPTER TWELVE

Sword and Breviary

ATHERS BIARD AND MASSÉ were the first missionaries belonging to a religious order to set out for New France. As such they were fully aware of their responsibilities. Although prepared for a difficult life, they were still encouraged by the thought that there were already twenty-one Indian converts. Illusion on that score had yet to give way to reality.

Father Biard, then forty-three, was not a man to shrink from reality, even though his life up till then had been the fairly sheltered one of a highly intelligent, scholarly member of the Society of Jesus. For he had taught grammar, arts, Hebrew, moral theology, and positive theology in various Jesuit colleges. He was very much the European man who respected the benefits of his civilization and felt little attraction for the charms of the wilderness. Montaigne-like views about the relativity of cultural and moral values were not for him. His standards were stern. He was severe with himself and others, often impatient and sardonic with those whom he considered stupid or who did not see things the way he did. Father Massé, making notes in his copy of Biard's *Relation* of 1616, bracketed one section with the observation 'sarcasms not necessary.'

For Father Biard was to be the first in a long line of distinguished Jesuits to write fascinating accounts of North America, and the first missionary to describe the Indians. However critical subsequent priests of his own order or the Récollets might be of 'barbaric' Indian ways and superstitions, none looses upon them quite such flashes of scorn as Father Biard. Yet his letters to his superiors and his *Relation* make very good reading: his prose is vigorous and lucid, and it is often

Portrait of a Jesuit

enlivened by quick dramatic touches, picturesque vocabulary, and images drawn from observation rather than books on rhetoric, though it is clear that the study of rhetoric lent a firm foundation to his style. At times one senses a tinge of self-righteousness. But then Father Biard was to be put in the position of having to defend himself and his order against some outrageous accusations. One also senses that he is conscious of exercising almost continual self-control. Charity for him was a carefully assumed mantle and not a natural skin, though like many reserved people he could be touched by the warmth of others. But the unsympathetic outsider might interpret his constant efforts to impose a new Adam upon the old as hypocrisy.

His companion, Father Massé, the son of a merchant baker in Lyons and then about thirty-five, was an altogether simpler character. When he was still quite young, the adventures of St Francis Xavier in the Indies had fired him with enthusiasm. His most ardent boyhood desire was to become a missionary and suffer in foreign lands. It was this that led him to the Jesuits. But his eyesight was weak and he almost did not make it through the period of probation. As it turned out, he was able to read well enough to complete his studies, though he expressed himself awkwardly on paper. His gifts lay in a practical rather than in an intellectual direction. He was so good with his hands that later, in Quebec, Father Lejeune dubbed him Père Utile (Father Useful). But generally he was known as Father Enemond. He took this name when a novice and he seems to have preferred it to the more formal Father Massé. Writing his obituary in 1646, a fellow Jesuit claimed that Father Enemond was naturally quick-tempered but had kept himself in check with mortifications of the body. When back in France and praying to return to 'my dear Canadas' (sic) he drew up a rigorous programme for himself that included hair-shirt, whip, fasting, and swallowing the spittle of others if he caught himself making an uncharitable remark.

There was to be plenty of mortification on board the *Grâce-de-Dieu* – and plenty of contempt later. But for the moment young Biencourt, however he felt about the Jesuits, behaved correctly and invited Father Biard to share his cabin. Simon Imbert, a failed tavern-keeper, now in the service of the Biencourts, later claimed that he gave up his bed to Father Massé. No one could then have foreseen the imbroglio in which the dubious Imbert would entangle them all within a year. And though this is anticipating, now is perhaps the time to mention that Imbert is in all likelihood the author of a *Factum* (an outline of accusations made preparatory to a lawsuit) written in the virulent style of the *Anticoton* and other anti-Jesuit pamphlets. In this *Factum*, printed in 1614, the Biencourts accuse the Jesuits of wrecking their enterprise at Port Royal.

At the beginning of the voyage those most suspicious of the Jesuits were Jean Daune (the captain), David de Bruges (the pilot), and their fellow Huguenots. Jesuits, they were convinced, were minions of the Pope whose main desire would be to lure them into the embraces of the scarlet woman of Rome. They requested that the priests make a solemn promise not to interfere with their religious beliefs and practices during the voyage. Father Biard vowed that they 'would live as in France,' that is, according to the stipulations of the Edict of Nantes. But this promise did not rule out formal debates on questions of religion.

The small ship was packed. There were thirty-six men in all, eighteen of whom Biencourt had signed on for the Habitation. If Hébert and Charles La Tour had not gone out with Poutrincourt the year before, they certainly joined young Biencourt on this voyage.

For the first two days after leaving Dieppe they had a fair wind. But then stormy January skies and seas prevailed and they were blown to the Isle of Wight. Bad weather kept them here for eighteen days. A passage from the *Factum* gives us a picture of life in port and some idea of the low blows its author aims at the Jesuits:

During this time a Dutch vessel having acknowledged the sieur de Biencourt's ship and entertained him, the sieur de Biencourt returned the courtesy. This was on the Sunday before Lent. And the next Tuesday, that is to say Shrove Tuesday, the three captains, English, Flemish, and Dutch, asked M. de Biencourt and Father Biard to dine on their ship; which they did, and drank to the health of the Kings of France and England, knee bared to the ground, according to that country's custom. Father Biard joined in willingly, and drank so heartily that the sailors ... and others took him up and carried him in their arms, after seeing him fall and bruise himself several times. He was put in a cabin where he spent the whole night flaying the fox,* as did a surgeon, Master Bernard Marot, a Basque, whom the sieur de Biencourt had ordered to be bound for fear he should injure himself or throw himself into the sea; for he was drunk, or as they say, had drunk like a lion. But as for Father Biard, he was

* This 'écorcher le renard' was a French slang expression meaning to vomit after a drinking bout.

merely swine-drunk and only needed to sleep after heaving up his entrails in witness of Jesuitical sobriety.

Now just as these two had been drinking companions, so did Father Biard wish to continue their association in doing penance. And in order to get the surgeon to apologize to the master of the vessel whom in his anger he had abused, Biard took him by the hand and led him on the deck in order to beg the master's pardon. And there, Father Biard, kneeling down, begged pardon of God in order to set an example to the surgeon. And in the presence of all the crew, who had been assembled at the call of the trumpet, he struck himself several blows, in penance for his drunkenness. Such is the conduct of good Jesuit fathers setting forth on a holy mission.

It is highly unlikely that Father Biard was ever drunk. But it is very probable, as Father Campeau points out, that he was seasick. And before finding his sea-legs, he possibly slipped, fell, and had to be helped up. One knows what malicious gossip can make of such incidents. As for the Marot story, Father Biard could well have thought it important that the Catholic surgeon apologize to the Huguenot master of the ship, and so went down upon his knees during the morning prayers to set an example of Christian repentance.

The ship did not leave the Isle of Wight until the 16th February, Ash Wednesday, the day after the carouse. They were at sea for a little more than three months, an exceptionally long time even in those days. High winds buffeted them, and for weeks on end they were numbed by the cold, relentlessly beaten and drenched by the waves.

Towards the end of March they drew near the Grand Banks where a violent west wind attacked them. Beyond the Grand Banks more trouble loomed. The sea was covered with enormous icebergs. They veered to the south only to find themselves breaking their way through a vast stretch of low ice. Young Biencourt here showed his mettle and, among the cries and alarms of the sailors, steered the ship safely through.

On the 1st May they passed Champlain, in the same terrifying predicament, on his way to Quebec. Just a few months before, he had married the twelve-year-old Hélène Boullé and was now off on his explorations again. He remembered this passage through the ice as one of his worst navigational experiences, and it occasioned some of the most vivid lines to be found in his *Voyages*.

At last on the 5th May the *Grâce-de-Dieu* sighted land and anchored off Canso. Here, according to Lescarbot, the unbaptized Indians ran away on seeing Biencourt, but the baptized came to greet him as a brother. Biencourt could proudly announce to the missionaries that the number of converts now extended beyond the original twenty-one.

After so long at sea, it was a relief to disembark and find themselves walking on firm ground once more. Father Biard brought out the sacred vessels and said his first Mass in the New World.

They re-embarked to follow the coastline round to Port Royal, making brief halts at various places. One of these was a Port St-Jean that seems to have been somewhere near La Have. Biencourt and Biard retained very different memories of this halt. There in the port, trading for furs, Biencourt saw that same Captain Chevalier whom Lescarbot had derided for greed and gluttony and whom Poutrincourt had forcibly detained at Port Royal in the summer of 1607. On this occasion Biencourt hoped to do some trading himself; otherwise the ship would have little to take back to France. Father Biard was with Biencourt in the long-boat as it pulled to shore. The Indians gathered about this new patriarch. Biard asked Biencourt to say that he had come to baptize and save them. He also wanted them to know that he wished to make them presents of everything he had. This Biencourt refused to translate, saying that he had come to barter goods, not give them away. Chevalier overheard. Delighted at getting his own back on a Biencourt, he was only too happy to serve as Father Biard's interpreter and smiled maliciously as the Indians showered reproaches on Biencourt for being meaner than his patriarch, who wanted to give, while he wanted only to trade. By this time any furs available were probably safely stowed away in Chevalier's own boat. Young Charles was not pleased. Were the missionaries bent on going their own way, ignoring the need to trade? And would they always be so prompt to make use of the services of Biencourt rivals?

Father Biard himself was much more interested in his first meeting with converts. Five among the Indians camped there, he was told, were Christians. He went up to speak to them and discovered that they could barely make the sign of the cross. What were their baptismal names? Patriarch, they replied. (It was the Patriarch who had given them the new names they had by now forgotten.) Were they Christians? They did not know what he meant. Had they been baptized? Oh yes, 'the

Patriarch has made us like the Normans.' This was discouraging enough but there was worse to come. Let us hear Father Biard describe this encounter himself:

The name of the *sagamore*, that is, the lord of port Saint John, is Cacagous, a man who is shrewd and cunning as are no others upon the coast; that is all that he brought back from France (for he has been in France); he told me he had been baptized in Bayonne, relating his story to me as one tells about going to a ball out of friendship. Whereupon, seeing how wicked he was, and wishing to try and arouse his conscience, I asked him how many wives he had. He answered that he had eight; and in fact he counted off seven to me who were there present, pointing them out with as much pride, instead of an equal degree of shame, as if I had asked him the number of his legitimate children.

Awful doubts as to the efficacy of Jessé Fleché's conversions began to assail Father Biard.

As we have seen, the *Grâce-de-Dieu* arrived at the Habitation on the 22nd May, the feast of Pentecost. Their arrival on the very day that commemorated the descent of the Holy Ghost in tongues of fire upon the first apostles seemed a happy augury to the missionaries. But they were not the only ones who had cause for jubilation. Biencourt and his men had at last arrived at their destination – four months now after leaving Dieppe. Poutrincourt could rejoice at seeing his son, learn how he and the ship had triumphed over wind and waves and ice. Those who had spent such a miserable winter at the Habitation were hugely relieved, assured now of a passage out of this wilderness, home to France. Father Biard says they were all so happy they felt as if they were in a dream.

In the morning Mass was celebrated. After the midday meal Poutrincourt went walking on the shore with Father Biard. It was a good time of year, the spring foliage a fresh green. Father Biard wondered why such a beautiful spot should be so little known. He listened sympathetically to Poutrincourt's account of all that the people at the Habitation had been through that winter. Busy with the unloading, men passed to and fro between the ship and the Habitation, calling out greetings, embracing one another in exuberant French fashion. Suddenly two who were out in a canoe capsized without anyone's noticing the accident except Poutrincourt and Father Biard. Gentleman and Jesuit began to signal with their hats to attract attention to the men struggling in the water, for the ship was too far away and the wind too loud for them to be heard if they called out. No one saw their frantic gestures. Together they fell upon their knees and prayed. One of the strugglers managed to throw himself upon the canoe, a boat came to the aid of the other, and both were saved. Another good augury, it seemed.

The *Grâce-de-Dieu* certainly arrived at a very opportune moment for Poutrincourt. But when he had time to think things over, he could not feel encouraged. First there was the news of the King's assassination, which he and his party now heard almost a year after the event. Poutrincourt felt he had lost his most likely supporter. For he had taken the royal flash of anger as a personal command. And since he had dutifully obeyed, he had expected some reward. The Queen did not seem to understand his position. True, there were the letters from the court that Charles had handed him, but in them was nothing but empty praise and a volley of exhortations to protect the good Jesuit fathers. And here in fact were the Jesuits themselves who had come to take the missionary work in hand – if not the whole enterprise – since they had won such favour at court! Financially he had lost, not gained, for his son had incurred further debts. And though young Biencourt had received the title of Vice-Admiral, Poutrincourt had not obtained the all-important monopoly of the fur trade in Acadia – a very severe set-back indeed. How was the Habitation to be maintained?

This was no theoretical question but a very pressing problem. During the long voyage nearly all the provisions on board the *Grâce-de-Dieu* had been used up. And now there were fifty-nine men at the Habitation to feed: the twenty-three who were already there and the thiry-six new arrivals. Membertou and his family continued to be frequent visitors. The most urgent task was to husband their resources and make further provision for the Habitation. This Poutrincourt could best do by setting sail immediately for France. Still, he should try to return with some furs and fish in order to finance the next voyage.

Before the *Grâce-de-Dieu* had been completely unloaded, canoes arrived containing a delegation of Etchemins from the Ste Croix region. They had a complaint to lodge: a certain Captain Le Coq from Honfleur had pillaged them and killed one of their women. Would

Poutrincourt come to see that justice was done? Also, he should know that in those parts there were men in ships from St Malo and La Rochelle, traders hostile to the Biencourts.

Here then was an occasion for Poutrincourt to outface these men and have his son's authority as Vice-Admiral recognized. He might also obtain some food from them, and engage in trade for furs with the Indians before returning to France. Within a very few days the *Grâce-de-Dieu* was off to a port called 'Pierre Blanche' (White Rock) somewhere near the mouth of the Ste Croix river. Father Biard went with Poutrincourt. On their arrival they found that Le Coq had decamped. But they encountered four other ships there, among them one from St Malo belonging to Robert Gravé and commanded by Captain La Salle, a relative of his. Called up one after the other, the captain of each vessel agreed to recognize Biencourt as Vice-Admiral and also to help Poutrincourt by supplying provisions for which he was to pay them back in France.

While this was going on, someone told Father Biard the story of Robert Gravé, who was hiding in the nearby woods for fear of Poutrincourt. He had spent the whole winter with the Indians. Here was an opportunity for the priest to play the peacemaker and reconcile the French. He begged Poutrincourt to forgive the young man for the sake of his father. Old Gravé's fame obviously travelled far. Poutrincourt was quite convinced that young Robert was out to wreck his enterprise. Still he promised, though reluctantly, to forgive him and forget the past if Father Biard could bring the young sinner to make a formal public apology for his misdemeanours.

Gravé, in his skins and moccasins – for he had taken to dressing like an Indian – must have felt some surprise on seeing the black-robed priest looking for him in the woods. As for Father Biard, he was greatly taken with Gravé. In a letter to Father Baltazar written a few weeks later, he described him as 'a young man of great physical and mental strength, excelled by none of the savages in the chase, in alertness and endurance, and in ability to speak their language.' This is unusually hyperbolic for Father Biard. Even after a year's total immersion in the Etchemin language, it is unlikely that Gravé, though obviously fluent, could speak quite as well as a native. But the young man showed himself repentant and malleable, allowed Father Biard to rejoice like the good shepherd on finding his lost sheep. Grateful to Father Biard for arranging a reconciliation, Gravé was no doubt also shrewd enough to realize that Father Biard's good will towards him was something of an asset. If there was to be rivalry for the fur trade between himself and the Biencourts, it would do him no harm to have the Jesuit on his side.

So, with some solemnity, Gravé made public amends to Poutrincourt and the cannon was sounded. The next day Mass was to be said on the shore of an island. Gravé obviously had not been able to make his Easter duties that year. He asked Father Biard to hear his confession next morning before Mass and amazed the Indian onlookers by kneeling on the shore for a long time, head bowed, murmuring to the Patriarch.

After Mass, Gravé asked Poutrincourt if he might invite Father Biard to dine on board his ship with him and La Salle. Poutrincourt consented. But La Salle, it seems, had not treated Biencourt with due deference and, as a proud, independent Breton, had shouted his defiance at the young Vice-Admiral. This the latter chose to interpret as an insult to the King. Irritated and full of his new importance, Biencourt put his men on board the ship and seized La Salle while the meal was in progress.

Father Biard, much upset, taxed Biencourt with acting in an unjust, unchristian manner. He shut himself away to pray and refused to eat or drink until La Salle should be set free. Finally, Poutrincourt gave in to his pleas and got his son to release La Salle and his ship. But by now both Biencourts were convinced that Father Biard had been won over to the side of the traders who came only for the furs. His actions surely declared that he was in league with them against the Biencourts. Yet, in their opinion, they were the true colonizers whose aim was to establish the authority of the King in this new country.

It was on this occasion that, according to the *Factum*, Poutrincourt attempted to put the Jesuit in his place and pronounced thus on the distinctions between the spiritual and the temporal: 'Father, I pray you leave me to do my duty, which I know very well, and hope to go to Paradise as well with my sword as you with your breviary. Show me the path to heaven: I will give you good guidance on earth.' This little speech smacks of something besides an attempt to separate the roles of Church and State. In Poutrincourt's family, particularly on the Salazar side, there had been some notable prelates and churchmen. But one gets the impression that for him, as for most medieval seigneurs, the household priest was something of a spiritual domestic whose services were to baptize, marry, bury, and pray for the family. This was not a role that Fathers Biard and Massé could be prepared to play. They were, after all, Jesuits, members of the 'light cavalry' of the post-Tridentine Church. They represented a new spiritual force that in France was, in the words of E.J. Pratt,

> Kindling the hearths and altars, changing vows
> Of rote into an alphabet of flame ...

This renewal of religious ardour was to have a strong influence on French society in the early part of the seventeenth century. So it is not uninteresting to note this clash between old feudal ways and a new, more fervent and rigorous spirit on the shores of New France.

The *Grâce-de-Dieu* returned to Port Royal in early June, after an absence of twelve days. There Father Biard found Father Massé installed in the cabin they were to share. If they took over Jessé Fleché's, it would have been the study where Lescarbot had spent his evenings reading and composing, withdrawn from the rowdy company. Father Biard describes it as so cramped that 'we can scarcely turn around when we have a table in it,' but then 'the other dwellings also, as is to be expected among new settlers, are by no means large or commodious.' In a brief letter to Aquaviva, Biard mentioned that 'we have been obliged to take a servant to do the drudgery. We could not dispense with one without a great deal of anxiety and trouble.' The chapel they found 'badly arranged, and in every way unsuited for religious services.' Poutrincourt offered them a quarter of the Habitation. He had not been able to roof it over himself. The Jesuits would have to do that. They, he must have thought, were the ones who had the means.

On the feast of Corpus Christi the fathers organized a procession with little Indian boys to bear the candles and swing the censers. Poutrincourt praised their efforts and also the ingenuity with which they decorated the makeshift chapel. Father Massé's deft hands had been busy.

Jessé Fleché was relieved to see the Jesuits. The winter had been very hard, and for some time, he told them, he had been waiting for the first opportunity to return to France. Father Biard diplomatically refers to him as a 'worthy man.' Did the Jesuits really manage to conceal from him the dismay they felt at his over-liberal use of holy water? Over the course of the year he had baptized about 140 Indians in all, though the Jesuits were never to obtain a 'register' of names. Fleché admitted that he had 'not been able to instruct them as he would have wished, because he did not know the language ...' So far there was no translation into the native tongue of the Creed, the Lord's Prayer, the Commandments, and the sacraments! The Jesuits resolved then and there that there would be no more baptisms without instruction and that they themselves would immediately set about learning the Micmac language.

In the meantime Father Biard applied to Biencourt to translate the Lord's Prayer, which he proceeded to teach Membertou. The old chief and shaman was the keenest of the new Christians, ambitious to learn as much as he could in order to become a preacher himself. When it came to 'Give us this day our daily bread,' Membertou objected: 'But ... if I did not ask [God] for anything but bread I should be without moose-meat or fish!' He had already, early that spring, made trial of the Christian God and had not found him wanting. For, one day, feeling very hungry, he had sent his daughter to see if the fish were running and had begun to pray. He had not been long on his knees when his daughter rushed back calling out that the fish had come. Membertou was reassured by such a speedy response to his prayer.

But he was the only so-called Christian in whom the Jesuits found a glimmer of faith, any real desire to adopt Christian ways of behaviour. Father Biard was much impressed by the fact that, even before becoming a Christian, Membertou had never had more than one wife at a time. Yet he attributed this as much to Membertou's common sense as to natural virtue! On the whole, Father Biard felt vastly discouraged. Baptism had not wrought the slightest change upon savage souls.

From the time of their arrival at Port Royal, Father Biard had in mind a letter to Father Baltazar, the Father Provincial in Paris. For he knew his superior would be particularly anxious to have an account of the Indians they had come to convert. For three weeks he observed them closely with a view to making a report. His conclusions were not of the most optimistic. The missionary's task was more daunting than he had imagined:

the country ... is only a forest, without other conveniences of life than those which will be brought from France, and what in time may be obtained from the soil after it has been cultivated. The nation is savage, wandering and full of bad habits; the people few and isolated. They are, I say, savage, haunting the woods, ignorant, lawless and rude: they are wanderers, with nothing to attach them to a place, neither homes nor relationship, neither possessions nor love of country; as a people they have bad habits, are extremely lazy, gluttonous, profane, treacherous, cruel in their revenge, and given up to all kinds of lewdness, men and women alike, the men having several wives and abandoning them to others, and the women only serving them as slaves, whom they strike and beat unmercifully, and who dare not complain; and after being half killed, if it so please the murderer, they must laugh and caress him.

We may well ask ourselves whether these are the same Micmacs whom Lescarbot knew and loved. Father Biard, it was true, was later to observe them more closely and somewhat modify his opinions.

What really stuck in Father Biard's gullet then was the good opinion these dirty, lazy, impious vagabonds had of themselves. First they had the audacity to claim that they were braver than the French simply because no revenge was taken on them for killing Basques and Malouins and damaging their ships. (This is something we have not heard of before.) Then they considered themselves superior because they were kind and generous to one another, unlike the envious, quarrelling, selfish French. More ingenious too: look how the French exclaimed over the things they made. (Generosity and ingenuity, we may remember, were qualities that Lescarbot had admired in the Indians.) To think, too, that they really imagined themselves to be richer than the French, since the latter went to such trouble to obtain their beaver skins! And some sagamo, hearing that the young King of France was yet unmarried, was gracious enough to consider giving him his daughter's hand in marriage. Father Biard found it hard to conceal his scorn.

How were they to deal with such vainglorious stupidity? Great success in conversions could not be counted on immediately. The missionaries would have many hardships to face and stood in great need of God's grace, prayers, and more material aid. As yet unaware of the Biencourts' mistrust of him, he put in a good word for Poutrincourt: 'a mild and upright Gentleman ... beloved and well-known in these parts ...' Both he and his son 'zealous in serving God ... honour and cherish us more than we deserve.'

Meanwhile Poutrincourt was making preparations for his return to France. It was now obvious to him that there would be no profits made on this voyage. If only the ship had arrived earlier so they could have done some trading! But then there was that story about the Huguenot merchants refusing to let the Jesuits embark. Rather than blame merchants, winds, and weather, Poutrincourt preferred to feed with suspicions his already established prejudices against the Jesuits. Here were the new men insidiously intriguing their way in, causing delays, and now wanting to 'have a finger in too many pies.' People do not like to feel beholden to those whom they resent and suspect. Poutrincourt could not accept the fact that if it had not been for the money provided by Jesuit supporters, the Biencourts would have been in serious difficulties. Leaving the Habitation in command of his twenty-year-old son, Poutrincourt no doubt warned him to be on his guard against those 'clever fellows.'

On the 11th June the *Grâce-de-Dieu* sailed with thirty-eight men on board, among them Simon Imbert. Messire Jessé Fleché, the sieurs Bertrand, Belot, and Jouy, and those who had wintered at the Habitation were overjoyed to find themselves on the ocean bound for home.

Somewhere along St Mary's Bay the ship was hailed by some Indians. They were looking for Poutrincourt and urgently requested his help. The ship dropped anchor while he went ashore with them to visit Actodin, Membertou's second son, known since his 'conversion' as Philippe. He was lying in his wigwam seriously ill. Poutrincourt could do nothing for him then but told him to go to the Habitation where he would be looked after.

The *Grâce-de-Dieu* had taken advantage of favourable winds and tides to leave before Father Biard had quite finished his correspondence. But he caught up with the ship in a long-boat and handed over the Jesuits' letters to be taken to France. Poutrincourt mentioned his visit to Actodin and told Father Biard to expect the sick man at the Habitation. Somewhere off the thickly wooded coast of Acadia, the gentleman and the Jesuit saw one another for the last time. Later each was to hear again of the other – though not in a way that would give either much pleasure.

CHAPTER THIRTEEN

Conflicts

ACK AT THE HABITATION, Father Biard waited for the sick man to arrive. As he did not, the priest, anxious about this new Christian, travelled five leagues to see him. He was horrified at what he found: the baptized Indian lying on his best robe, about to make his funeral oration while his relatives were ready with song, dance, and the slaughter of his dogs to help dispatch him into the next world. Father Biard vehemently interrupted these, to him, shocking proceedings and insisted that Actodin/Philippe should be immediately taken to Port Royal.

There his life was despaired of. As a last resort the Jesuits laid upon him their precious relic, the bone from St Lawrence's skull. He recovered – though the Jesuits prudently stopped short of crying miracle. It was the kind of gesture, however, likely to impress the Indians, for whom bones, like everything else in the material world, had a spiritual aura. (They greatly respected the bones of the beavers they killed and never threw them to their dogs.) Indeed Catholicism, in some regards, was closer to Indian religious practices than Father Biard would have ever wanted to admit. And here we may note that Silas Rand, the Protestant missionary and lexicographer who was to work among these same Micmacs in the nineteenth century, would have considered the 'Papists' quite as guilty of 'superstition' as the Indians.

After this the colony settled into its daily routine. With no Lescarbot to record it, we cannot tell what exactly Biencourt set his men to do. Hébert took up again the planting and gardening that he so much enjoyed. The harvest from the few acres under cultivation was good and the priests made hosts from some of the home-grown and home-ground wheat. They themselves continued their usual offices, said Mass every day, sometimes led processions on Sundays, administered the sacraments, tried to give a Christian tone to the settlement. But they had no reason to congratulate themselves on their parishioners. These were, for the most part, rough, blaspheming men used to living and drinking hard. Such men would have had almost no religious education. With sinking hearts the priests observed that they knew nothing about the beliefs of their religion, did not even have simple faith and jeered at the efficacy of prayer. Did it really help, the sailors scoffed, to call on the saints if they were in danger of drowning? (Father Biard righteously observed that a certain man who had sneered at this practice received his just deserts, for he was carried out to sea by a wind and never seen again.) One of the men's great jokes was to get the Micmac women, really quite decorous but used to a much more unclothed language, to call out obscenities to them in French. The Jesuits could but tighten their lips and shake their heads. How could they count on such people to set a good example to the heathen?

The priests' most urgent task was to learn Micmac in order to be able to instruct the Indians. They were, of course, used to learning other languages, but without the aid of formal grammars and dictionaries they did not know how to begin. At first Biencourt put himself at their disposal every day as interpreter. But though he knew enough to 'communicate,' as the modern phrase goes, it was not nearly enough to communicate the mysteries of the faith.

The Jesuits then resolved to learn the language from the Indians themselves. This entailed coaxing them – the 'stupid natives,' Father Biard calls them – into becoming their teachers. Did the Indians intuitively sense this prospective pupil's contempt for them? For they made reluctant pedagogues. Before lessons began, they would, to Father Biard's great annoyance, first ask to be fed – not unnaturally, as they were, after all, taking time off from one of their major, even holy, occupations, which was to procure food. And then, even when supplying the priests with words and phrases, they would amuse themselves and their friends by slipping in ribaldries that the priests then solemnly enunciated as 'beautiful sentences from the Gospel' – a trick encountered by missionaries all over the world.

So, despite bribing, miming, and charades, there was little that the priests were able to get from the Indians. After many gestures and signs they could not find the equivalent of the phrase that was absolutely basic to Christian faith: *Credo*, I believe. Father Biard began to suspect that their language was as limited as themselves. He pressed harder. There was no difficulty in finding words for concrete things like *good, strong, red, black, large, hard*. But as to the 'abstract, internal, spiritual ... *goodness, strength, redness, blackness* – they do not know what they are.' He tried to get translations for 'all the virtues ... *wisdom, fidelity, justice, mercy, gratitude, piety*.' All they could come up with were expressions like '*happy, tender love, good heart*.' Father Biard had hit upon one of the main differences between the European turn of mind and 'la Pensée sauvage' – though one can hardly expect him to be a Lévi-Strauss before his time and appreciate that their intelligence was of a different, not a lesser, order.

In all his exasperation one solution presented itself to Father Biard. News had reached Port Royal that young Gravé intended to spend another winter on the Saint John River. Now this was someone who was really fluent in the native language (though it would be the Etchemin rather than the Micmac dialect), and also grateful and well disposed to the frustrated priest. Who better to help him translate prayers and draw up a catechism? Why should he not go and spend the winter with him? On hearing of Father Biard's proposal, Biencourt bristled. Here was the head of the mission calmly suggesting that he make his centre the Saint John River and attach himself to a rival. And it was this same Gravé who had already tried to diminish the Biencourts in Secoudun's eyes! Biencourt took the proposal as a personal insult, a vote of no confidence in the Port Royal enterprise. If Father Biard went over to Gravé, the Biencourts would lose all credit as colonizers. For Father Biard, of course, this was of no importance. Mission work came first. The main reason they were all there was to convert the Indians. A more understanding priest might have appreciated Biencourt's point of view. A more mature man than Biencourt might have realized how Father Biard saw things and handled the matter more sensibly. But Biencourt was young and angry and said touchily that if it was a question of translating prayers, he could do that as well as Gravé. And, wrote Father Biard later, he took such offence that 'we had to yield to him, to have peace.'

Indeed, at this point we may wonder at Poutrincourt's wisdom in leaving his twenty-year-old son in charge of the Habitation instead of the older Hébert. But such an arrangement would have run counter to notions of precedence and family pride, of which both Biencourts had a fair share. Besides, it was Biencourt who held the appointment as Vice-Admiral, the only title that gave any of them something of an official position. A summary of events in Acadia (written in English in 1624) describes Biencourt as 'being a youth at that time of more courage than circumspectnesse,' and a certain heedless, headstrong recklessness does seem to have been another family trait. Yet he was to show himself capable on occasion of keeping his head when his older followers were losing theirs – unfortunately for himself, not often enough. Dressed in his little brief authority, he was too young to wear it with complete ease, keener on flashing it about than on getting things done, more conscious of his role than his duties. He certainly wanted the Port Royal enterprise to succeed, was prepared to be forceful and energetic, but let impulse and envy get in the way even of his own self-interest. A little more calculation would have shown him that he had more to gain than lose by making friends of the Jesuits. He, of all people, should have known what powerful protectors they had at court. But alerted by his father and Lescarbot, he was mistrustful, suspected that they were out for total control, reacted irritably to anything that suggested they were not whole-heartedly behind him. Besides, he resented their influence in getting the last expedition afloat, preferred not to think about it.

Towards the end of August Biencourt realized that the storehouse at Port Royal was sadly bare. So he set off for the Ste Croix area in search of a ship that he knew was on the point of departure for France. On this he placed one of his men with letters to his father urging him to send provisions before winter set in.

Then he turned his attention to a certain Captain Plâtrier, a Huguenot, who had bravely decided to spend the winter with some of his men on the island of Ste Croix, the first Europeans to do so since that disastrous winter seven years before. Biencourt's intention, however, was not to compliment the captain on his courage, but to exact from him nothing less than a fifth of his furs. What was Biencourt up to here? The fifth (the *quint*) was a feudal tax imposed by seigneurs on vassals taking over lands in their domain. We can only conclude that, after de Monts' withdrawal, the lordly Biencourts had come to consider the whole of the Fundy region to be their territory. Plâtrier, as a new vassal, would have to pay his dues.

But he might resist. Sailing up the Ste Croix river, Father Biard, who was with the party, had himself put off on the rocks at the tip of the island. He refused, he said, to be involved in fights between Frenchmen. His fears were unfounded. Plâtrier proved apologetic, amenable, not to say abject. Of course he would acknowledge Biencourt as his seigneur. But furs? He had none to give him. Two English fishing boats had captured him and stripped him of his pelts. And then these 'maudits Anglais' had waved papers in his face which, they said, were letters from their King claiming this territory for England.

Biencourt was indignant. He knew very well from his father that in 1604 Henri IV had appointed de Monts as Lieutenant-Governor over all this area from the fortieth to the forty-sixth parallel. It was the French who had the prior claim. He vowed he would do his best to protect Plâtrier and oppose the English. But, he told the captain, he himself had other enemies – and French ones at that! Robert Gravé and some fellow Malouins were spending the winter on an island in the Saint John River. Biencourt fully expected trouble from them. In true feudal fashion, Plâtrier immediately promised to assist him should any quarrel arise. And he helped the young Vice-Admiral recover a long-boat that had been left near the mouth of the Ste Croix.

On the 8th September Biencourt and his company were back at Port Royal. Father Massé met them with the bad news that Membertou had arrived at the Habitation very ill with dysentery. He had put him in Father Biard's bed and was looking after him as best he could. The priests were anxious to show this first-baptized of the Indians what true Christian charity was. Hébert brought him food and medicine but they took upon themselves all the menial tasks of nursing him. Chopping and carrying wood to keep a good fire burning in order to offset the bad smell was the most onerous.

Some days later Membertou's wife and daughter came to be with him. As the little cabin could not contain them all, Father Biard asked Biencourt to have Membertou carried to one of the empty rooms in the Habitation. Biencourt had him taken to his wigwam outside the fort. There the priests and Hébert continued to visit him. But every day he grew weaker. Young Biencourt prompted him to avail himself of the consolations offered to dying Christians, so Membertou meekly made a general confession to Father Biard of all the sins he had committed since his youth.

By this time other members of the old chief's family had assembled. On the 17th September, a time of chillier winds and turning leaves, Membertou began his funeral oration, a sort of last will and testament. Something that was very much on his mind was Poutrincourt's promise to have him buried with his ancestors at the entrance to Port Royal.

Father Biard was startled and firmly told Membertou that as a Christian he could not be buried with heathens. Membertou replied that then his people would stop coming to the Habitation, since they avoided places that reminded them of death and their dead. The priest protested that unless Membertou were buried with Christians, other Indians would not think that his conversion had been sincere. At this point Biencourt, who was acting as interpreter, interposed with the suggestion that the priest could bless the ancestral burial place, and, in this way, Membertou would be laid to rest in hallowed ground. But no, declared Father Biard, that would not do. For first they would have to disinter all the heathen bodies and that would surely scandalize the Indians and turn them against the French.

Biencourt shrugged his shoulders at this quibble. Was it really necessary to dig up the heathen dead? Membertou, feeling he had Biencourt on his side, would not give way. Father Biard took a strong line: if Membertou persisted in this request, he, Father Biard, would not be present at his funeral. On that determined note, he left the birchbark wigwam and walked sternly back to the fort.

Later that evening, however, thinking that his vehemence might be taken for anger, he returned with Father Massé. The two priests, bearing a consecrated wafer and holy oils and reciting the penitential psalms, administered Extreme Unction to the dying man.

It is not unlikely that Biencourt spent that evening complaining to his relatives, Hébert and Charles La Tour. For the priest's attitude had irritated the young commander. Who was this meddling, self-important Jesuit, he might have fumed then as he did later to his father, to come and interfere with the sieur de Poutrincourt's promises?

The next morning, Sunday the 18th September, Membertou sent for Father Biard and Biencourt and continued his oration. Father Biard's admonitions and his administering of the last sacraments had had their effect. Membertou now declared that he had changed his mind and wished to be buried in Christian ground. But, he appealed to his people, would they still come to Port Royal and pray for him there?

And would Biencourt make his grave 'wide and honourable' as his brother Poutrincourt had promised?

Membertou's sight, which had always been remarkably clear, was now growing dim. He told Biencourt he felt that the end was coming. He said he was sorry not to see Poutrincourt before his death, since he owed him so much. (It is from Biencourt himself, of course, and not Biard that we have this.) And he begged his sons to respect the French sagamo as a father, to remain at peace with Biencourt and be their allies against any hostile Indians. He then gave his blessing to his family with Father Biard 'dictating the words and guiding his hand.' Biencourt took Membertou and his children by the hand, promised to avoid all disputes with the sons, love them as his father had loved Membertou, and care for his wife as best he could. (Indeed, one day they were to become closer to him than his own family in France.)

About three or four that afternoon, while everyone was at Vespers, news came that the end was very near. The tall old chief, who had been considered one of the most cunning and treacherous leaders on those shores, died peacefully in the arms of Father Biard. Biencourt ordered that an all-night vigil should be kept. The next day they buried Membertou with all the pomp and ceremony the little colony could muster, the men carrying arms, 'drums beating as in a funeral procession for captains.' Over his grave, Christian fashion, they placed a large cross. From it, in accordance with Indian custom, they hung his bows and arrows. Biencourt gave a funeral feast for the family. Following tradition, the Indians never referred to him again as Membertou; he became 'the great Sagamo.'

On the 3rd October, when the leaves blazed red and orange and gold among the dark evergreens, Biencourt set out again in the long-boat that Plâtrier had helped him find. His most urgent task was to find food. Five years before, he had been to Saco in Almouchiquois country. He knew that the Indians there grew corn and hoped to visit them and obtain some by barter. Once again Father Biard accompanied him, as did Hébert, Charles La Tour, two Indians, and fifteen other Frenchmen. Father Massé remained alone at the Habitation with Valentin Pajot. A couple of men who had been left to plough the fields near the river occasionally looked in to see them.

Before setting his course for Saco, however, hot-headed Biencourt had other business in mind. He intended paying a call on Robert Gravé who, with one Captain Merveille, was wintering on an island in the Saint John River. From them he was determined to exact one-fifth of their furs. He had heard rumours that Gravé was out to defy him, even kill him – though we might well wonder whether these rumours were not just wild suppositions made by Biencourt's men when in their cups.

They crossed the Bay of Fundy to the mouth of the Saint John River. Here an Indian, Antoine Betmain, came to see them with his wife and child. Since his baptism, he told them, he had felt more at peace, freed from the torments inflicted by evil spirits. He asked if the patriarch would baptize his wife and child too. But this new patriarch replied that he could not until he had given them the proper instruction. Request and answer were made through Biencourt, who noted that the new dispensation was no baptism without catechization – Jesuit fashion, of course.

They got past the reversing falls and sailed up-river. By this time Biencourt and his men were stirring themselves for action. After they had gone about four and a half leagues, it grew dark. Just one and a half leagues further on lay their destination – an island called Eménénic (now identified as Catons Island) where the Malouins had erected a rough habitation for the winter. The tension grew as the distance lessened. Then a dramatic spectacle burst upon them, a magnificent flashing display of the northern lights that had taken on a red glow – as indeed they do when there is a large influx of solar particles hitting atomic oxygen in the upper atmosphere. Everyone took this as a baleful portent. The Indians cried out that there would be war.

On arrival they fired a salute from their falconet which was duly answered by the Malouins. Though almost primed for blood-letting, they passed the night peacefully enough anchored opposite the settlement. The next morning two Malouins appeared on the bank of the river, signalling to them that they had nothing to fear by disembarking. Gravé and Merveille, they said, had been gone three days and no one knew when they would be back. Father Biard said Mass.

But Biencourt was convinced that the Malouins intended treachery. After Mass he suddenly clapped a band of armed men around the little habitation. Some of the Malouins crumpled, began to despair of their lives. Others raged and called out threats. Biencourt would see: Gravé and Merveille were bringing back a horde of Indians with them; Gravé would get his revenge on Biencourt for this assault; he wore a huge knife hung around his neck and could run faster than any Frenchman. Biencourt took these taunts as justifying his pre-emptive strike.

By the end of the day both parties were inflamed with words and probably flushed with wine. It was quite dark when Merveille returned to the island to be challenged by one of Biencourt's sentries. Thinking that this was a joke on the part of one of his men, he made a mocking reply and was answered with a shot which he realized was fired in good earnest. Merveille staggered into a net that was stretched around a little garden. Men with naked swords bore down on him, seized him, and took him into the house.

Exhausted from his recent journey, Merveille was overcome with terror. What with sickness and losses, he had had a particularly bad year, and a short while before an Indian had predicted that he would not last out the winter. Now, it seemed, his last moment had come. He threw himself in front of the fire moaning and groaning, while his triumphing captors yelled over him. Father Biard, finding it impossible to get himself heard, knelt down beside a bench and began to pray. Suddenly Merveille looked up, saw him (had heaven sent this priest to him in his hour of need?), ran towards him and begged him to hear his confession. While Father Biard was attempting to soothe the distraught captain, the men glared at them – were these two hatching some plot? – then glanced suspiciously round the room. A certain La France rushed forward, picked up a loaded firearm that was near the bench, and called to Biencourt to look out. Biencourt, who had been pacing about the room, spun round. La France excitedly repeated the accusation. Merveille, he claimed, had made towards the priest only in order to seize hold of his weapon. In despair the captain protested that he had had no chance to see, let alone prime, the firearm. Biencourt's men yelled their disbelief, the Malouins screamed back that it was a frame-up. Biencourt had Merveille and three of the most hostile Malouins bound with rope for the night.

The wretched captain could not sleep and complained that his hands were too tightly tied. Father Biard begged Biencourt to have him untied and to allow him to sleep in one of the built-in beds. He, Father Biard, promised that he would stand guard at the door so Merveille could not escape. Biencourt relented. Merveille inside on the bed and Father Biard at the door spent the rest of the night in prayer while around them the uproar continued, voices loud in accusation, warnings, oaths. Obviously, everyone felt that the red sign in the sky had foretold that blood would be shed and was acting accordingly.

But Father Biard's prayers were answered. No one was killed or even injured. The orgy of screams and threats had worked a cathartic effect upon the men, who, at last exhausted, subsided. By morning all was quiet. In the afternoon Gravé returned and peace was made between the two parties. It is not clear what specific arrangements they came to, except that Biencourt does not appear to have got his furs. He borrowed a ship from Merveille and also took away with him one of the Malouins. A legal document of 1619 mentions an agreement made on the 9th October 1611 between Biencourt and one Groult who, we know, was associated with the Gravé family. For some reason, Biencourt gave one-fifth of his trade goods to Groult, perhaps in exchange for provisions or furs.

With Gravé and Merveille Father Biard found himself among friends. Merveille and others went to confession and received communion. Gravé invited the priest to stay and spend the winter with them. Father Biard thanked him and replied that he could not accept the invitation just then. Biencourt was off on a dangerous journey and he felt it his duty to be with him. Besides, it was important for him to visit the native peoples, let them see him and hear his Christian message. But he hoped to be able to take up their invitation another time, especially as Gravé, with his knowledge of the Etchemin language, could help him in drawing up a catechism. He was touched by the gratitude and friendliness of these Malouins, pleased to think he had been of service to them. Some weeks later, when drawing up an end-of-year report for Father Baltazar, he wrote, 'in truth I love these honest people with all my heart.' Biencourt was not unaware that the priest's preference was for his rivals.

As they sailed towards the Kennebec, Biencourt, with Plâtrier's story in mind, turned his thoughts from Gravé to the English. These usurpers, he told his men, would have to be dealt with firmly. But they did not meet any English ships. The first evidence they had of the English presence was Fort St George, which George Popham had constructed four years earlier, the same year that de Monts had pulled out of Port Royal. After one winter, as we have heard, the English abandoned it. When Biencourt's group arrived at the mouth of the

Kennebec on the 28th October, it was beginning to take on the look of an interesting ruin. At first the French gaped with admiration at the fort with its trenches, ramparts, and bastions, for it was a much more sophisticated feat of engineering than their own humble Habitation. But then they began to see the disadvantages of its situation and principally the infertile nature of the soil – 'nothing but stones and rocks.' Was it Hébert who remarked on that particular drawback?

A strong wind was blowing on their third day there. Biencourt discussed the matter in council and it was agreed that they should explore the Kennebec. Three leagues up-river – probably near today's Bath – they dropped anchor. While waiting for the tide they saw coming towards them six Almouchiquois canoes containing twenty-four well-armed Indians, but both parties were wary of an encounter. That evening French and Almouchiquois camped and made their fires on opposite sides of the broad river. Father Biard has left a vivid evocation of this night in the wilderness:

All night there was continual haranguing, singing and dancing, for such is the kind of life all these people lead when they are brought together. Now as we supposed that probably their songs and dances were invocations to the devil, to oppose the power of this cursed tyrant, I had our people sing some sacred hymns, as the *Salve*, the *Ave Maris Stella*, and others. But when they once got into the way of singing, the spiritual songs being exhausted, they took up others with which they were familiar. When they came to the end of these, as the French are natural mimics, they began to mimic the singing and dancing of the Almouchiquois who were upon the bank, succeeding in it so well that the Almouchiquois stopped to listen to them; and then our people stopped and the others immediately began again. It was really very comical, for you would have said that they were two choirs which had a thorough understanding with each other, and scarcely could you distinguish the real Almouchiquois from their imitators.

It is rather touching to find the usually stern Father Biard forgetting, in his amusement at the scene, that the French might be imitating devil worshipers. And something of this Jesuit's sense of drama vividly shows through.

The next day these Almouchiquois offered to guide them along another branch of the river to see the great chief Météourmite. He, they

said, would supply them with corn. This chief was not an Almouchiquois himself but a leader of a Kennebec tribe. As we have seen, he had
met de Monts and Champlain in the summer of 1605 and had shown
himself willing to make an alliance with the French. Biencourt accepted
the offers to lead him to this chief. But he was on his guard. He sent a
small boat in advance to make soundings. The water became shallower
and shallower. The man making the soundings called out to the ship to
cast anchor. They looked around. The Almouchiquois had disappeared. They had been led into a trap.

Returning the way they had come, they met Météourmite himself
with a band of followers coming to look for them. The crew, frightened
and angry, wanted to attack. Biencourt restrained himself and them,
and among the suspicious growls and curses of his men, greeted the
chief politely. Météourmite, as it turned out, did not altogether
approve of the Almouchiquois either. He invited the French to visit his
encampment, and put some of his own men aboard the French ship to
show them the way. It was a hair-raising voyage 'through such perilous
heights and narrow passes that we never expected to escape from them,'
wrote Father Biard. It looks as though, like de Monts and Champlain,
they had found themselves in the Back River channel of the Kennebec
at the mercy of its strong tidal currents.

When they arrived at Météourmite's impressive encampment,
Biencourt, attended by his armed followers, went to parley with the
chief who sat in lone splendour in his wigwam encircled on the outside
by forty young braves. The unarmed priest was conducted to the
largest wigwam where he found eighty people. The sight of this
audience stimulated Father Biard's pronounced taste for the dramatic.
Falling on his knees, he recited the Lord's Prayer, the *Ave Maria*, and
the *Credo*. The Indians applauded with their ceremonious 'Ho! Ho!
Ho!' The Jesuit then distributed crosses and holy pictures, which he
got their receivers to kiss, and blessed the children presented to him.
Here, at last, with this attentive, appreciative crowd was evangelical
work as he had imagined it to be!

Meanwhile Biencourt had learnt from Météourmite that he had little
corn but that his Indians would be prepared to barter their furs for
French trade goods. The following morning Father Biard went off to an
island to say Mass, taking a boy with him as server. The men, still
suspicious, arranged a place in the middle of the deck for the Indians.

With their weapons near at hand they waited for them to come aboard. A whole horde surged forward, pushing and shoving. Someone screamed to them to go back but could not be heard above the yell of the Indians. It seemed like an invasion. Some of the crew reached for their weapons and took aim. Several times Biencourt was on the point of giving the signal for his men to attack. But he remembered Father Biard defenceless on the island. If any Indian were harmed, the unarmed priest could expect no mercy. It was a lucky thought that no doubt saved the life of everyone there. All the goodwill that Champlain had first established and the French subsequently fostered would have vanished with the first shot fired – as they recognized themselves once the panic was over. Météourmite and other chiefs, seeing the danger, hurriedly called to their followers to return to the shore.

That evening Météourmite sent some of his men to apologize and to say that it was not they but some Almouchiquois who had caused all the trouble. Again, as on the occasion of de Monts' visit, Météourmite declared himself friendly to the French – but not the English. And the French found themselves treated to tales about the brief English settlement at Fort St George. The Indians had liked Popham, though it was rumoured that the Almouchiquois had put him to death by magic. But the next captain, Raleigh Gilbert, proved so ferocious to the Indians that they took their revenge by killing eleven Englishmen. The narrators, however, reassured their visitors that the French were different: 'they flattered us,' Father Biard later wrote in his *Relation*, 'saying that they loved us very much, because they knew we would not close our doors to the Savages as the English did, and that we would not drive them from our table with blows from a club, nor set our dogs upon them.' Also the French feasted them and brought them good things from France. Here we are at the very origin of what has become a commonplace of pioneer history: French friendliness compared with English hostility to the Indians. As for Father Biard, his head rang: 'These people are, I believe, the greatest speechmakers in the world; nothing can be done without speeches.'

By this time it was about the 4th or the 5th November and too late to go to Saco. Biencourt felt that he should do something to assert French dominion so decided to visit the island of Eméténic, where the English who had captured Plâtrier made their summer headquarters. There on the shore Biencourt raised a cross with the arms of France carved upon it. They found some boats pulled up on the beach. The crew were all for burning them. Biencourt saw that they were just fishing vessels that could not be used to attack the French and ordered his men to let them be. Father Biard, who secretly thought that Biencourt was too easily influenced by his unruly men, was impressed. In his end-of-year letter-report to Father Baltazar he made a special point of commending him as 'kind and humane.'

On the 6th they sailed towards the Penobscot, a river that Father Biard found very beautiful even though it was not the fabulous Norumbega of which he, like Champlain, had heard. Sailing up the river they turned off into a tributary which was probably Long Pond. It was a spot that Father Biard was to remember with great pleasure and wish to return to. At the confluence (New Orland) they met a large assembly: three hundred Indians, eighty canoes and a boat, eighteen wigwams. The great chief was Bessabez, with whom Champlain had made that first important alliance fairly near here at Bangor seven years before. (Following Champlain, Father Biard was later to refer to the region as Kadesquit.) The Jesuit was greatly taken with Bessabez. In fact, in the course of this journey he had begun to regard the Indians with some traces of respect. He too was now drawing comparisons between French and Indians to the advantage of the latter. A few weeks later, in the report mentioned above, he wrote: 'I confess we often see in these Savages natural and graceful qualities which will make anyone but a shameless person blush, when they compare them to the greater part of the French who come over here.' He was obviously finding his brawling, blasphemous travelling companions more than a little trying.

Just as on the Kennebec, Father Biard had the opportunity to address the assembled Indians and to meet others. Champlain had had rosaries among his trade goods, so these Indians were not unfamiliar with the crosses that the priest presented to the sick when he went to visit. Amongst these was a man who had been ill for four months. Two days after being blessed he was well enough to go on board the ship to trade, his cross around his neck. For Father Biard this was mission work indeed.

Biencourt had less reason to rejoice. Any bartering they did was for furs not food. Of this they were still desperately short. On the way back to Port Royal they called in at Ste Croix Island. Plâtrier, as obliging or as intimidated as ever, lent them two barrels of peas or beans.

While there Father Biard realized that he was not very far from the Saint John River. He approached Biencourt and asked him to arrange for him to go there so he could spend the winter working on his catechism with Gravé. Again the young man's hackles rose. Would this Jesuit never see how insulting such an arrangement was? Finally he agreed that the priest could go, but only if he kept and fed the sailors who would take him to the Saint John. This was obviously impossible, and Father Biard resigned himself to returning to Port Royal and so forgoing his project and the more sympathetic company of Gravé and Merveille.

On the 18th November they were back at the Habitation. From the point of view of obtaining provisions, the long journey had been almost a complete waste of time. Snow fell on the 26th. If a ship did not arrive soon from France, a tough winter lay ahead.

CHAPTER FOURTEEN

Excommunication

EDNESDAY, 10TH AUGUST, 1611, SAINT-GERMAIN: ... [the King] went to the Queen's apartment, where he met the sieur de Poutrincourt who was giving her the news of Port Royal, his dwelling in Canada.' So runs an entry that Hérouard, Louis XIII's chief physician, made in his meticulously kept diary. It shows that, on his return to France, Poutrincourt lost no time in bringing the conversion of the Indians once again to the royal attention. He announced that well over a hundred had been baptized in the year he had spent in the New World. And he mentioned, too, the names of all the noble personages who were their godparents. The Queen no doubt commended him for his zeal, asked solicitously about the Jesuit fathers, and did not detain him any further. Once again he had drawn a blank from the court that thanked him for his trouble in making New France something of a reality but gave him nothing.

Nor was he to find much support elsewhere. Of course there was always Lescarbot, who would praise his efforts, encourage him, perhaps publish an account of the latest occurrences. Obliging and interested as ever, Lescarbot picked up his quill to write his *Relation Dernière*. In this he brought the story of the colonization up to date. And to stir the consciences of the godparents, he mentioned them all by name. This little book seems to have been ready by the middle of September. But it did not reach the printer until November and was issued in 1612. In it Lescarbot heavily underlines Poutrincourt's zeal for conversions. He also dwelt on the special 'effects of God's grace in New France,' from sieur Bertrand's relief from gout to the 'strange and incredible' perseverance shown by both de Monts and Poutrincourt in their efforts to establish colonies. About this time, too, he prepared a second edition of his History – with additions. But all this activity, which would waft Lescarbot some windy fame, brought Poutrincourt nothing in the way of immediate material aid. And if he did not send provisions soon, the people at the Habitation would starve.

Finally Poutrincourt approached Madame de Guercheville. Unless he could find funds to support Port Royal, he told her, the good work of conversion could not go on. The great lady agreed to become a partner in his enterprise if the Jesuits and Robin did not object. Father Baltazar, representing his order, was only too pleased. Now that Robin was back among the distractions of Paris, his brief flare of interest in the New World had vanished. Madame de Guercheville's deference to his wishes was only a matter of form. With her husband's permission, she entered into a contract with Poutrincourt. Later she told the Jesuits that one of her reasons for doing so was that she suspected Poutrincourt was not as appreciative of them as he might be. He had obviously not answered her concerned and affectionate inquiries about the fathers with the right degree of enthusiasm. She hoped her intervention would bring him to a sense of what he owed them.

Madame de Guercheville agreed to furnish three thousand livres for the loading of the ship and in return was to receive half the profits from this venture. Alarmed that the great lady might want a share in territory as well as profits, Poutrincourt had it written into the contract that he reserved for himself Port Royal and the 'adjacent lands as far and as wide as they may extend.' As we have noted, the Biencourts had begun to look upon the Bay of Fundy area as *their* domain.

Madame de Guercheville was amazed to find Poutrincourt laying claim to territory beyond Port Royal. She asked to see the relevant documents proving his claim. Put on the spot, Poutrincourt awkwardly replied that he had left them at Port Royal. Madame la Marquise's mistrust of the impoverished provincial nobleman deepened. She saw de Monts, who was able to assure her that Poutrincourt's domain did not extend beyond Port Royal. And he agreed to transfer to Madame de Guercheville herself all his rights in New France based upon Henri iv's commission of 1603. To make doubly sure, the lady also secured letters from the King that made her mistress of all the territory de Monts had claimed as New France except, of course, Port Royal. And hers this vast territory was to remain, in name anyway, until she ceded her rights in 1627 when Richelieu founded the Company of One Hundred Associates. Poutrincourt had grasped at too much and now found himself firmly circumscribed. As Father Biard later put it, with perhaps excusable triumph: 'in this way, he, who was thought to be so shrewd, found himself, against his choice, locked up and confined as in a prison within his Port Royal.'

By now Madame de Guercheville's suspicions were thoroughly aroused. She entrusted her three thousand livres not to Poutrincourt himself but to a Jesuit lay brother, Gilbert de Thet, who was being sent out to help the priests. Brother Gilbert was then about thirty-six, but still a little naïve and impetuous. He had orders to give the money to a Dieppe merchant, Jacques Baudouin, who was to make the necessary purchases of food and merchandise. Poutrincourt went to see Brother Gilbert and relieved him of twelve hundred livres in exchange for a receipt. So only eighteen hundred livres went on the cargo. The ship, however, was not Poutrincourt's *Grâce-de-Dieu* but one belonging to Captain Nicolas L'Abbé the younger, of Dieppe. The author of the *Factum* claims that Poutrincourt spent four thousand livres on this expedition and makes no mention whatsoever of Madame de Guercheville's contribution. We have no means of knowing whether Poutrincourt simply appropriated the twelve hundred livres or whether some of this went on expenses other than cargo.

In charge of provisions and catering on board went Simon Imbert. He was, we may remember, a failed tavern keeper now in Poutrincourt's employ and the probable author of the *Factum*. He was also, one suspects, a pretty unsavoury character. His taste in reading matter was for scurrilous and sensational anti-Jesuit stories. For entertainment on the voyage he took with him a copy of the notorious *Anticoton*. For reasons we shall soon discover, it is most likely that Brother Gilbert kept a watchful eye on Imbert's ways with casks and barrels, while Imbert's ears were alert for any remark by Brother Gilbert that might betray Jesuit ambition, intrigue, and treachery.

Captain L'Abbé's ship sailed at the end of November, just as the snow was beginning to fall at Port Royal. Food at the Habitation was now in such short supply that everyone was severely rationed. Father Biard lists specific quantities: 'There was given to each individual for the entire week only about ten ounces of bread, half a pound of lard, three bowls of peas or beans, and one of prunes.' Poor fare, indeed. What, one wonders, had happened to the game and wildfowl that were so plentiful at the time of the Order of Good Cheer? Occasionally some of Membertou's family came to see them and treated them to a present of game. Deep snows meant good hunting for the Indians. But there were no other visitors. The little colony turned in upon itself. The meagre diet and the enforced inactivity made the men edgy and irritable. Biencourt noticed the Jesuits inciting them to piety with gifts of rosaries and holy pictures. At the same time, he was to tell his father, they urged *him* to exercise a more severe discipline over his men. The young commander felt it unfair that they should coax with carrots and tell him to use the stick.

But his principal grievance, now that he had time to think things over, was the small number of Indians the Jesuits had baptized: four children, a very sick old woman, and a little girl. This last the priests lodged in one of the cabins. They looked after her, instructed her, and baptized her. The name they chose for her was that of their patroness, Antoinette du Pons, 'who may rejoice that already her name is in heaven, for a few days after baptism this chosen soul flew away to that glorious place.' Biencourt was not impressed. Numbers talked. As far as he was concerned the whole venture would lose credibility unless more Indians were converted. Why should the Jesuits make difficulties where Jessé Flcché had found none?

Indeed it was the conduct of the so-called converted that, from the first, had set the Jesuits against baptism on request. For the neophytes knew nothing about their new faith. They had accepted baptism merely as 'a sign of friendship with the Normans.' If they did come to church, it was for all the wrong reasons. Father Biard felt, too, that it was unjust to the Indians to baptize them without making them fully aware of what conduct would be expected of them as Christians. For the priests had incurred much resentment when they told baptized polygamists that they were now duty-bound to give up all but one wife. The Indians went off protesting that this was not what they had bargained for when accepting to have the holy water poured over them.

In trying to persuade Biencourt that the Jesuits were only doing their duty in *not* baptizing, Father Biard attempted sweet reasonableness that had a knowing sting in the tail. The Jesuits, he told Biencourt, were content with bringing forth fruit in patience. Biencourt need have no fear for the Indians' salvation. If they should die unbaptized but repentant and desirous of baptism, they could still be saved. Let the young commander pray and also make it possible for the Jesuits to instruct the Indians in their native tongue. Biencourt knew what *that* meant. He should let Father Biard go to live with Gravé!

Biencourt was further outraged when, on Christmas Day, Father Biard preached in his room. For, on this occasion the priest roundly declared that the Jesuits would not baptize the Indians without first thoroughly instructing them. And he added that if the French there had not already been baptized, they themselves could not qualify for baptism as they knew so little about their faith. It was not a tactful point to make, though no doubt true. Lescarbot himself in his preaching days there had observed that his listeners 'had not known a single principle of the Christian doctrine.' And we may remember that he had remarked that it was in such ignorance that most Christians lived. Biencourt's own interpretation of the Jesuits' reluctance to sprinkle the 'saving waters' was that, as they had not been there at the beginning, they wanted to discount everything that had been achieved before their arrival.

The priests themselves were very discouraged. There seemed little they could do for the rough, mocking French sailors and artisans whom they saw day after day, let alone the Indians whom they saw only sporadically. Both priests fell ill, one after the other. Their servant left them and they had to do all their own tedious daily chores: chop wood, cook, mend their clothes. In his end-of-year letters to his superiors, Aquaviva in Rome and Baltazar in Paris, Father Biard held out few hopes for a successful mission. But, as usual, he was politely complimentary to the Biencourts, father and son.

And yet – and yet – the Jesuits were beginning to have serious doubts about the whole enterprise. What exactly was Poutrincourt doing attempting to found a colony when he did not have the resources to maintain it? Could something really solid be established in the present hand-to-mouth way? According to Biencourt, they inquired into his family's affairs. What they picked up was not encouraging: debts, lawsuits in France. Would Poutrincourt not be better advised to set his own house in order first before embarking on a reckless venture overseas? (This was not a question that had particularly bothered the King when he had angrily stirred Poutrincourt into action.)

But it was Biencourt's venture too. He had begun to look on Port

Royal as his patrimony. The Jesuits' scepticism about the success of the enterprise called the Biencourts into question as colonizers and as men. The priests may have thought that their solicitude was well meant. All Biencourt could see was that Jesuit lack of support could invalidate what his father had begun and make his endeavours look worthless. Again the Biencourt honour was at stake. He himself sensed the priests' doubts, and felt that he was being watched, weighed in the balance, and found wanting.

Father Biard was to write that during this difficult period the Jesuits did their best to console everyone in public and private. The Gospel for the Sunday that fell on the 15th January dealt with the wedding feast at Cana. Father Biard took as his text: *Vinum non habent* – they have no wine. And he exhorted the company to take the Blessed Virgin as their advocate for all their spiritual and material needs. Then, after Mass, he pointed to the men and said laughingly to Biencourt, 'Vinum non habent.' He had, he claimed, a premonition that help would soon arrive. And he asked Biencourt to let the men have the little wine that was left. So Biencourt gave orders for the barrel to be emptied. The men, wrote Father Biard, 'were delighted, and, in their joy after drinking, said, "Now, truly, we have the courage to wait and see if the Father is a Prophet."' The Father had hazarded a lucky guess. A week later, on the 23rd January, the ship arrived. Captain L'Abbé had taken just two months to make the winter journey.

The ship brought only a small quantity of supplies, says Father Biard. But the people at the Habitation were saved from starvation for that winter at least. There must have been livestock on the ship as well – pigs, sheep, poultry, pigeons? – for Father Massé described Captain L'Abbé as having 'like a wise Noah in his ark, preserved species of animals, so they could propagate others in this land.' The Jesuits were happy to have the companionship of Brother Gilbert. And there was a servant for them, a boy called Guillaume Crito.

The provisions came as a great relief to Biencourt. Here was proof of his father's competence! A letter from Poutrincourt did nothing to destroy this illusion, for he did not mention to his son the contract he had made with Madame de Guercheville and her contribution of three thousand livres. It was Imbert who gave Biencourt that unwelcome piece of news – unwelcome because Biencourt would have preferred his family to be independent of this patroness of the Jesuits. Imbert also brought the embarrassing news that the same lady had taken over as her seigneury all Acadia except Port Royal. Biencourt began to feel more resentful than ever towards the Jesuits.

But whatever the undercurrents of suspicion or mistrust, life at the Habitation during most of February flowed on smoothly enough. At council meetings the Jesuits were even invited to discuss the future of the colony. According to the *Factum*, on one occasion when the three Jesuits, Biencourt, Hébert, and Imbert were present, there was talk of bringing Madame de Poutrincourt out to Port Royal. Father Biard is reported as suggesting that the Queen would surely give her a handsome present if she went to take leave of Her Majesty before coming to New France.

But Brother Gilbert, as agent for Madame de Guercheville and the Jesuits, had something disquieting to report. With Father Biard he went to see Biencourt. For he was uneasy about Imbert and his handling of affairs, was anxious to know whether Imbert had given Biencourt a true account of his stewardship. Biencourt admitted that Imbert had not delivered to him any bills or receipts. There was nothing to show exactly how Madame de Guercheville's money had been used. The Jesuits insisted that they did not want to accuse Imbert of anything without careful inquiry. But Imbert had claimed that some of the goods belonged to him personally. And at Dieppe he had sold some wheat, one of the most urgently needed commodities at the Habitation. He had also claimed that seven barrels of ship's biscuits had been consumed on the voyage, though Brother Gilbert could account for five only. Was Imbert holding back two barrels for himself? Brother Gilbert asked Biencourt to look into this matter but with the utmost discretion. According to Father Biard – and Father Massé confirms this – Biencourt himself said that the Jesuits could not have put their request more tactfully.

But Biencourt delayed making the proper sort of investigation. He was angry with Imbert for getting him into this position and giving the Jesuits reason to find fault with one of the Biencourts' men. Imbert became so upset by the young commander's 'ill-looks' that he took to his bed. There the Jesuits came to visit him, one of their duties being to visit the sick. But about the beginning of March he was well enough to be outside helping Hébert who was taking advantage of an early thaw to prepare a little garden for spring. Biencourt passed by. Imbert, seizing his opportunity, asked if he could accompany him on his walk. Biencourt nodded. Imbert followed him and anxiously plied him with questions. Was anything wrong? Why should the young master treat him with such coolness?

Biencourt abruptly asked him to tell the truth and account for the missing wheat, the barrels of ship's biscuit, the goods that the Jesuits 'accused' him of appropriating for himself. Imbert's answer came trippingly off his tongue: M. de Poutrincourt had permitted him to bring out eight barrels of ship's biscuit and a hogshead of wine to do a little trading for himself; it was Jacques Baudouin, the Dieppe agent, who had sold some corn to defray expenses; only nincty barrels of ship's biscuit had gone on board and, as eighty-five were delivered at Port Royal, five indeed had been consumed on the voyage. He did not produce any memorandum nor did Biencourt ask for any more material proof. No doubt because he wanted to, he simply accepted Imbert's explanations.

But now Imbert felt he was fighting for his life and quickly deployed diversionary tactics. He had done so much for the Jesuits – he had journeyed to Eu to fetch them, he had given up his bed on the ship to Father Massé – and now, he lamented, they were out to destroy him with false accusations. For all his trouble his only reward would be the gallows! Could not Biencourt see that 'these people were full of ambition and hypocrisy?' Look how they had worked upon Madame de Guercheville to make herself mistress of Acadia and squeeze Poutrincourt out of his seigneury! It was a conspiracy, a deliberate plot to destroy the authority of the Biencourts in New France. And had he not already told Biencourt the scandalous story of Brother Gilbert?

One day while still at sea on their way to Port Royal, Imbert and the Jesuit brother had been talking with Captain L'Abbé in his cabin. Imbert happened to speak with regret of the death of Henri iv. At that, Imbert claimed, 'the Jesuit began to say that the King's assassination had been a very fortunate blow struck for Christianity, that without it Christendom would have been lost ... and that France would never be subject to any country but Spain.' Now what did Biencourt make of such a treasonable statement? And Imbert strummed away at the old refrain – all Jesuits were Spaniards at heart. If they were against Biencourt, it was because they were enemies of France and agents for Spain. And so Imbert supplied Biencourt with a grand justification for all his suspicions and hostilities: the Jesuits were potential traitors. There is nothing like patriotism to work men up into a lather of self-righteous indignation.

Imbert, sure then of having Biencourt on his side, went off to find Father Massé. He complained bitterly of the Jesuits' injustice. Father Massé had promised him letters of recommendation in France. This was a terrible way of recommending him. Brother Gilbert no doubt was the informer. But what of Brother Gilbert's strange views about the assassination of the King? Should they not be looked into? And he repeated again what he had told Biencourt.

Father Massé in alarm went to consult Father Biard. The Jesuits were in a difficult situation. Biencourt had not conducted a discreet investigation; he had merely blurted out to Imbert that the Jesuits had accused him of theft. And now Imbert, in retaliation and to deflect inquiry into his own activities, was accusing Brother Gilbert of making treasonable statements. Father Biard could appreciate the seriousness of this accusation. All the current defamatory pamphlets like the *Anticoton* blamed the Jesuits for Henri's assassination. Polemicists would seize on this story: Jesuit Brother Claims King's Death a Blow Struck for Christianity; France Shall Have No Master but Spain. It was a story that had to be scotched immediately. Biencourt was obviously not disposed to do the Jesuits justice. Father Biard would have to see to it himself.

A measure of the seriousness of the affair is that today we do not have Father Biard's version of it, only a vague metaphoric mention of vapours, thick clouds, winds, tempests, and whirlwinds ravaging the fruits and hopes of a first clearing. In his *Relation* of 1616 he did write a whole chapter on the crisis and also, it seems, a passage on Imbert as author of the *Factum*. But chapter and passage were cut by the Jesuit censors five years after this incident took place. Father Biard might prove Brother Gilbert innocent (by 1616 Brother Gilbert was dead anyway), but the censors knew how people repeated old proverbs about no smoke without fire. Detractors of the Jesuits were still around waiting to pounce, even though less was heard about Jesuit responsibility for Henri's death. It would be imprudent to touch on that sensitive subject again even in order to vindicate the Jesuits. So Father Biard had almost complete discretion forced upon him. In trying to put together a coherent sequence of events, we have mainly the *Factum* to go by.

Its author continues the story thus:

On leaving Father Massé, Imbert went to see the sieur de Biencourt and found him with the sieur Hébert to whom he was complaining that the Jesuits showed ill-will towards his best servants and yet looked with such favour on people he had trouble with, like Du Pont [Gravé], Merveille, La Salle and others. While this was happening, Biard, having conferred with Massé, entered, called to Imbert, and, in the presence of the said gentlemen and Hébert, said to him: 'Raise your hand.'

'What!' said Imbert, 'I was expecting you to do me satisfaction for the false accusation you put upon me and now you want to try me?'

That was precisely what Father Biard wanted. And according to him, Imbert was tried and found guilty. For in his Latin version of the 1616 *Relation* he speaks of falsehoods which 'it was easy for our brethren to refute; and once, twice, and a third time they so plainly and completely disproved them, before Biencourt, in the hearing of the whole settlement, that Imbert was rendered speechless by the final refutation, and was so reduced that he did not hesitate to claim, for the sake of excusing his wickedness, that these slanders had been uttered by him while much intoxicated.'

But in the course of all the uproar much else had been said. At one point there was so much noise and shouting that, according to the *Factum*, Hébert left his medicines and distillations and came out of his cabin to remark that 'the Jesuits' conduct would make more heretics than converts among the savages.' Brother Gilbert was indignant and

turning to the priests, he said to them, 'Fathers, do you hear that? After feeding these people here, all they can do is find fault with you.' And, speaking to the sieur de Biencourt, they said, 'Well, is it not true that we are feeding all of you, so you and your men are subject to us?' – 'Do you hear that, Monsieur?' said Hébert, 'These newcomers would like to lay down the law to those who came first.' – 'Yes,' said Gilbert du Thet, 'erunt ultimi primi,' – that is the last shall be first. 'But,' said the Jesuit Biard, 'suppose Gilbert did say that if the King had not been killed, Christendom would have been lost, that it was a happy stroke from heaven, that France would never escape the power of Spain, are those terrible words?' – 'Ha!' said the sieur de Biencourt, 'I do not understand your rhetoric. I shall refer it all to the King and the gentlemen of his Council, who will be better able to interpret it than I.'

Then Imbert began to complain of such abuse, saying he would go to France and report their behaviour to the King, to the Parlement and to the Sorbonne and he would learn if they could have him executed for having revealed something of import to the King's service.

In such an account much is obviously distorted and exaggerated, the most considerable omission being that of Imbert's confession. But it does give some idea of the highly charged atmosphere, the hidden resentments bursting forth. Biencourt seems to have kept from his men, he even seems to have kept from himself, the extent of his indebtedness to the Jesuits. By virtue of the contract, they were his business associates, not his private chaplains or dependants. Yet it was as such that they were viewed at the Habitation. The Jesuits naturally resented this.

Now the Jesuits had another and a very serious grievance. Father Biard requested from Biencourt a report of the inquiry which had proved Brother Gilbert innocent and Imbert a drunken slanderer. But this Biencourt refused to give him, though Father Biard asked for it repeatedly.

L'Abbé's ship was soon to leave for France. While furs and timber were being loaded, quills flew furiously. On the 10th March Father Massé wrote a letter to Madame de Guercheville. Imbert drew up a memoir on the way the Jesuits had conducted themselves in New France. He also wrote out a copy of a declaration he had made to Biencourt of Brother Gilbert's allegedly treasonable speech. This copy, signed by Imbert and witnesses, and not the report of the inquiry proving Gilbert innocent, was to be sent to Poutrincourt. Besides a long complaint of the Jesuits, their past and present offences, Biencourt had business affairs to write to his father about. With this letter he enclosed a memorandum for the Jesuits accounting for the previous voyage in which they had been partners, also receipts for wages given his men 'whom I have paid or satisfied, or nearly so.' He wrote that he had not had much luck with trade this year – only 377 beaver pelts, 52 moose skins, and with these he was also sending some wood.

On Sunday 11th March, the first Sunday in Lent, the Jesuits did not say Mass. Brother Gilbert had been expecting to return to France. But on that day Biencourt ordered his chest to be taken off the ship. Was it Imbert who suggested that it be searched for treasonable material? Three letters were found and read, copies and commentary later placed in the *Factum*. If this is the sort of thing the Jesuits write, exclaimed Imbert, when their letters are handled by honest people who distrust them, what must they not commit to paper when they have their own accomplices as messengers! For two of the letters contained remarks that stung Biencourt to the quick and that Imbert described with horrified delight as inciting to 'rebellion.'

On the 29th February Father Massé had written a brief letter to the father of Captain L'Abbé, thanking him for alms given the Jesuits when they were in Dieppe and offering to write a letter of recommendation for his son, the captain. For 'his piety, his prudence in trading, his courage in difficulties, his knowledge of the sea and his diligence in accomplishing tasks have made us blush for the men at the Habitation, who have not his abilities. It should be he and his men in command of this work; but then your abbey* would be deprived of a very necessary leader.' So now Biencourt knew what the Jesuits would say about him in France! Was this not tantamount to 'recommending' that the L'Abbé family oust the Biencourts from Port Royal? He probably noticed the date. Father Massé had made this odious comparison even before the real trouble had blown up.

Father Massé's second letter, written on the 10th March to Madame de Guercheville, is clumsy and elaborate in style. Yet the message is clear. The New World seemed to open its arms to ask for the protection of Madame la Marquise's 'greatness ... but alas! the prince of darkness of this world' is already 'armed and in the field.' And 'those who had come thinking to combat him are destroying themselves, grow weaker every day and are not far from beating a retreat. I see no hope, unless your magnanimity should come to our aid or continue the pursuit with new forces in another place.' So it was true! The Jesuits did not think Port Royal worth maintaining. They wanted to start a new mission elsewhere. This was disloyal – treacherous.

In the third letter Brother Gilbert asked his correspondent to remember him to the Abbess of Montmartre and the Sister Bursar – sure proof, sneered Imbert suggestively, that the Jesuits are not 'such eunuchs for the sake of the kingdom of heaven and not so dead to the world that they make no wishes concerning it.'

What the Jesuits did wish then was that at least one, if not two, of

* This, of course, is a play of words on the name 'L'Abbé,' which in French means 'abbot.'

them should return to France, principally to answer any allegations Imbert should make against Brother Gilbert. They made this wish known to Biencourt. He flatly refused to allow any of them to leave or send anything over on the ship. It was a quite unjust and unreasonable decision and one that, in the long run, was quite counter to his own self-interest. He had no authority over the comings and goings of the Jesuits. The King and Queen Regent had merely commended them to his care. Yet by now he was beyond reason. For he lashed himself into the belief that the Jesuits were potential traitors and that it was his duty to keep an eye on them. With no superior force to check him, he let the high horse of his authority run away with him.

The Jesuits were outraged by Biencourt's injustice. They were not prepared to give in easily. Late in the afternoon of the 13th March Charles La Tour and Valentin Pajot were in the woods about a quarter of a league from the Habitation. They saw movement on the waters of the port. A boat from Captain L'Abbé's ship pulled to shore. Into it climbed two black-robed figures, Father Biard and Father Massé. They were rowed to the ship. The two young men raced back to the Habitation to tell Biencourt what they had seen.

Biencourt was furious. So Captain L'Abbé was in collusion with the Jesuits, aiding and abetting them to depart without his permission! This was not to be tolerated. Captain L'Abbé was at the Habitation. Biencourt told him that he would detain him there until the priests were off the ship. L'Abbé sent Michel Morel, the master of the ship (the same Morel who had been Gravé's captain on the *Bonne Renommée*?), to ask the fathers to return to the Habitation. The priest told Morel that they had come to drink with Captain L'Abbé on his ship and they would not leave until they had seen him. Morel returned to the Habitation with this message. Biencourt insisted that L'Abbé should get the Jesuits off his ship. L'Abbé sent another of his officers, Jean Pointel, to persuade them to leave. By this time the priests had locked themselves in the captain's cabin. Anyone who dared lay a hand on them, they warned, would be excommunicated. Intimidated, Pointel returned to shore. L'Abbé, again at Biencourt's insistence, ordered Pointel to pay no attention to the threat of excommunication and to break open the cabin door. Pointel and some sailors returned to the ship. The door went down and beyond it were the two priests pronouncing anathemas upon them. Pointel managed, we do not learn how, to get Father Massé to leave with him. Father Biard remained 'lying belly up behind a chest threatening to excommunicate anyone who should touch him.'

In a letter to his father, written the following day, Biencourt gave an account of his interview with Father Massé:

I sent for Father Enemond to speak to me. He replied that, when he had spoken to God, he would come. When he came before me with his square bonnet, I asked him why he was scheming to leave without my permission, since he was in my charge in this country. He answered that he did not recognize my position and that he had greater power and authority delegated to him by the King in this country than I had, and that he excommunicated me, protesting against all the wrongs that had been done him and his companion, Father Biard. I made him withdraw, seeing there was no reason to be had from him, since he was beside himself with anger. I called all there to bear witness to the arrogance the said Enemond had shown me, and the scant account he took of the King's officers.

Biencourt held no commission from the King, yet he had really come to believe that he represented the Crown. We might note how his hostility to Father Massé focuses on the priest's 'square bonnet,' headgear being one of the most ancient symbols of authority. It is a small detail that vividly points up the young man's resentment of the Jesuits.

In the course of all these comings and goings, as night closed around ship and Habitation, Father Biard managed to write a letter of protest. Perhaps he had already written it before he lay down behind the chest. For a man who was very angry, it is a cogent and coherent piece of writing, addressed to both Biencourt and Captain L'Abbé. In it he emphasized the Jesuits' priestly dignity and right to freedom of movement, also the fact that they were Biencourt's business partners, *not* his vassals. He demanded justice for Brother Gilbert and finally warned Biencourt against appropriating profits that should be shared with the Jesuits and Madame de Guercheville. (Father Campeau believes that the priest issued this last warning because he suspected Biencourt of paying off his own men with furs that should have gone to the company as a whole. We may remember that Biencourt had written to his father to say that he had satisfied his men 'or nearly so.')

Having managed to dislodge Father Massé, Biencourt was determined to have Father Biard too. L'Abbé's sailors rowed once again to the ship and returned with the letter but – no Father Biard. A sailor handed the 'brutal thunderbolt' to Biencourt. At this point Hébert is said to have exclaimed, 'Don't read it. It is only meant to deceive and frighten you.' One rather wonders whether Biencourt ever did read it. L'Abbé's men then suggested that one of Biencourt's officers should go with them and try to break down the resistance of the formidable Father Biard. More men in a small boat or canoe paddled over the chilly March waters between Habitation and ship, among them Hébert, as Biencourt's official representative.

The *Factum*, which is highly untrustworthy, claims that Louis Membertou, on seeing this disturbance, remarked, 'Your patriarchs don't like you, so they cannot be of any use. Let us deal with them; we shall soon rid you of them.' If this is true, Biencourt still had enough sense to prevent that. 'Take care you do not,' he is supposed to have replied, 'they are holy people and I am responsible to the King for them.' Holy people – and treated in this way? The French must still have seemed very strange to the Indians.

In the end, perhaps because he was concerned about L'Abbé, Father Biard told Morel, the master of the ship, that he would not leave on Hébert's orders, but that he would go to shore with Morel. Confronting Biencourt, the furious priest demanded that L'Abbé should be set free. He was entirely free, Biencourt replied. Why, Father Biard then asked, might *he* not board L'Abbé's ship? The only answer he got was that being 'overwrought' ('travaillé') he should retire. Young Biencourt had proved to his own satisfaction who was master at the Habitation.

The next morning L'Abbé came to ask Biencourt if he could speak to the Jesuits alone. He was obviously troubled by the part he had been forced to play in the events of the previous day and probably secretly sympathetic to the Jesuits. Biencourt was in no mood to let L'Abbé and the priests plot 'rebellion.' If L'Abbé had come to take leave of the Jesuits, let him do it in the presence of others. L'Abbé knocked at the priests' door, and asked them if they would not be saying Mass that day. Not for people who were excommunicated, came the reply. But would he take letters back to France and faithfully promise not to show them to anyone? Hostile figures in the courtyard, suspicious eyes fixed upon the little group at the doorway made it obvious he could not. Until the ship sailed, the Jesuits went on trying to see L'Abbé alone. Biencourt's men proved too vigilant.

And Biencourt, in writing to his father, felt he had cause to congratulate himself on doing his duty: 'I have kept these Fathers from roaming around, as they wanted to do, until the King, their Provincial or General orders me to send them back. Also they might use some underhand means on the ship to have it go where they wish.' To Spain? In order to sell Port Royal to the Spaniards? In seeing Fathers Biard and Massé as Jesuit hijackers, Biencourt was letting his imagination run as wild as his exercise of power.

But anti-Jesuit propaganda, his own prejudices and suspicions, his desire to command, and more than a touch of self-deception had done their work. In place of Pierre Biard, Enemond Massé, and Gilbert du Thet, Biencourt could see only two grotesques in square bonnets and their functionary conspiring to thwart his authority and take over his domain. Concluding his letter, he wrote: 'I beg you, monsieur mon père, to waste no time in showing up the wickedness of these Jesuits and to trust them as little as possible.'

CHAPTER FIFTEEN

Alarms, Excursions, and Expeditions

BIENCOURT MIGHT WARN HIS FATHER to be on his guard against the Jesuits. But others were just as mistrustful of the Biencourts. No sooner had L'Abbé's ship put in at Dieppe – probably early in the summer – than it was seized for liquidation under judicial supervision. The instigator of this action was probably Madame de Guercheville's agent in Dieppe, the merchant Jacques Baudouin. Not only was the merchandise taken into custody but also, says the *Factum*, 'The very clothes of the passengers were sold and they could not retrieve them since they had not reclaimed them in time.' Were these 'clothes' furs that Baudouin regarded as belonging to the company? The *Factum* had no doubts about who was to blame for this dire act: the Jesuits, of course, acting under cover of the name of their powerful patroness.

Despite his animosity to the Jesuits, Imbert could not have felt on strong enough ground to pursue his case against Brother Gilbert. Captain L'Abbé, it appears, took it upon himself to make a sworn statement to a magistrate in Dieppe declaring the absent Jesuit brother innocent of making any treasonable statement.

Poutrincourt, however, heard a very different story when Imbert visited him to deliver Biencourt's letters and make his report. With considerable relish the ex-tavern-keeper piled tale upon tale to illustrate the hypocrisy of the Jesuits, their malice towards himself, their 'rebellion' against the Biencourts, their intrigues, their ambition, their treachery. If Imbert were guilty of malversation, as seems likely, it was important for him to focus all Poutrincourt's anger upon the Jesuits. Poutrincourt listened to it all, his prejudices and indignation fed by

Imbert's venom. He now had no doubts about the Jesuits' intentions. They were bent upon his destruction. He was incensed at the excommunication and the wickedness of the so-called pastors in not attending to their flock.

Meanwhile Father Coton, Father Baltazar, and Madame de Guercheville were amazed and disturbed at not receiving any letters from the priests. But Captain L'Abbé had a brother at the Jesuit college of Eu, and sailors had tales to tell. Stories got around: the Jesuit fathers at Port Royal were being starved to death; they had been nearly killed; they had had chains put on their feet. Rumours filtered through from Normandy to the court in Paris. Some reached the ears of no less a personage than the Chancellor of France, Brûlart de Sillery, who was then still close to the Queen Regent. This notable dignitary of the kingdom, the Minister of Justice no less, encountered Poutrincourt and taxed him with charges of impious cruelty. The unhappy sieur staggered under this blow dealt at his reputation. What were the Jesuits trying to do to him? He went to see the Bishop of Amiens to complain about 'such fabrications.' What could be done to have the disgraceful sentence of excommunication declared invalid? He fastened on other prelates as well. How could he shake himself free from the Society of Jesus who were hounding him to his ruin?

According to the *Factum*, 'his distress was such on seeing his labours, his expenses and his honour rendered useless by the calumny of people in whom he had trusted ...' But the sentence is incomplete. The next one mentions an illness. Did Poutrincourt appear to go mad? Lescarbot describes his friend as succumbing to a sickness 'which came near to ending him completely.' Was this, as Father Campeau has suggested, a nervous breakdown or a severe depression, which in those days would certainly have been thought of as madness? In March 1610 Poutrincourt had squeezed his resources to the utmost and set off for Port Royal to prove himself to the King. All he had acquired in two years was not fame, let alone fortune, but debts and disgrace. And something would still have to be done to send supplies out to Port Royal before winter. One can quite see why he might have cracked under the strain.

Meanwhile his son at Port Royal was doing little better in advancing the Biencourt fortunes. Relations between the Jesuits and the men of the Habitation had been completely severed. The priests said Mass in an 'attic,' probably the top part of their cabin where they stored provisions. It must have been a lonely life, cut off from the usual activities of spring: the planting, the fishing, the expeditions. Even if they could repeat to themselves 'Blessed are you when men revile and persecute you,' they could not be completely insensitive to the atmosphere of hostility that surrounded them. In the margin of his copy of Father Biard's 1616 *Relation*, Father Massé suggested that a book should be devoted to the rupture at the Habitation. And he mentioned 'the insults and wretchedness that we had to endure because of the hatred the calumniator stirred up against us among the French.' Poor Father Massé had prayed to be treated with contempt, but this was more than he had bargained for.

Some time in April Biencourt sailed to the Penobscot to trade. He hoped, too, to settle differences that had arisen between the Indians there and the Micmacs of Port Royal and Cape Breton. Perhaps with that end in view, he had some Penobscot Indians with him on his boat as he returned to Port Royal. Somewhere near the Ste Croix River he became involved in a fracas with his old enemy, Chevalier. In the course of this, one of his own men dropped a piece of lit tow-rope onto a barrel of gunpowder. Biencourt's ship went up in flames, some of the Indians were burnt, and all his ammunition, provisions, and furs, as well as merchandise belonging to his faithful vassal, Plâtrier, were lost.

It was a signal triumph for Breton independence. Chevalier must have crowed – so much for Biencourt's high-handedness and Lescarbot's jibes! Gravé and La Salle, who were also there watching the hostilities, may well have smiled quietly to themselves, though they do not seem to have taken advantage of young Biencourt's wretched situation. Someone must have helped the humiliated Vice-Admiral and his men limp back to Port Royal.

By June the Jesuits felt their seclusion and inactivity weighing heavily upon them. It was now midsummer and they had to make plans. If there was to be a reconciliation, they would have to take the first step. It would mean crawling to Biencourt, but this could be taken as an exercise in humility. How else were they to break the deadlock?

Father Biard accordingly approached Biencourt to make his apologies and ask him to forget the past. The quarrel had been occasioned, he claimed, by Biencourt's false suspicions of the Jesuits. But let them now show in what affectionate regard they held their commander.

In return Father Biard had to listen to Biencourt discoursing long and loftily on *his* neglect of his duties, pointing out where he had failed as a priest and as a Christian. It must have been one of the hardest penances Father Biard ever had to bear. But he was meekness itself. He told Biencourt that he was quite right. It was the devil, 'the author of all evil,' who had stirred up discord. But now that God had given him the grace to effect a reconciliation, he would like to say Mass in the chapel. And he asked Biencourt to get all his men to attend. For the first time in over three months priests and men gathered together.

Having shown the proper submission to the autocratic young commander, Father Biard lost little time in getting to his real purpose. After Mass he approached Biencourt and asked him if he would permit Brother Gilbert to leave for France on one of the ships that were then in the Ste Croix area. Biencourt consented on condition that Father Biard exempt him in writing from all responsibility for Brother Gilbert. The hot-headed young commander was very solemn about his obligations to keep the Jesuits tucked under his wing! Father Biard was only too happy to do so and Brother Gilbert somehow found his way to a ship that would return to France later in the season.

The two priests meanwhile decided to make as thorough a study of the Micmac language as possible. It was summer. Why should not one of them go to live with the Indians during those warmer months, as indeed Gravé had done for a whole year? The priest might then observe their ways and customs as he travelled about with them. Father Massé was particularly keen to go, and the men at the settlement, who seem to have had some say in the matter, favoured him for this mission as the more practical of the two priests.

With capable Father Massé went the Jesuits' servant, Crito, to help him and to serve Mass. Their native host and guide was Louis Membertou, who, says Father Biard, was very pleased to have them. This is the first time that a French missionary took to the nomadic life of the Indians, and bravely attempted to accommodate himself to a difficult, alien way of life. Others were to follow suit and leave fascinating accounts of their adventures: Brother Gabriel Sagard and Father Le Clerq of the Récollets, Father Le Jeune, the heroic Father Brébeuf, and other contributors to the *Jesuit Relations*. Father Massé, however, was a man of deeds not words. He wrote no account himself of his experiences, though many of his observations were probably incorporated in the survey of the 'savages' with which Father Biard introduced his *Relation* of 1616. But in the margin of his copy of this *Relation*, next to his colleague's elegantly brief summing-up of the hardships he, Father Massé, had endured that summer, he wrote that there was much else to tell and that some of his reports had been misunderstood. Experience, he realized, is much more complex than neat analysis allows.

Father Massé and Crito shared the life of Louis and his family for more than two months from the end of June until early September. With them they passed over the Bay of Fundy to the Saint John River. (Those who take the ferry from Digby to Saint John for the two-hour crossing might try to imagine what it was like tossing about in a light birch-bark canoe.) The priest and his servant found the way of life extremely hard. Though it was the season when food was plentiful, the diet did not agree with them. They grew thin and pale, their legs became heavy and they turned feverish. At one time Father Massé felt he was losing his sight, which had always been weak. Finally, however, both he and Crito recovered, though we cannot tell how much progress he made in the language. Later Father Biard said that they began to put together a little catechism. However, Father Massé did have the satisfaction of baptizing some sick Indians just before they died.

At the Habitation, Father Biard was receiving more formal linguistic instruction from a good-natured Indian who was happy to stay with him – but only for so long as the priest would feed and wait on him. For cooking and serving food was women's work. (One interesting facet of Father Biard's complex character is his irritation with Indian men, his pity for the women who did all the work and whom he considered badly treated.) The lessons lasted for three weeks only, as Father Biard ran out of food. He did have some reserves as we shall see, but these were strictly emergency rations.

Someone who was still seriously concerned about the Jesuits and their almost certain lack of provisions at Port Royal was Madame de Guercheville. She too had heard the stories about their being detained at Port Royal against their will. She took the initiative of organizing another expedition to be led by her own agent, the Norman René Le Coq, sieur de La Saussaie. At her lady-in-waiting's prompting the Queen wrote a chilly letter dated 7th August to Biencourt. In it the Queen notified Biencourt that she had now charged La Saussaie with protection of the Jesuits. Biencourt was to help them whether 'they wished to continue their stay where you are, go elsewhere or return.' The Queen enjoined him to treat them carefully 'as people to whom I am attached as much for their merits and piety as for other good considerations.' It was about this time as well that Father Coton received fifteen hundred livres, the annual royal contribution made to the Jesuit mission in Canada.

Madame de Guercheville obviously had her suspicions. But she still had heard nothing definite about Biencourt's usage of the Jesuits. Since she was arranging for a voyage to take supplies to Port Royal, she felt Poutrincourt should share the burden of the expenses. So La Saussaie journeyed to Poutrincourt's barony at St Just and found that gentleman just recovering from his sickness. Having made a low, elaborate bow, La Saussaie explained that Madame de Guercheville was prepared to make another contract with him for the relief of Port Royal. Poutrincourt dispiritedly replied that he did not have any funds available. Still, he agreed to go to Paris to see what could be done. As leader of the new expedition, La Saussaie also took the opportunity of asking Poutrincourt for any maps or charts he might have of the coasts of New France. Poutrincourt obliged, but later felt that they had been pried out of him.

Mid-August found both Poutrincourt and La Saussaie in Paris, the feudal seigneur appropriately lodged in the Quartier Latin, the more medieval part of the city, and La Saussaie near the Jesuit house in the Marais, a new quarter distinguished by order and elegance and about to become the most fashionable district in Paris.

The *Factum* alleges that once in Paris, Poutrincourt saw Father Coton, to whom he suggested that the Jesuits should put up the money for this new expedition as he, Poutrincourt, had already spent much more than the Jesuits. If this interview did take place, Father Coton would surely have asked Poutrincourt what news there was of the priests at Port Royal. Had Poutrincourt not received a letter from his son? It would have been an embarrassing question for Poutrincourt to answer. On the question of funding, Father Coton coldly replied that the Jesuits had no money. He, too, had come to mistrust this 'noted Catholic.'

La Saussaie put Poutrincourt in touch with one Louis Beauxhoste. We know little about this personage except that on the 17th August he lent Poutrincourt 750 livres. To obtain this Poutrincourt and his wife had to agree to the drawing up of a bond, engaging their persons and their property and promising repayment within two months. On the same day and before the same notary, Poutrincourt and La Saussaie signed a contract. La Saussaie recognized receiving the 750 livres. Madame de Guercheville was to contribute another 750 livres and La Saussaie was to superintend the fitting-out of a small ship at Le Havre which was to sail for Port Royal. There Biencourt was to hand over the furs to La Saussaie. The latter would then bring them back to Le Havre or Dieppe for sale. Profits were to be evenly divided. La Saussaie was expected to keep an exact account of expenses and profits. Poutrincourt left the notary's rooms relieved and resentful – relieved that Port Royal would receive provisions before the winter, resentful at having to find the money to redeem his bond while the Jesuits could do so much 'under the borrowed name of a lady.' For he managed to persuade himself that the Jesuits had ingratiated themselves with the great lady and were using her as cover for 'their secret enterprise.' And this, Imbert had assured him, was none other than to oust him from Port Royal.

La Saussaie entrusted preparations for the voyage to a fitter-out from Rouen called Simon Lemaistre. But before the expedition could get under way, some time in late September or early October, Brother Gilbert arrived in Dieppe. Here at last was an eyewitness of events at Port Royal with news of 'Our Men' for the Jesuits at Eu, for Father Coton and Father Baltazar in Paris, for Madame de Guercheville and the Queen. They soon had the whole story: Biencourt's autocratic ways, his injustice and ingratitude to the Jesuits, his envy, his recklessness, his questionable accounts – and his men! Port Royal was not what he, Brother Gilbert, could term a Christian colony. The conversions were merely nominal. Most of the Indians had been quite unaffected by baptism and had sunk back into their superstitious ways. And yet, he reported, the priests still felt that they had made some impression on the Indians. Life in the wilderness was hard, but, if they managed to imprint the word of God upon the hearts of these poor savages, they asked for nothing better than to dedicate themselves to good works in New France. Brother Gilbert had letters from the priests suggesting that, if there were funds available, they might go elsewhere along the coast, which now belonged to Madame de Guercheville. Father Biard was especially attracted to Kadesquit, that beautiful spot on the Penobscot near today's Bangor where he had encountered Bessabez and an encouraging number of well-disposed Indians.

Indignant, outraged – one can imagine what she had to say on the subject of little nobles – Madame de Guercheville countermanded her order to La Saussaie. There could be no joint expedition with people like the Biencourts. She was, however, willing to subsidize another, still with La Saussaie as leader. But as the aim was to set up a new colony elsewhere, it would have to be organized on a much larger scale. New preparations for this, with Lemaistre as fitter-out and busy Brother Gilbert as supervisor, took all winter.

So, to Poutrincourt's desperation, there were the perfidious Jesuits at work again. No motion was made to return to him his investment of 750 livres. On the 17th October his bond to Beauxhoste fell due. On the 4th November he saw Imbert and signed a document acknowledging his debt of 1,000 livres to Imbert for services rendered on voyages over the last two years. It was a large amount. On this occasion, Poutrincourt must have talked over his new troubles with the sycophantic Imbert, a man never slow to encourage anti-Jesuit indignation in his employer. Perhaps it was Imbert who suggested to Poutrincourt that not Beauxhoste but the Society of Jesus was his real creditor. It was the Jesuits surely who had lent him money under cover of Beauxhoste, only to get it taken away from him by La Saussaie and so maliciously land him in a trap. Was it not La Saussaie who had put forward Beauxhoste as lender? And was not La Saussaie an agent for the Jesuits, nay 'their Lieutenant-General in their secret enterprise'? Poutrincourt's paranoia was such that he took this story of tortuous intrigue for the truth, and proceeded to act on it.

Convinced that the man behind it all was Father Coton, Poutrincourt had him summoned before a civil magistrate on the very next day, the 5th November. This priest, Poutrincourt claimed, should answer for La Saussaie, who had made off with his money and had then backed out of the expedition, leaving him with neither money nor goods. On the 16th November the case was heard. Father Coton said he knew nothing of La Saussaie – who was indeed Madame de Guercheville's agent. If La Saussaie had money that Poutrincourt had entrusted to him, the priest coolly argued, Poutrincourt could surely get it back. By this time Father Coton's sympathy for Poutrincourt would have been somewhat scant. The court required Poutrincourt to obtain further documentation to back up his case against Beauxhoste and the Jesuits.

We now get a brief glimpse of the long-suffering Claude Pajot,

Madame de Poutrincourt. Her husband might rave on about Jesuit plots and talk of proving it in court. Her bourgeois common sense told her that a bond was a bond and that they would be obliged to redeem it. How many more court cases would her impetuous husband plunge himself into? How much more would they owe in lawyer's fees? And finally, where would his obsession with that wilderness across the ocean land her and her family? All she could see for the constant drain on their resources over the last three years was debts, debts, and more debts. Then there had been her husband's illness – his madness? – from which he had just recovered. Unless she did something they would all face ruin. We have no idea whether there were angry scenes, recriminations, disputes in which the aristocratic (quixotic?) notion of 'honour' flashed and clashed against solid bourgeois notions of respectable prosperity. What we do know is that on the 21st November she requested an inquiry into the terms of her marriage contract with a view to obtaining a legal separation of property from her spouse. She must have felt justified in taking this action when, on the 19th December, the court declared against Poutrincourt on the Beauxhoste matter. Together they owed the merchant 750 livres and interest, and the court ordered that they should pay it.

By now Poutrincourt was anxious about his son and the people at Port Royal. He himself had endured one bad winter there and knew how rigorous it could be. So he hurried to Dieppe to see what could be done about refitting the *Grâce-de-Dieu*. An unpleasant surprise awaited him. An agent for Simon Lemaistre, the Rouen outfitter, had him arrested and imprisoned for defaulting on his bond which Beauxhoste had transferred to Lemaistre. It is a curious story. Surely Lemaistre, holding goods worth 750 livres bought with money given to him by La Saussaie on Poutrincourt's behalf, should have been able to pay off the bond. But – if the *Factum* is right – Lemaistre, document in hand, realized he was in a superior position legally and let the full force of the law fall upon the unhappy gentleman. Could Madame de Guercheville have intimated to La Saussaie, and he to his agents, that it was unnecessary to treat her former business partner with too much consideration?

It is uncertain how long Poutrincourt was in prison, or exactly what conditions he lived in: dungeon or merely detention. But whether among the rats or just confined in a shabby room, he had time to brood over this new trick that the 'Jesuits' had playcd on him. How much further would they go in their desire to reduce and humiliate him?

On the 16th January, after making offers, declarations, and an appeal, Poutrincourt was released on consideration of his rank. A week later, however, he found himself sentenced by a magistrate of Le Havre to pay the debt. Somehow – we do not know how – the money was found. Did Lemaistre perhaps hand over to him the goods that had been bought on his behalf? He also obtained enough to have the *Grâce-de-Dieu* partially fitted out and taken to La Rochelle. But with all these set-backs, Poutrincourt was unable to send out provisions to Port Royal until the late spring of 1613.

Meanwhile, at Port Royal, Biencourt had been so sure that a ship would arrive before winter set in that he had rashly traded nearly all his provisions for furs. By the 1st November he realized that nothing was likely to arrive. The Jesuits were now in a position to show Christian charity and heap coals of fire upon the improvident young gentleman. For they had reserved some grain in their storeroom and now cheerfully offered this for general use.

In *his* account of the winter of 1612–13, the only one we have, Father Biard is understandably more interested in stressing the Jesuit contribution than in describing the colony as a whole. Many questions one would like to ask remain unanswered. Was this grain their only food? Did they not try shellfish again? If they made bread, they would not have worried about dysentery. Did they go hunting? Did Member-tou's family again come to share their kill with them? What of their domestic animals? How were they fed? If the colony had been on the verge of starvation, would they not have sacrificed pigeons, hens, a pig? For towards the end of 1613 there were, we know, pigs, horses, and foals at the Habitation. Were some of these offspring of the animals Captain L'Abbé had brought with him 'for future propagation,' or were they sent out by Poutrincourt in the summer of 1613? Was there much sickness, any death over that winter? How severe a winter was it? It certainly was not a time of ease and plenty. But was it quite as terrible as one might think on reading Father Biard?

Father Biard's personal victory that winter was to prove that 'intellectuals' like the Jesuits were superior in organizational ability and practical accomplishment to so-called men of action. Had not Poutrin-court put them off in the first place by saying that they were men of learning unfitted for dealing with the hardships of a life in the wilds? Now they were in a position to show what they could do. The first task they set themselves was to build a boat, while the men of the settlement sat around the fire and scoffed. But in this, when spring came, the Jesuits were able to go out looking for roots, acorns, and fish. 'And thus,' wrote Father Biard, 'we were butting against time (as the saying is) with our shoulders, or rather with our hands and feet, dragging on our miserable lives until the arrival of the ship.'

In Rome the Jesuit General, Father Aquaviva, had eventually learnt from Father Baltazar about the unfortunate state of the Canadian mission. He had heard, too, of the plan to set up a new one elsewhere under the aegis of Madame de Guercheville. He was alarmed at the thought of Our Men 'boldly nay rashly' wandering about in a wilderness insufficiently explored by French soldiers and merchants. Early in January 1613 he wrote to Father Baltazar to say that the Jesuits should be recalled until such time as something more was known about the region. By the time Father Baltazar received this notification, preparations had gone too far. It would be tactless to turn down royal support for a Jesuit overseas mission. On the 26th March 1613 Aquaviva wrote again to Baltazar to say that he was surprised to hear that, in spite of his letter of advice, two more Jesuits were going out. The Father General was worried lest they should be vainly exposed to yet graver dangers. His misgivings were to prove completely justified.

But his disapprobation came too late, for two weeks earlier, on the 12th March, the ship, the *Jonas*, had already sailed from Honfleur. The captain of this other *Jonas* (at least fifty tons lighter than Lescarbot's) was Fleury of Abbeville and the pilot Israel Bailleul of Rouen, who was – surprisingly for this very Catholic voyage – a Huguenot. We may remember that he had gone to Ste Croix on the *Bonne Renommée* with Gravé in the summer of 1605.

In command of the expedition as civil and military leader was low-bowing La Saussaie. In her enthusiasm Madame de Guercheville does not seem to have pondered the fact that he had no experience whatsoever of voyages to and along the coasts of New France – a point that Champlain acidly noted when, in 1632, he described this venture.

La Saussaie had a vision of establishing and supervising an idyllic agricultural settlement. Perhaps he had been reading Lescarbot. He took with him seeds of various sorts as well as exotica like apricot and peach trees. Horses went too, and goats, as well as enough provisions for a year or more. Madame de Guercheville had stinted on nothing. Second in command to La Saussaie was Nicolas de La Mothe, who was to show himself to be a pluckier man than his leader. One Ronseré, whom Father Biard described as the ensign, seems to have had some fighting experience. For these more military-minded gentlemen there were cannon and ammunition and the Queen herself contributed four large tents.

One of the more curious personages on board was the interpreter. This was a certain Jean-Jacques Simon, who must at some time have been on ships bartering along the Acadian coast in order to qualify for the post. He was either ill or a hypochondriac, for he stipulated that he would go on the expedition only if he were assured of the services of a physician, a surgeon, and an apothecary, all of whom Brother Gilbert did indeed manage to engage for him. For his services he was advanced one hundred livres.

The two accompanying Jesuits were Father Quentin and Brother Gilbert. Father Jacques Quentin was then in his early forties. While Bursar at the college of Eu, he had met Fathers Biard and Massé. He seems to have been a competent administrator and a brave man, but nothing of his personality glimmers through Father Biard's recital of their subsequent adventures together. With him went the indefatigable Brother Gilbert. Orders were that they were to return to France with the ship if the two priests at Port Royal were still alive. Apparently some dark doubts had been expressed on that score!

On leaving Honfleur, Brother Gilbert, who, like Father Biard, seems to have had a taste for the dramatic, made a solemn prayer with the whole crew as audience. (*Tableaux vivants* were much in vogue in Jesuit colleges.) As the wind filled the sails, he 'raised his hands and eyes to Heaven, praying God that he might never again return to France.' His dearest wish, he exclaimed, was to die while working for the conversion of the 'savages.'

In the meantime Poutrincourt was desperately trying to get his own relief expedition afloat. As always, the trouble was financial. On the 2nd March his wife formally renounced all community of property with him. On the 9th the court declared the separation of property final. Poutrincourt was ordered to allow her half the lands and seigneuries of Guibermesnil and Marcilly – a portion to which she was entitled by the marriage contract of August 1590. He was also expected to return to her the 19,545 livres he had spent of the money she had inherited from her parents. They seem to have agreed to put Guibermesnil in Picardy up for auction, for by the 10th May it had been sold despite the protest of their lawyer, Nicolas Desnoyers, to whom they owed 12,000 livres in fees.

And indeed Desnoyers had been of some service to Poutrincourt in suing, on his behalf, Eric of Lorraine, the Bishop of Verdun, for the debts that Poutrincourt and the Paris merchant Fortunat du Gué had incurred in 1608 when Poutrincourt had first attempted to organize his own expedition to Port Royal. On the 22nd April Eric's nephew, Charles, now himself Bishop of Verdun, decided, with his uncle's authorization, to settle the matter out of court. The old bishop assured his nephew that he had promised Poutrincourt nothing. But he was willing to pay Poutrincourt thirty-five hundred livres and du Gué one thousand livres in exchange for the papers and documents on which they based their claim – even though Charles maintained that these papers would not be judged sufficient evidence in a court of law. At this point Poutrincourt and du Gué were only too glad to get what they could, and signed the transaction.

With thirty-five hundred livres in hand Poutrincourt was now in a position to do something about his ship at La Rochelle. For years he had been claiming from Macain and Georges, the fitters-out there, the seven hundred pounds of gunpowder he had taken out with him on de Monts' 1604 expedition and which he had left at Ste Croix. When de Monts' company had been dissolved, Poutrincourt seems to have thought that this should be returned to him as part of his salary for the year he had acted as commander at Port Royal. But Macain and Georges had been slow to acknowledge his claims. Now, however, since he did not appear quite so destitute, they were prepared to negotiate with him and help him send provisions out to Port Royal. On 2nd May a contract was drawn up between Poutrincourt and the Rochelais merchants. In this Poutrincourt's representatives acknowledged receiving on his behalf, from Macain and Georges, 420 livres lent at a rate of 25 per cent interest. All furs were, on the return journey, to be handed over to the two merchants. From this time on, the Biencourt family were firmly associated with the Rochelais.

On the 5th May the *Grâce-de-Dieu* sailed for Port Royal. On the 13th

Poutrincourt wrote to his friend Lescarbot, who, since 1612, had been attached to the French ambassador in Switzerland. In his letter he gave *his* version of the troubles at Port Royal, the excommunication, his subsequent dealings with Father Coton, La Saussaie, and Beauxhoste, and his imprisonment. But, he exclaimed, at last the ship was on her way: 'May God have her in his keeping! I do what I can to free myself from the miseries of these parts.'

CHAPTER SIXTEEN

Virginia Triumphant

ON THE 16TH MAY 1613, Madame de Guercheville's *Jonas* anchored off Cape La Have, which the French had named and Champlain mapped and charted almost nine years earlier to the day. The voyagers went on land, erected a cross, and on it placed the arms of Madame de Guercheville, the new seigneuresse of the coasts.

Their next stopping place was Port Royal. Here they found the Habitation almost empty. Biencourt and his men were away, fishing or visiting the Indians. But the two priests were there with their boy, Crito, to thank God for their deliverance, give their deliverers a rapturous welcome, gather together relic, altar vessels, and their few belongings. In charge of the fort was Hébert. So it was to him that La Saussaie delivered the cool royal command 'to release the Jesuits and to let them go wherever they pleased.' Twelve years later Hébert was to meet Father Massé at Quebec. The first encounter may have been chilly, but some years later Guillaume de Caen, of the company then in charge of Quebec, was to complain that Hébert and the Jesuits were in league against him, plotting his downfall. Time and circumstances make for strange changes in alliance.

The *Jonas* hovered in the basin for another five days waiting for a good wind. Then, at last, a good north-easterly wind filled the sails and took Fathers Biard and Massé away from the place where prospects might please, but man, to Jesuit missionaries anyway, had proved vile. It must have been with an enormous sense of relief that they sailed out past the Gut through which, just two years earlier, they had entered with such high hopes.

Their charity might have been sorely tested, but they still had faith and hope. Father Biard asked the captain to set his course for Kadesquit, near Orland, on the Penobscot, the most propitious place for settlement and mission work he had encountered. But the weather changed and for two days and nights they veered to and fro in the thick, dark fog among breakers and rocks, praying and making vows. At last the fog disappeared and before them rose the shining peaks of Mount Desert Island. Bailleul, the pilot, steered them eastward into a wide port – Frenchman Bay. Again they raised a cross and Mass was sung. Since God's hand had reached out to save them, they called this place St Sauveur.

God might save them from the perils of the sea, but nothing, it seemed, could save them from human wrangling. Pilot and crew now maintained that they had arrived at their destination, which was, they had been told, a port in Acadia. But Father Biard was eager to go up the Penobscot. La Saussaie explained to the crew that Kadesquit on that river was the port intended, and not the one where they now found themselves. Bailleul was indignant. He was a pilot, he protested, not an explorer, and no large ship had ever been up the Penobscot. (Champlain, it will be remembered, had explored that coast and the river in a pinnace.) And anyway, Bailleul and the sailors claimed, pointing at the map, Kadesquit was in *Norumbega* not *Acadie*. Father Biard's heart sank: 'reasons here, reasons there; nothing but argument, a bad augury for the future.'

The inhabitants of the coast had seen the French ship. Smoke signals arose from the shore. Bailleul was of the party that went to meet the Indians, to whom he mentioned that the Port Royal Jesuits were on the ship. Some remembered the patriarch who had been on the Penobscot with Biencourt nearly two years before and said they would like to see him again. Father Biard immediately went on shore to ask the way to Kadesquit. But the Indians were reluctant to let him leave so soon. If he wished to stay in these regions, why not remain with them? This place was just as good as, if not superior to, Kadesquit. Then they invited him to go and see their chief, Asticou, who they alleged was very ill. If Father Biard did not come to see him, he would die without being baptized and so would not go to heaven. And Father Biard would be to blame. These Indians obviously knew their missionary. Nothing now could keep Father Biard away. With La Mothe, the lieutenant, and Simon, the interpreter, he travelled three leagues by canoe to visit the sick chief.

As it turned out this was a ruse, but a successful one. Asticou was suffering from nothing more than a cold. But once there, the French surveyed the spot. They were very much impressed. Even Father Biard, whose heart was set on the Penobscot, found it attractive and promising. There was cleared land, fertile soil, rivers, streams, and a hill that sloped up from a safe harbour which was sheltered by large Mount Desert Island and other smaller islands at the entrance. (Going by these and other indications, Father Campeau has very plausibly suggested that this spot was at today's Lamoyne Township near Bar Harbour airport, that they had first anchored off West or South Gouldsboro, and that the small islands would be the Porcupine Islands.) La Saussaie and others came to inspect the place. All agreed that they were not likely to find a finer spot.

And then what Father Biard saw as a 'very evident' sign confirmed them in the belief that the good Lord favoured their designs and intended them to stay. On their way back to the ship, the group was delayed by wails of mourning. In dramatic circumstances, with a 'great crowd of Savages drawn up in regular order, standing in the open air,' Father Biard baptized a dying child. After the ceremony the priest handed the child to the mother and the child immediately began sucking hungrily at her breast. It was a moment of triumph for Father Biard: 'These good people looked upon him as though he were more than man, trembling before him, and seeming to have been strongly touched by God.'

So the French brought the *Jonas* three leagues west to the site of the new colony. After raising another cross, La Saussaie had foundations for a fort traced and dug. That done, he turned his attention to the rich, dark earth and called his men away from construction in favour of cultivation. He was eager to see how crops would fare. As for a habitation, he said, tents were all they would need to live in over the summer. His immediate subordinates, La Mothe and Ronseré were uneasy. It was all very well to plough, till the soil, and plant seeds. But was it necessary? They already had a good supply of food. What really came first was housing and defence.

In the warm summer weather tempers rose as they argued over what mattered most for survival: food or shelter. While they argued, the men idled and neglected both. Captain Fleury, too, grew anxious. About the 17th June, three weeks after their arrival at St Sauveur, he asked La

Saussaie to have goods and armaments taken off the ship. And he protested that he would not be responsible for them if some misfortune befell the *Jonas*. La Saussaie asked him to have patience and keep them on the ship since he had as yet no suitable place to store them.

Towards the end of June, Fleury grew even more alarmed. English warships, he heard, were roaming the region. He urged La Saussaie to have the ten cannon on board taken on shore to defend the colony. Men in La Saussaie's following jeered and said such rumours were mere scare stories. Fleury eventually knew the questionable triumph of being right. For an English ship from Virginia *was* prowling the sea near the new colony.

This is an appropriate place to say something about the English colony developing to the south of the French habitations. In 1607, the year that de Monts was obliged to pull out of Acadia, the English had set up their rough, triangular, palisaded fort of Jamestown on the marshy banks of the James river. This was the germ of what was to be both the British Empire and the United States of America. But these swelling imperial themes had a strained, sickly start. By Christmas of 1607, within six months of arrival only 38 of the original 105 settlers were alive. Colonizers starved in a country where game, fish, and berries abounded. Reinforcements in 1609 proved disastrous. There was not enough food to go around. Between October 1609 and March 1610 – at the time Poutrincourt was planning to reoccupy Port Royal – nearly 500 people died. During this period, known as the 'starving time,' people ate roots, snakes, vermin, boots, shoes, and the corpses of Indians stewed with herbs. One man killed his wife, salted her, and had actually eaten part of her before he was found out and executed.

Sixty living cadavers were just on the point of abandoning the colony when a new governor, Lord Delaware, arrived. He and his successors, Sir Thomas Gates and the Marshal, Sir Thomas Dale, set the colony on its feet by introducing severe measures known as *Lawes Divine, Morall and Martiall*. Within two short years these measures and other more positive inducements had improved the tone and muscle of the colony. In 1612 a certain John Rolfe began to experiment with the planting of tobacco, raising the milder West Indian species instead of the harsh indigenous sort. King James, who detested the practice of smoking, might have grimaced. After 1614 the 'joviall weed' was to flourish in Virginia and, with it, many Virginians.

One of the adventurous men of the tough new regime was Captain Samuel Argall. He was a bold navigator, the first to shorten the voyage from England to Virginia by sailing direct instead of by way of the West Indies. In 1610 he had arrived at the Chesapeake within nine weeks of leaving England. The early months of 1613 found him busy building a frigate, trading for corn with the Indians, and exploring the rivers of the region. The great chief Powhatan, who feared for the survival of his people, had captured some Englishmen and seized English arms and tools. Argall conceived the audacious plan of abducting his daughter, the beautiful Pocahontas, and holding her to ransom. The strategem succeeded. The English recovered their men and their hardware. Pocahontas had already shown a certain tenderness for Englishmen. A year later the enterprising John Rolfe fell in love with the captured princess, married her, and later took her to England where she was presented at court.

But the romance of Pocahontas lay in the future. Argall's next task after abducting her was to provide food for the colony. For he was determined it should not know another 'starvation time.' He decided to sail up the coast to the group of islands off the Kennebec which the English used as a base for summer fishing. Early in the summer of 1613 he set off in his frigate, the *Treasurer*, a 130-tonner that sported fourteen large cannon. The crew consisted of sixty unkempt but well-trained men, each equipped with a musket. For English ships were always on the look-out for hostile Spanish vessels. (And indeed, the Spanish ambassador in England was assiduous in his reports on the growth of the Virginian colony, which it was in Spanish interests to destroy.)

Fog, rain, and the current drove the *Treasurer* north-east of the islands. On the 2nd July some Indians sighted her off Mount Desert Island. Taking this English frigate to be a French ship in search of the *Jonas*, they went out to tell Argall and his men that a ship belonging to their countrymen was anchored not far off. On their guard at first, the English soon saw that these 'savages' were well intentioned. Clad in their skins, they bowed and greeted them with gestures that the bluff English recognized as being elaborately French. They also caught the word 'Normandia.' The English had little food left, the crew were in rags, and Argall loved loot. What an unexpected prize this might be! Using sign language, the English asked how large the other ship was, how many men were on board, how many cannon. They looked excitedly at the raised arms and fingers of the answering Indians. The French ship, it appeared, was much smaller than the *Treasurer*, less well manned and equipped. It could be theirs for the taking. Let the Indians lead them to their fellow countrymen!

One helpful Indian stayed on board to show the way. With a good wind behind them, the *Treasurer* sailed into the bay. The guide pointed to the *Jonas* anchored behind some islands. The English could just make out the tents on shore. Then the Indian noticed them draping red flags round the decks, preparing the cannon, getting ready their muskets. The mood of exhilaration turned to one of tension. Too late, the horrified Indian saw he had been misled.

From the shore the French saw this strange ship bearing down upon them. They were puzzled and anxious, not sure what to do. Bailleul, the pilot, took fourteen of his sailors out in a boat and around an island to reconnoitre. La Saussaie decided to stay on shore and kept most of the men with him. They took up their arms. But La Mothe, Ronseré, and other sturdier characters, among whom was Brother Gilbert, went to join Captain Fleury on the *Jonas*. There were ten men in all to defend her.

With trumpets blowing and drums beating the *Treasurer* advanced. From the *Jonas* the French called out a greeting and were answered with cannon and musket shot. Captain Fleury shouted an order for someone to fire the cannon. Brother Gilbert bravely lit the match but, unused to such exercises, did not train the cannon upon the English ship, so the shot went wide. The *Treasurer* drew close, ready to grapple, but Captain Fleury managed to pay out cable and draw his ship into shallower water.

The English then fired their muskets upon the French. Brother Gilbert fell, badly wounded. Captain Fleury and three others were also hit. That left six unwounded men against sixty. What could the French do but surrender? Two jumped into the water to swim for shore. The English fired upon them; their bodies thrashed upon the water, then disappeared.

The victors boarded the *Jonas*. Argall called for his surgeon on the *Treasurer* to come and tend the wounded. Then the English rowed to shore. Here La Saussaie and his men had taken refuge in the fort, probably a palisade built round the foundations that had been dug. Argall's lieutenant, Turner – or Turnel, according to Father Biard – was a well-educated man with a knowledge of Greek and Latin as well as French and other languages. So the English had no trouble in making themselves understood. They called upon La Saussaie to yield. La

Saussaie asked for time to take counsel and then stole off into the woods. Argall sent a party to search for him, and took advantage of his absence to seize the chests. Unseen by the French he picked the lock, carefully removed the royal commissions and patents, put everything else back just as carefully, then locked the chests again.

Next day La Saussaie returned to the tents. Argall had already conceived a low opinion of this leader who ran away from danger, but first played with his mouse by making polite inquiries. So La Saussaie claimed they had been sent by their King? The four tents were a personal gift from His Majesty? Argall would in no way want to cause trouble between James of England and Louis of France. So could he see La Saussaie's commission? La Saussaie, who had his keys with him, replied that the letters were in his chests. When these were brought, Argall asked him to look carefully to see whether they had been tampered with. La Saussaie replied that everything was in order. He unlocked his chests, looked, searched more frantically, but could not find the letters.

This was the opportunity that Argall was waiting for. He frowned. His voice and manner hardened. These French, he declared, were nothing but imposters and worse – outlaws, pirates who deserved to die. This having been decided, it was now virtue on his part to set his men on to plundering the ship, while the French looked on helpless.

Father Biard heard that Brother Gilbert was hurt and sent a message to Argall asking that all the wounded be brought to shore. Argall gave his permission. Just twenty-four hours after he had fallen, Brother Gilbert died a painful but uncomplaining death in the arms of the Jesuit fathers. The prayer he had made at Dieppe was answered. The French buried him at the foot of the cross.

Argall's threats left the French very uneasy about their fate. They were completely at the mercy of the English, who, having looted the ship, now took to snatching the clothes off their backs. What did Argall plan to do with them? Exterminate them? Since the colony was being founded to further Jesuit missionary work, the priests decided to see whether Jesuit prestige might affect Argall's attitude. At any rate, the announcement of their presence might prevent the English captain from allowing plunder to lead to murder. So Fathers Biard and Massé went to see him on the *Treasurer*. They explained that they were not only priests but Jesuits and asked him to help the French return home. Argall does not seem to have had the usual Protestant antipathy towards the Society of Jesus. He courteously heard them out but confessed himself surprised at seeing the Jesuits associate themselves with 'marauders.' This challenge unloosened all the eloquence of the articulate and logical Father Biard, who proved that the French were there in good faith and to perform good works. Argall gave way to him point by point, but still held the trump card which he coolly proceeded to play. Well knowing where the all-important commissions were, he shook his head: 'Certainly ... there has been some fault, as far as I can see, for your letters going astray' – the 'fault,' as he gleefully knew, being all his own. Still, he promised to consider the matter of their return to France, and invited the priests to dine with him every day.

If Argall *had* been devising a swift death for his captives, someone else deterred him besides the Jesuits. Bailleul and his fourteen men were still at large. They might testify against him if he permitted any such atrocity. And just the fact that they were out of his grasp irritated Argall like 'a thorn in his side,' said Father Biard, watching him at dinner. But Bailleul managed to visit the French stealthily by night, in order to talk over what could be done. He assured the Jesuits that, Huguenot though he was, they could count on him if they wished to escape. The priests were grateful but replied that they could not think of their own safety until they had seen what became of the other colonists. Father Biard warned Bailleul to be on his guard: Argall was desperate to catch him. Bailleul decided to try to put the English off his track. The next couple of days he came into view of the English, but not within range of their cannon. Then he made a great show of setting off to find a fishing ship, taunting the enraged English, calling out that they would not get him this time, they would have to wait. But he and his men did not go far, just anchored their boat behind some islands. Perhaps his conscience was troubling him. Having been absent from the fray, he was now anxious to do what he could for his companions. Disguised as an Indian, he ranged along the shore, watching and waiting. His skins, moccasions, and face-paint were, in all likelihood, provided by the sympathetic Indians in the neighbourhood. For at night, when the English had withdrawn to their ship, they too came to visit their French friends. The guide was particularly upset at being the unwitting cause of their misfortune. They asked what they could do for the French and offered to take them in their canoes wherever they wanted to go. Two chiefs, Bessabez from the Penobscot and one

Aguigueou, were visiting Asticou. Ever since 1605, when Weymouth had captured five Indians to take to England, Bessabez had not been well disposed to the English. The three sagamos offered to take ten men each, feed and keep them with them until the next summer. Then they could go looking for French fishing vessels to take them home and so escape 'falling into the hand of the wicked Ingrés.' The French were grateful for Indian compassion. Even though their vocabulary might lack the abstract noun for that and other qualities, Father Biard was beginning to modify even further his opinion of these 'rude barbarians' whom he now took to calling 'these good Savages.' And ever after he was to praise their generosity. Still, the French could not imagine surviving a whole winter with the Indians, however kind. Father Massé and Crito had fared badly enough over one summer. On the other hand, what did the English have in store for them? Death – or slavery?

Finally Argall and Turner offered terms to La Saussaie. The English would take the captured *Jonas*. The French could take the long-boat and 'go where God directed us.' Father Biard was horrified at these terms. Did the pusillanimous La Saussaie realize what he was condemning them all to? He hurried off to remonstrate with Argall. The long-boat could not possibly hold thirty men, still less convey them over so many leagues to some place such as Canso where they might meet French fishing ships. This 'was plainly throwing us into the jaws of death and despair.' Argall shrugged. La Saussaie had made no difficulties about accepting the offer. Still, if some workmen would go to Virginia with him and put in a year there, he was willing to take them. Three agreed to go, as did Nicolas de La Mothe, for whom Argall had developed a liking.

Others joined La Mothe, among them Captain Fleury, who was unwilling to abandon his ship, especially since he was led to hope he might recover her. Father Biard suggested that en route for Virginia, a small party of Jesuits – that is, two priests and their assistants – should be taken to one of the islands in the Monhegan group. There they would ask English fishermen to take them back to Europe. So fifteen men in all remained with Argall.

The other fifteen, with La Saussaie in charge, were to go off in the long-boat. Simon (the interpreter) and his three medical attendants must have been in this group. (One wonders how the hypochondriac's health fared in these fraught days.) They had a choice of which priest should accompany them, so they chose Father Massé, no doubt because of his practical talents. Since he was likely to reach France before Fathers Biard and Quentin, he took with him the sacred vessels and the relic. Argall gave them a few provisions. Without a map, they were delivered to the mercy of the waves. Only a couple of them knew anything about sailing.

But Bailleul, who was keeping an alert watch, saw them set off. Still dressed in Indian skins, he managed to signal to them from the shore, and unseen by the English, climbed aboard and directed them to where his boat and his fourteen sailors lay hidden. The situation now seemed more hopeful. They exchanged places so that there would be an even distribution of sailors and passengers. And the two boats sailed off together with a pilot to guide them and a number of experienced men as crew.

Often hungry and hampered by bad weather, they did eventually find ships from St Malo on the coast near Halifax, one of them belonging to that old friend of the Jesuits, Robert Gravé. On the way they met and received help from two other friends. At Cap Fourchu (Yarmouth) Louis Membertou treated them to a most welcome feast of moose meat and pressed his former guest, Father Massé, to come and live with him and his family. The priest was very touched but said he had to remain with his companions. Then, near Port Mouton, they encountered four canoes. In one was the younger son of that Panounias whose death in 1606 had led Membertou on the warpath against the Almouchiquois. On his father's death he had changed his name and now went by a French one, Roland. He and the others recognized Father Massé, and, seeing the plight the French were in, gave a whole ship's biscuit to the priest and half to the others. Deprived of bread for three weeks, the grateful French fell upon it ravenously. Hearing about this incident many months later, Father Biard was to comment on the irony of the situation: 'Savages freely furnishing bread to the French.'

The journey back to France on two small ships proved horrifying, but at last, about mid-October, they arrived at St Malo. The town treated them to a grand welcome. Bishop, governor, magistrates, merchants, and citizens greeted, lodged, fêted, questioned, and listened to the thirty men who had returned from the other side of the ocean after so many near encounters with death. La Saussaie made a formal deposition describing the unwarranted attack of the English upon the French at St Sauveur. The diplomatic machinery that was set up to deal with such violations slowly ground into motion.

Safely back in France, Father Massé must often have wondered about his fellow Jesuits. Their odyssey was eventually to prove longer and more perilous than his. It was a small fleet that sailed for Virginia out of Frenchman Bay: the *Treasurer*, the *Jonas*, and a long-boat of twelve tons that the English also captured from the French. With it went a splendid haul: horses, goats, tents, clothing, furs, cannon, ammunition, agricultural tools, and a good supply of provisions.

The Jesuits were on the *Jonas*, which now had Turner as captain. However, he did not take them to look for an English fishing ship as promised but made straight for Jamestown. The French anxiously asked themselves what sort of welcome they would get there. For they had heard terrible tales of the severe Marshal, Sir Thomas Dale. He was supposed, however, to be friendly to the French, as he owed his early promotion to a French monarch, Henri iv. The latter had recommended him for a captaincy when he was fighting with French forces in the Netherlands against Spain. But now, ten years later, Dale was to do his best to wipe out all sign of what de Monts and the French had accomplished for the French monarchy in Acadia.

Sailing up-river through the luxuriant forests of Virginia, they reached Jamestown. It was with a stern countenance that the Marshal listened to Argall's account of the capture of these French 'pirates' who had dared to settle on territory claimed by England. He had little compunction about sending English sinners to the gallows. What would he not do to foreigners whom he considered criminals? The French could already see themselves 'ignominiously walk[ing] up a ladder to be let down disgracefully by a rope.' At this point Argall's gentlemanly conscience strode to the fore. He told Sir Thomas very firmly that he had given his word of honour to his prisoners that they would not be executed. Sir Thomas scoffed at the idea of treating marauders with honour. Argall then confessed that they did have some sort of charter from the King of France, and he produced the royal letters that he had filched from La Saussaie's trunks. So now the French knew what had become of them! To ignore these patents and hang the French might cause a diplomatic incident, for England and France were not at war. The French prisoners could breathe more freely.

The Council of Virginia, composed of Sir Thomas Gates (the

Governor), Sir Thomas Dale, Argall, and others met to decide their fate. The English now knew that they held the whip hand and, inspecting the French commission, felt they could afford to ignore it. This commission expressly gave the date of Henri IV's charter to de Monts as the 18th November 1603, whereas James' first charter dated back only to April 1606. Nevertheless, the Council had no trouble in working themselves up into a righteous froth of indignation about French usurpation. Had not Cabot in the fifteenth century claimed the whole of North America for England? Comparing the two charters, the Council could have seen that Henri's charter claimed the coast from the fortieth to the forty-sixth parallel, and that their own later charter of 1612 claimed only two hundred miles of coast north of Virginia – that is, as far as today's Atlantic City. But, playing fast and loose with latitudes, they maintained that they had a right to the whole coast as far as Cape Breton.

So Argall, whose capture of the French at St Sauveur had not been authorized by the Council, now found himself retroactively justified. The Council also commissioned him to return north to plunder all French ships and burn all settlements. The English had heard of both Ste Croix and Port Royal – from charts and papers, or from some of the French themselves? On this punitive expedition Argall was to take with him some of his prisoners. They would be allowed to return to France with their defeated fellow countrymen. In their moment of triumph the Virginians were prepared to crown their success with a sense of their own magnanimity.

Encouraged by his first exploit against the French, scenting more action and renown and, above all, plunder, Argall sailed from Jamestown with his fleet of three ships. With him in the *Treasurer* went Fleury and four other Frenchmen. The Jesuits and their boy were again on the *Jonas*, commanded by Turner.

Argall had little difficulty in finding St Sauveur. There the foliage had already been touched by the fall. The English carried out their orders. Flames redder than the turning leaves flared briefly over the rudimentary fortifications. The priests winced as they saw the crosses pulled down. Under one of these lay Brother Gilbert. Then the English raised another adorned with the name of King James and his coat of arms to show that this country was now theirs. (In actual fact, French occupation of this region was to continue sporadically for some time, one of the most fascinating commanders concerned being the colourful Baron de St-Castin.)

Argall then sailed up the coast in search of Ste Croix. Father Biard was the only one in the group who knew exactly where the island was situated. Argall interrogated him. But much to his displeasure, the priest refused to give anything away. The enterprising captain, however, was not easily put off. He had in his possession the maps that Poutrincourt had given to La Saussaie. By consulting them and observing the coastline, he was able to find the Ste Croix River and sail up it to the island. There he appropriated a good pile of salt. Then he set fire to all that remained of the settlement which de Monts had built that busy summer nine years earlier. Presumably any crosses marking the graves of the men who had died there in the first winter were destroyed. Argall was not tender about such things. But over the years the buried bones were to surface and bear mute witness to former French habitation of the island.

Apart from the salt, Argall had as yet no booty. But there was still Port Royal. Though he needed a guide, he did not look to the French for help. Instead he scoured the countryside in search of an Indian and managed to find one, 'by dint,' wrote Father Biard, 'of much running about, lying in ambush, enquiring, and skillful manoeuvring.'

Father Biard had by now become quite friendly with the well-educated Turner. In order to draw the English away from Port Royal, he suggested to the lieutenant that the English might be going to a great deal of trouble for very little reward. It was now October and late in the season. The Habitation, he stressed, was very meagrely supplied. Turner believed him and put this argument to Argall. But the Captain had got his guide. Greedy for any loot that might come his way, he was determined to make for Port Royal.

We have no account of the summer Biencourt and his men had spent at Port Royal. But subsequent allusions indicate that it had been a good one. Indeed, to those there it may have seemed that the departure of the Jesuits marked a turning point in the fortunes of the colony. For Poutrincourt's *Grâce-de-Dieu* had arrived, bringing provisions and perhaps more seed and livestock. Agriculture was not neglected. Men had been ploughing, planting, and cultivating wheat. The ship returned to France with a good cargo of furs and some men. One of these was Hébert, who was in La Rochelle in December that year signing a contract on behalf of young Biencourt and helping Poutrin-court organize yet another expedition to Port Royal. This, with Poutrincourt himself in command, was to leave that same month. With the aid of Macain and Georges, the Biencourts were determined to keep their colony going. They were beginning to think they might succeed.

Friendly with the Indians and feeling they had no cause to fear, the French no longer kept constant watch at the Habitation as in their early days there. On the 31st October, when Argall's little fleet arrived at Port Royal, young Biencourt and most of his men were away visiting the Indians on Long Island. Others were tilling the fields on the Annapolis River. The three ships entered the port by moonlight. Next day the tide was against them so they did not arrive in front of the settlement until ten or eleven in the morning. An English account of the raid claims that when Argall and forty of his best men landed on a meadow, they heard a cannon shot fired from the fort, either to warn them off or to warn others of their arrival. They hurried to the fort and found it empty – of men but not of goods. Shoes and clothing lay scattered about. There were utensils, a good store of food. Argall could triumph. So this was what Turner, prompted by the Jesuit, would have him miss! As punishment for his foolish credulity, Argall allowed his lieutenant a smaller share of the plunder than usual. Turner smarted at this insult and – blamed the priest.

When all available booty had been seized, Argall ordered the Habitation to be stripped of everything the Virginians might use down to the very locks. When just the empty husk of the Habitation remained, it was set alight. On a huge stone nearby the French had engraved the fleur-de-lys, the triangular hillocks of de Monts' coat of arms, and the Biencourt lion. Wielding hammer and pick, Argall's men smashed at it until these proud symbols of French dominion were effaced. And that was the end of the Habitation where, for eight years on the edge of the wilderness, Frenchmen had lived and worked, planted and feasted, prayed, play-acted, dreamed and quarrelled.

But there was also livestock for the taking. The English rounded up pigs feeding on acorns in a wood and drove them grunting and squealing towards the *Treasurer*. They found horses and colts, and led or chased them to the shore. Some were embarked on the *Treasurer*, others on the *Jonas*. (Lescarbot, who got his information from Poutrincourt, mentions that there were cows too.)

Argall and his men then went up towards the mouth of the river where the French had their wheatfields. Biencourt's men, who were there ploughing, made off up a hill, but the English managed to seize their boat. Argall also had some of the wheat collected to take back to Virginia, but ordered the rest to be destroyed. The mill, which he could not reach because of the ebbing tide, and also the barns, he left intact.

In the midst of all this looting and burning, another drama was being played out. At the wheatfields with Argall was Father Biard, who twice, he wrote later in his *Relation*, went down on his knees and begged the English captain to have pity on the French, leave them their boat and some food for the winter. From their hillside the angry, bewildered French caught sight of a black robe and recognized the priest who, as they saw it, had despised, excommunicated and then deserted them. It must be none other than this sanctimonious, hypocritical traitor who had brought the English to Port Royal. They hurled at him a volley of abuse, every curse at their command, and called on the English to kill this villainous Jesuit. Argall looked at Father Biard curiously. Why should these French feel such hatred for one of their own priests?

With the fields now burned black, the Habitation a heap of charred sticks under a grim November sky, and their ships laden with livestock and plunder, the English prepared to sail for Virginia. But bad weather kept them a few more days near the narrow entrance to the port. At this juncture Biencourt arrived from Long Island, for news of the raid and the conflagrations had spread quickly down the coast. Filled with rage and despair, he demanded to see the English leader. Argall agreed to a parley after declining Biencourt's offer to take him on in single combat. That, for Argall, was a piece of medieval nonsense.

In the course of their two-hour meeting, Biencourt tried another tack. Would Argall take him under his protection and let him hold Port Royal under English sovereignty? In return he offered him one half of the furs that he promised to collect together in a certain port, and also gave him samples of metal, assuring him that they came from rich mines. Was this a genuine offer and was Biencourt attempting to survive by accepting English rule? For some historians this would make him the first Acadian. It is quite probable, however, that he was stalling for time and hoping to get help from his Micmac allies so they might surprise the English in some port or at some so-called mine. But the abductor of Pocahontas was too wily for that and peremptorily refused to treat.

Some of Biencourt's Micmac friends were, in fact, there in the woods. Over the years they had seen how the French had taken it upon themselves to try and reconcile warring tribes of Indians. So now one Micmac, distressed for his friend, thought he might act as arbitrator between Biencourt and Argall, whom he took to be a Frenchman. He rushed towards them and appealed to them in a mixture of French and Micmac to make peace. He was so intense, so earnest, and made such wonderful rhetorical gestures that both Argall and Biencourt burst out laughing.

But as far as Father Biard was concerned, Biencourt was in no laughing mood. It must surely have been this priest, so ill intentioned towards the Biencourts, who had set the English upon Port Royal! In all probability Argall did nothing to discourage this belief. He bore Father Biard a grudge for refusing to help him find Ste Croix. What did he care if these French blamed the priest for the destruction of Port Royal? It is always an advantage to see one's enemy divided, and Argall, as we know, was not above playing little games. As for Biencourt, he had by now heard of the Beauxhoste bond and his father's imprisonment. This most recent blow, struck just when they were struggling to their feet, was surely the culmination of the plot woven by the Jesuits against the Biencourts! And that square-bonneted bogey, now with the English, was one of the chief agents in working their ruin.

Biencourt broke out in vehement denunciation of the priest who was, he told Argall, a 'pernicious Jesuit ... a true and native Spaniard,' a criminal well known in France, 'a fugitive from justice ... the cause of a great deal of scandal at Port Royal.' Let Argall be on his guard. This priest had done terrible things to the French, so 'there could not be the slightest doubt that he would do something still worse to the English.' Argall was amazed. Father Biard, a native Spaniard? Not only Biencourt but about five of his followers eagerly signed a written charge testifying that this was so, the most damaging accusation they knew they could make to the Englishman. They urged that Argall 'put on shore and desert Father Biard.' Young Biencourt's fury against the Jesuits now reached its peak. If he could only get his hands on the priest, he would hang him! Obviously he had found a scapegoat on whom he could lay all the responsibility for his terrible loss.

Father Biard was now in danger of his life. Turner became even more hostile, furious with himself for being such a poor judge of character as to let himself be taken in by a dissembling Spaniard. Argall was so angry that he did indeed threaten to abandon the priest on some deserted shore. His followers, however, advised that he be taken back to Virginia. There the stern Marshal would know what to do with a Jesuit – and a Spaniard to boot!

As for Father Biard, he was appalled at such lies. How could Biencourt, whom he later, in his *Relation*, referred to discreetly as 'a Frenchman,' hate him so much as to be willing to perjure his immortal soul to have him killed? How could he be so possessed of the devil, 'so desperately given up to and enslaved by sin'? It obviously never occurred to him that Biencourt considered him responsible for the destruction of all his hopes.

Father Biard had never been happy at Port Royal. But, writing of the burning of the Habitation, he exclaimed that it was a 'truly pitiable thing, for in an hour or two the work of several worthy people, during a number of years, was reduced to ashes.' With many memories in mind, he prayed, 'may our Lord grant that this same fire has so completely destroyed all sins, which may have been committed in this place, that they may never again arise in any other place, nor ever provoke the just and dreadful vengeance of our God.'

Argall, however, was not particularly burdened by a feeling of sin as he sailed for Virginia. He had every reason to feel jubilant. St Sauveur, Ste Croix, Port Royal were all destroyed. No more French colonies would dare to settle on territory where he had planted English crosses. And yet – Acadia was not quite dead.

Staying On

HE IRONY is that at the very time the Port Royal Habitation crackled in flames and then collapsed into ash, Poutrincourt must have been considering that, at long last Fortune was gracing him with a steady smile. During the course of 1613, as we have seen, the *Grâce-de-Dieu* had been to Port Royal and had returned with Hébert and a good cargo. In the fall Poutrincourt's affairs took a definite turn for the better. He signed an agreement with Georges of La Rochelle, accepting three hundred pounds of the gunpowder he had claimed. His differences with the firm of Macain and Georges were at an end, and, for reasons we shall look into later, the two Rochelais merchants now showed themselves interested in backing Biencourt enterprise in Acadia. Together with Hébert, who was acting on Charles' behalf, Poutrincourt entered into negotiations for another expedition to Port Royal. The final agreement was drawn up on the 26th December. Five days later, on the 31st, their ship *La Prime*, a seventy-tonner, captained by François Soreau, sailed from La Rochelle with Poutrincourt and Hébert on board. Accompanying them was David Lomeron, a nephew of the brothers-in-law Macain and Georges.

Poutrincourt would have been in high spirits. He could not have anticipated that this, his fourth voyage to the New World, was to be his last. Among several satisfactions was the prospect of returning to Port Royal unpolluted by those pestilential Jesuits. In late summer Hébert had brought news of their departure on Madame de Guercheville's *Jonas*. That to Poutrincourt spelt relief. But he still fumed when he thought of the excommunication and his imprisonment. Probably in the course of 1613, strengthened by the thought of his improving fortunes, he asked Imbert to draw up a *Factum*. With the intention of instituting legal proceedings, he put together all the letters and documents he had concerning the affair. These would reveal the Jesuits for what they were: 'subtle foxes ... chameleons ... false pastors,' equivocators, usurers, traitors, power-hungry regicides. It was something Poutrincourt would have 'to show his friends and dispose his judges to render him justice.' Imbert was still busy on this when news reached France of the destruction by the Virginians of St Sauveur, that rival colony. Poutrincourt savoured a most unchristian sense of gloating triumph. On leaving La Rochelle, he might have reflected that while the little *Prime* was battling her way through wintry seas, Providence – and Imbert – were working *for* him against the Jesuits.

That Providence was on *their* side was a thought that occurred again and again to two of these detested Jesuits, Fathers Biard and Quentin, also somewhere on the stormy Atlantic, surviving incredible perils. On leaving Port Royal, the *Jonas*, commanded by Turner, had been blown off course, and the decision was taken to sail east rather than to Virginia – where the priests would indeed have received short shrift. Later, anchored off Faial on the Azores, they and their boy, Crito, obligingly hid in the hold for days on end and so protected their Protestant pillagers and captors from being hanged by the Portuguese. It was a nerve-racking ordeal, but Father Biard was not unhappy to show the heretics that Jesuits, far from being slippery equivocators, were men of their word. About mid-February 1614, in rags and tatters, they reached Milford Haven in Wales, and towards the end of April at last set foot again on French soil to be warmly welcomed by Calais dignitaries.

But no cannon boomed and echoed at Port Royal when Poutrincourt arrived there in March. What faced him was complete and utter disaster. Nothing was left of the Habitation except the charred mess that showed grey and black through the melting snow. Gaunt, sick, and starving, Biencourt and his men told their story: the unexpected pounce of the enemy led by that traitor Biard and their terrible sufferings over the worst months of the year. The mill had been left untouched, so they had managed to turn it into a rough shelter. As for food, they had been reduced to eating roots, grass, the buds of trees, the lichen on rocks. Even some of the strongest among them had died. We are not told explicitly, but it is likely that Membertou's family had done something to keep the rest alive. In the retelling of the story one name rang out: Father Biard. How could the English possibly have made their way to Port Royal if he had not been their guide? Poutrincourt now had no doubts. It was Jesuit envy and intrigue that had crushed him, accomplished the ruin of all his New World hopes.

What were the Biencourts to do? Poutrincourt might despair, but, assured now of support from La Rochelle, his son was determined not to give up. It was over three years since he had seen France. What did he have to return to but the life of a small country seigneur – hunting, lawsuits, and debts? In spite of all the hardships in the New World he liked the sea, the sense of space around him, the opportunities to dominate and command. He chose to stay. With Lomeron he began to work out an agreement. He would remain in Acadia to trade with the Indians, while Lomeron, as his secretary, would make an annual voyage from La Rochelle, bringing out merchandise and supplies and taking back furs and fish to France. As Vice-Admiral, Biencourt could exercise a certain control over the area. For he had the right to examine charter-parties and confiscate the goods of those who did not have the proper papers. However, Biencourt and Lomeron did not reach this agreement immediately.

At this point it should be mentioned that relations between the merchants and traders of Rouen and St Malo and those of La Rochelle had worsened. In 1613, before Champlain had had time to organize a single company under the aegis of the new Viceroy, Condé, small companies from various ports obtained passports giving them the right to trade that year on the St Lawrence. A Rochelais ship, *Le Soleil*, was wrecked fifteen leagues below Tadoussac, her provisions, trade goods, and beaver skins joyfully looted by their rivals, the men of Rouen and St Malo, who made a considerable profit. If Lomeron had decided to come out to Port Royal with Poutrincourt early in 1614, it was possibly with a view to making Acadia the exclusive area for La Rochelle trading operations. For the Rochelais might find the St Lawrence closed to them – as indeed they did. But for some years now, as we know, Robert Gravé of the opposing Breton-Norman faction had been coming every year to trade in Acadian waters. And about the time the *Prime* and Poutrincourt put in at Port Royal, a Gravé ship, too, anchored off the devastated Habitation, though whether commanded by Robert or his redoubtable father we cannot tell. This visit triggered off a series of dramatic incidents that can only be pieced together from scant inventories of legal documents.

The *Prime* arrived at Port Royal on either the 17th or the 27th March. (In his deposition to the Admiralty at La Rochelle, Poutrincourt gives both dates.) On the 25th March (that is, either two days before Poutrincourt's arrival or eight days after), Biencourt made a written pact with the Gravés there. In this they agreed to go half shares on the furs obtained by trading with the Indians. It is fascinating to note those old rivals, the Biencourts and the Gravés, going into business together. But we cannot tell under what circumstances this deal was made, whether before or after the arrival of Poutrincourt and the *Prime*. If before, it was a deal Biencourt might have made out of sheer desperation. But then Poutrincourt himself, after his arrival, also made an agreement with Gravé – again in desperation?

The partnership did not last long. On the 22nd April, Lomeron, armed with a copy of Biencourt's commission as Vice-Admiral, went on board Gravé's ship and later drew up a report. Some quarrel obviously broke out which put an end to this all-too-brief association. Did Lomeron, intent on capturing Acadian trade for La Rochelle, question Gravé's right to be there? Was the Gravé – as seems likely – hot-tempered old François? Did he rage at Biencourt pretensions? Nevertheless – to complicate matters still further – on the 24th April Biencourt signed yet *another* agreement with Gravé. But finally on the 20th April, Biencourt made out a 'certificate' that infuriated the Normans. At this point the latter must have cocked a snook at their rivals and sailed out of Port Royal.

In early May the Norman ship, the one-hundred-tonner *Saint-François*, was trading on the Saint John River. Her captain was one Jean Groult. It will be remembered that Biencourt had given one-fifth of his trade goods to a Groult at the Saint John River on the 9th October after the disturbed night there. Merveille, too, another of the actors in that episode, was on the *Saint-François*.

Back at Port Royal the Biencourt-Rochelais faction seethed with indignation, and, as is characteristic of the Biencourts, indignation of the highly righteous sort. They were, as we have noticed, sticklers about procedures and liked to invest their actions with all due forms of legality. On this occasion Biencourt constituted Antoine Michelin judge for his 'admiralty,' and Michelin, on the 9th May, solemnly pronounced a sentence of confiscation upon the *Saint-François*. On what grounds we can only conjecture – probably refusal to recognize Biencourt's authority as Vice-Admiral. Thereupon Poutrincourt, Biencourt, Lomeron, and Hébert went on an expedition to the Saint John. On the 17th May, with no Father Biard to restrain them, they seized goods and furs from the *Saint-François*. Another ship, the sixty-ton *Don-de-Dieu* trading for the Rouen merchant Lucas Legendre, was also boarded some time that summer by the men of the *Prime*, who triumphantly confiscated provisions and merchandise. Altogether 642 skins of beaver, otter, and moose, taken from the Biencourt faction's Norman rivals, found their way to Macain and Georges. The Admiralty of Rouen later charged these Rochelais merchants with receiving stolen goods.

In his report on this incident, dated 7th June, Poutrincourt styled himself 'great Sagamo of the Souriquois and Etchemins and adjacent lands.' This self-conferred title makes it clear that Poutrincourt continued to regard himself as seigneur of territory beyond Port Royal, ingeniously basing his claim on Indian election rather than on the authority of the French crown. So in spite of the loss of the Habitation, we can see that it was not an altogether wretched, uneventful spring for the Biencourts, who showed themselves to be remarkably resilient. Still, it is frustrating to have nothing but a skeletal outline of events gleaned from court cases. Some of this litigation lasted nearly twenty years, the widows of the men concerned, among them Madame de Poutrincourt, continuing in French courts battles begun thousands of miles away at sea. The cries and curses, the passions and jealousies of rival traders became the busy scratch of quills drawing up dry legal statements.

Such incidents were to become increasingly common. For years the Rochelais traders and those from Normandy and St Malo attacked and looted one another's ships in Acadian waters. Among the Normans, Biencourt's old rival Robert Gravé was prominent. He kept on making his annual voyages to Acadia until, in 1619, he took off for the East Indies where he met his death at a fairly early age.

To us, viewing events from a distance, it might seem incredible that the French should start quarrelling among themselves just a few months after Port Royal was sacked and looted by the English. One can only suppose that competitors in the thick of things found it difficult to see that regional rivalries made for national weakness. The English, who were beginning to establish colonies nearby and whose interest in the area was increasing, could not be sorry to hear that the French were at each other's throats and furs. Still, however deplorable the situation seems to us today, we have a sneaking suspicion that for many of the men concerned it was a way of life they preferred to any other. After all, ice hockey had yet to be invented.

When Poutrincourt returned to France in the summer of 1614, he left his Port Royal estate entirely in his son's charge. For several years young Biencourt made Port Royal his base, though he was, in fact, more of a rover than a settler. With him were his second-in-command, Charles La Tour, and a handful of men. A good part of their lives must have been spent with the Indians, hunting and fishing. The Micmacs did not approve of casual encounters between their women and the French who came and went on ships. But as these Frenchmen were now practically living with them, it seems likely that they began to countenance marriages between these men and their girls – unions unblessed, of course, by any priest. The first child we actually hear of was a daughter born to La Tour in 1626. But it is not improbable that the blood of the Biencourts ran in the veins of other Micmac children.

Every summer the industrious but shadowy Lomeron would arrive with a ship from La Rochelle: the *Prime*, the *Fortune*, the *Charles*, the *Plaisir*, the *Jehan*. The ship would be unloaded then reloaded with a cargo of furs and fish. With Lomeron as his agent, Biencourt borrowed largish sums of money, eight thousand livres in 1616, for example, for the fitting-out of the *Fortune*. His yearly profits enabled him to pay off each debt before incurring another. This busy summer period was made busier by the constant policing of the waters: Captain Soreau, who had come out with the *Prime* in 1614, was also captain of the *Fortune* in 1616 with orders to arm his ship 'to defend himself or attack ships from Normandy and other places ... that would not recognize the said Biencourt as Vice-Admiral.' Behind that one phrase lie all the fun and games of looking out for and pouncing upon rival ships.

It would have been in 1616 that news reached Biencourt of his father's death late in the previous year. He died as he had often lived, recklessly: 'a buckler on his arm, his drawn sword in his left hand and a pistol in his right,' shouting 'Kill, kill! God save the King and Poutrincourt.' Involved in the civil disturbances in France, he hoped to render himself illustrious by some notable military exploit. For the old flame of ambition leaped again within the disappointed nobleman. But he only succeeded in getting himself shot down by his own Royalist allies, whom he suspected of plotting to wrench renown and the governorship of Méry-sur-Seine from his grasp. Another fancied plot? A fit of madness akin to the sickness that came near to ending him when he had heard of the Jesuit excommunication at Port Royal? It was a sad and inglorious end for a man who loved glory, a victim in death as well as in life of his desperate desire for distinction.

But Lescarbot mourned his friend and composed a Latin epitaph for him to be placed on his tomb at St Just. In it he made discreet mention of his 'emulous search for military glory.' He claims he had another epitaph sent to Port Royal – through Lomeron? – to be 'graven on marble and on the trees.' It is addressed to the Indians, Poutrincourt's 'converts':

> Dear children of God, my neophytes.
>   Dwellers in New France,
>   Followers of Christ,
>   Who are mine.
> I am that great Sagamos of yours,
>   DE POUTRINCOURT,
>   Known above the stars,
> In whom was once your hope.
> If envy has robbed you of me,
>   Lament.
> My valour took me from you,
> To give my glory to another
>   I could not brook.
>   Again lament.

This epitaph is all of a piece with the romantic vision that Lescarbot and Poutrincourt had once entertained of an idyllic New France. Both had dreamed of Port Royal as the replica of a French domain, handsome manor house surrounded by smiling fields and pastures, carillons of church bells ringing out on high days and holidays, the tawny-skinned inhabitants emerging devoutly from their wigwams to pray. As usual, reality is tougher, grimier, more various than the dreams in which it has its beginning.

Young Biencourt still had his dreams. Like his father he took to describing himself in documents as 'great Sagamo of the Souriquois and Etchemins and adjacent lands.' Yet, however satisfied with status and business profits, he was not happy at seeing what had been a colony reduced to a trading-post. Besides, how much longer could Acadia hold out even as a mere trading-post, given the rate at which the aggressive and enterprising English were sending out colonists? In the summer of 1618 the English boldly captured a ship from Dieppe. Biencourt heard, too, that a fleet with five hundred men and a number of women had put in quite near him for a supply of wood and fresh water. He may even have seen them himself. Why were the French so behindhand when they had started first? His mother's family had connections with the city councillors of Paris. On the 1st September he took up a pen to appeal to City Hall.

Unless something was done soon, he urged, Paris would be buying her codfish from England instead of getting it from New France. But this could be prevented by the erection of two or three forts along the coast and by settling more French in the country. Here was room for those who could not make a living in Paris: sturdy beggars, members of large and needy families. For 'the soil here is good for tilling, gentlemen, game is plentiful, fish abounds.' And he proudly added that he 'would not exchange this land for Peru if once it were properly inhabited.' Paris had long been interested in navigation, as the ship on the city's coat of arms could testify. A little expenditure on the part of the authorities of Paris and the glory of establishing the name of God and of France here in Acadia would be theirs. They would have the co-operation of Biencourt and his men, who knew the country, the coast, and the native language. If the country had been neglected by the French, it was because of 'ignorance and the malice of merchants.' It was the old, old cry: no help for colonizers. Again he appealed to the councillors to consider English intentions and ambitions.

There were some stirrings in Paris at this call to action, but nothing got underway.

Biencourt's fears were to prove quite justified. In 1620 the *Mayflower* put into the bay that fifteen years earlier Champlain had named Port St Louis. The pilgrim fathers called it Plymouth, thus establishing *their* link between old world and new. In 1621 Sir William Alexander, seeing a New France, a New Spain, a New Holland, and a New England, decided that there should be a New Scotland as well. James granted him a considerable portion of territory that took in all of today's Nova Scotia, New Brunswick, and Gaspesia. This, of course, constituted a direct threat to the French trading-posts in Acadia. But confrontation was delayed. The Scots did not settle at Port Royal until 1628 or 1629.

Besides his connection with the Huguenot merchants of La Rochelle, Biencourt meanwhile had also formed associations with two companies in Bordeaux. One, a Catholic company, arranged for four Récollets from the Province of Aquitaine to go to Acadia in 1620. Their centre seems to have been Eménénic Island (Catons Island) on the Saint John. But one priest established himself at Port Royal while another made his way to Miscou. It was seven years since Biencourt had seen a priest, but he does not seem to have been anxious to have one near him. From 1618 on, he had been spending less time at Port Royal. His headquarters became the trading-post at Cape Negro on the south shore – though here he was really poaching on Madame de Guercheville's preserves.

In 1623 he died, aged about thirty-one, without those consolations of religion that he had told Membertou were so important for a Christian. But La Tour, his companion for about twelve years, was with him when he died. To him, as his lieutenant, Biencourt bequeathed his position as leader in Acadia. (The actual fief of Port Royal went to his younger brother, Jacques de Biencourt.) Twenty-three years later, in 1646, La Tour was in Quebec. He arrived just a few months after Father Massé's death there. The notice on Father Massé in the *Relation* of 1646 mentions the persecution to which he and Father Biard had been subjected at Port Royal. Yet 'one of the principal among those who treated them ill, dying afterwards without assistance of any Ecclesiastic, said, with regret and grief, that he was paying severely for the torments that he had caused these poor Fathers to suffer.' This penitent can be none other than Biencourt, and the story, true or invented, could have come only from La Tour. If invented, he probably told it to ingratiate himself and to deflect Jesuit reproaches, for he himself had been one of the persecutors. But it could be true. In his last moments – and had he not told Membertou carefully to examine his conscience? – Biencourt might have thought of the Jesuits. With final clarity he might have seen through the mists of his self-deception and admitted to himself that his square-bonneted bogeys were largely figments of his prejudices, fears, and suspicions.

When writing of the founding of new settlements, Father Biard had delivered judgment on the Biencourt enterprise in his usual energetic and acerbic style:

I shall only suggest that it is great folly for small companies to go there, who picture to themselves Baronies, and I know not what great fiefs and demesnes for three or four thousand crowns, which they will have to sink in that country. It would be still worse if this foolish idea would occur to people who flee from the ruin of their families in France: for to such covetous people it invariably happens, not that, being one-eyed, they would be kings among the blind, but that being blind, they would go to throw themselves into a wretched pit; and possibly instead of a Christian stronghold, they would found a den of thieves, a nest of brigands, a receptacle for parasites, a refuge for rogues, a hotbed of scandal and all wickedness.

Now Biencourt was certainly no Champlain. Yet he does have the distinction of being the first Frenchman to commit himself entirely to Acadia. He had a good share of the Biencourt swagger and lust for glory. He often showed himself to be belligerent and high-handed. But he also had Biencourt tenacity. Madame de Guercheville's grandson, La Rochefoucauld, wrote of perseverance that it is something one cannot praise or blame. For it is simply the persistence of the tastes and feelings one has. Biencourt's tastes and feelings caused him to cling to the harsh but freer way of life in the New World. Micmac friendship, the goodwill built up between Indians and French over the course of several years, enabled him to do so. But if he had not remained at Port Royal after 1613 to assert French presence, it is possible that this territory would not have been returned to France by the Treaty of St Germain-en-Laye in 1632. Acadia as we know it today, and the tough, humorous Acadians who, like Biencourt, learned simply to hang on, would never have existed.

As it was, after Biencourt's death, ships no longer made the annual voyage from La Rochelle or Bordeaux. The companies in Bordeaux folded. The Récollets left Acadia for Quebec, then France. La Tour and a handful of Frenchmen found themselves absorbed more and more into the rhythms of Indian life, the chase on snowshoes after moose in winter, the spearing of salmon in the light of birch-bark flames in the summer. They endured the stinging, choking smoke in the wigwams; they cleansed themselves in sweat baths; they feasted. Indian women withdrew to the woods to give birth to their children, a little paler than the others of the tribe. But it was not a way of life that brought La Tour complete satisfaction. He too felt stirrings of ambition for himself and for France. But that is another story.

SOURCES

THIS NARRATIVE is based primarily on the writings of three men: Samuel Champlain, Marc Lescarbot, and Father Pierre Biard. In part I I have drawn mainly on Champlain and Lescarbot; in part II on Lescarbot and Father Biard. The edition of Champlain's writings that I have used is the well known *Works of Samuel de Champlain in Six Volumes*, which, with an English translation, was published by the Champlain Society of Toronto under the general editorship of H.P. Biggar. The volumes that are most important for Champlain's Acadian adventures are I, III, IV. Volume I: 1599–1607 (Toronto 1922) contains *Des Sauvages*, an account of Champlain's 1603 journey to the St Lawrence, translated and edited by H.H. Langton, and also *Les Voyages du Sieur de Champlain Xaintongeois* book I (Paris 1613), with translation, notes, and introduction by W.F. Ganong. It is in this that we find the fullest relation of French activities in Acadia between 1604 and 1613. Volume III contains books I and II of *Les Voyages de la Nouvelle France Occidentale, dicte Canada, faits par le Sr. de Champlain Xaintongeois ... et toutes les Descouvertes qu'il a faites en ce pais depuis l'an 1603, jusques en l'an 1629* (Paris 1632), written for and dedicated to Cardinal Richelieu. Book II of this is largely a retelling, with some changes, of Champlain's 1613 *Voyages*. Volume IV of the Champlain Society edition contains books III and IV of Champlain's 1632 *Voyages*. In book III there is an account of the hostilities between the Jesuits and the Biencourts, but it is essentially nothing more than a very brief résumé of Father Biard's *Relation* of 1616. The other volumes of Champlain's *Works* are naturally of great interest, but, as they have little direct bearing on the story of Acadian settlement, they have been used mainly for background. All quotations in English from Champlain's works are taken from this Champlain Society edition.

From the Champlain Society we also have an edition of Lescarbot's *Histoire de la Nouvelle France*, in three volumes with English translations, notes, and appendices by W.L. Grant (Toronto 1907, 1911, 1914). The third volume also contains, untranslated, Lescarbot's collection of verse relating to New France, his *Muses de la Nouvelle France*. The first edition of Lescarbot's *Histoire* appeared in France in 1609, was reprinted in 1611–12 with some amendments and again in 1618 with amendments and additions. In 1609 an English translation of the main body of the first edition appeared, made by Pierre Erondelle. This has been reprinted under the title *Nova Francia* in the *Broadway Travellers* series (New York and London: Harper 1928). When quoting Lescarbot I have used one or other of these translations, depending on whether clarity or colourfulness seemed appropriate. Two other works by Lescarbot which are important to this story are his *Conversion des Sauvages* (Paris 1610), reprinted with English translation in Thwaites' *Jesuit Relations* II 51–113, and his *Relation Dernière* (Paris 1612), also reprinted with English translation in *Jesuit Relations* II 119–87.

All Father Biard's writings relating to Acadia – his *Relation* of 1616, the Latin version of his experiences as a missionary, his letters both in French and Latin to his superiors – have been reprinted with English translations and will be found in the first four volumes of *The Jesuit Relations and allied documents: travels and explorations of the Jesuit missionaries in New France, 1610–1791*, edited by Reuben Gold Thwaites, 73 volumes (Cleveland 1896–1901). It is from these translations that I quote.

A fascinating collection of texts and documents, some published for the first time, has been made by Father Lucien Campeau SJ and published as *Monumenta Novae Franciae* (Rome and Quebec). The first volume, *La Première Mission d'Acadie*, appeared in 1967, the second, *Etablissement à Québec*, in 1979. These are works of distinguished scholarship, meticulously annotated and containing many interesting insights. Though I do not look at events from quite the same point of view as Father Campeau, who is naturally anxious to vindicate the Jesuits on every score, I would like to acknowledge that in part II of this work I am particularly indebted to his close study of and comments on the documents he has put together. One of the documents he reprints (I 320–406) is the somewhat rare *Factum* (Paris 1614), first reprinted in a limited edition by Gabriel Marcel (Paris 1887). Though unreliable as a relation of events – it is scurrilously anti-Jesuit – the attitudes and point of view presented are an important part of the story. I have quoted from it with due caution, advising the reader to approach it with the necessary fistful of salt. But this *Factum* also contains some authentic material – letters, for example, reproduced as written – which are not found elsewhere and which cast an interesting light on the situation. As the *Factum* has never been published in an English edition, all translations from it are my own. Again I would like to stress that any student wishing to make a special study of hostilities between Jesuits and gentlemen could not make a better start than with Father Campeau's impressive work.

Another book of documents on which I have drawn heavily for information and anecdotes is the *Noveaux documents sur Champlain et son époque*, issued by the Canadian Department of Archives, ed Robert Le Blant and René Baudry (vol I, 1560–1622, Ottawa 1967). It was fascinating to see how many vivid inferences and incidents could be drawn from dry-looking legal documents.

Two important sources of information regarding ships that left and returned to Norman ports and the men who sailed in them are *Documents relatifs à la marine normande* ... ed Charles and Paul Bréard (Rouen 1889) and *Nouvelles Glanes historiques normandes* ... ed Edouard Gosselin (Rouen 1873).

These are the main primary sources I have used for my narration. Others will be indicated in Notes and References.

Abbreviations for works above most often quoted in the text:

HNF   *History of New France* (Lescarbot)
JR   *Jesuit Relations* (ed Thwaites)
MNF I   *Monumenta Novae Franciae I: La Première Mission d'Acadie* (ed Campeau)
ND   *Nouveaux documents* (ed Le Blant and Baudry)
NF   *Nova Francia* (Lescarbot, tr Erondelle)
WSC   *Works of Samuel de Champlain*

My secondary sources have been useful for information, background, an understanding of place and period.

For the European background I have consulted Fernand Braudel's *Les Structures du quotidien: le possible et l'impossible* (Paris 1979), translated by Siân Reynolds as *The Structures of Everyday Life: The Limits of the Possible* (New York 1981); Henri Hauser's *La Prépondérance espagnole 1559–1600* (Paris 1933); Henri Lapeyre's *Les Monarchies européennes du XVIe siècle* (Paris 1967); John Lough's *An Introduction to Seventeenth-Century France* (London 1954); Donald H. Pennington's *Seventeenth-Century Europe* (London 1970); Victor L. Tapié's *La France de Louis XIII et de Richelieu* (Paris 1952), translated by D. McN. Lockie as *France in the Age of Louis XIII and Richelieu* (London 1974), a signally useful work; Frances A. Yates' *Astraea: The Imperial Theme in the Sixteenth Century* (London 1975).

General histories that concern the New World in connection with the Old are W.J. Eccles' *France in America* (New York 1972); F.-X. Garneau's *Histoire du Canada*, 6 vols (Montreal 1944); Samuel Eliot Morison's lively *The European Discovery of America: The Northern Voyages A.D. 500–1600* (New York 1971). A great classic, readable as ever after well over a hundred years, is Francis Parkman's *Pioneers of France in the New World, Part II*, first published in Boston in 1865. The edition I have consulted is the Frontenac Edition (Toronto 1899). The general work on the early history of Canada that I found most helpful and cannot recommend too highly is vols 1 and 2 of Marcel Trudel's *Histoire de la Nouvelle-France* (Montreal 1963, 1966). This has been abridged for an English edition, *The Beginnings of New France 1524–1663* (Toronto 1973), translation by Patricia Claxton. Excellent as a work of reference, it also has the merit of being pleasantly written.

Works that more specifically concern the area known as 'Acadie' are John Bartlet Brebner's *New England's Outpost: Acadia before the Conquest of Canada* (New York 1927); Candide de Nant's *Page glorieuse de l'épopée canadienne: une mission capucine en Acadie* (Montreal 1927); Naomi E.S. Griffiths' *The Acadians: Creation of a People* (Toronto 1973); Emile Lauvrière's *La Tragédie d'un peuple: histoire du peuple acadien de ses origines à nos jours 2 vols* (Paris 1922); Beamish Murdoch's *A History of Nova Scotia, or Acadia*, 3 vols (Halifax 1865–7); Edme Rameau de Saint-Père's *Une Colonie féodale en Amérique, L'Acadie*, 2 vols (Paris-Montreal 1889); John Graham Reid's *Acadia, Maine, and New Scotland: Marginal Colonies in the Seventeenth Century* (Toronto 1981), the most up-to-date of works on this period; Robert Rumilly's *Histoire des Acadiens*, 2 vols (Montreal 1955).

Works consulted on trade and fishing are Henry Percival Biggar's *The Early Trading Companies of New France: A Contribution to the History of Commerce and Discovery in North America* (Toronto 1901), which is particularly good on de Monts' company; two books by Harold Adams Innis: *The Codfisheries: The History of an International Economy* (revised edition, Toronto 1954), and *The Fur Trade in Canada: An Introduction to Canadian Economic History* (revised edition, Toronto 1970); and Charles de La Morandière's *Histoire de la pêche française de la morue dans l'Amérique septentrionale (des origines à 1789)*, 2 vols (Paris 1962).

Brief biographies of the main characters in this narrative can be found in the *Dictionary of Canadian Biography*, vol I (1000–1700) (Toronto and Quebec 1967).

There are also several biographies of Champlain, the most outstanding historical personage in this story. Morris Bishop's *Champlain: The Life of*

Fortitude (New York 1948; Toronto 1963) is written with style and relish. Unfortunately, though it is obviously based on careful research and a good knowledge of the period, it has neither notes nor a bibliography. Samuel Eliot Morison's *Samuel de Champlain: Father of New France* (Boston and Toronto 1972) is also very readable and contains much that is useful and interesting by way of scholarly apparatus. As is to be expected of a Rear Admiral who was also a highly distinguished historian, Morison is particularly good on Champlain as navigator and explorer.

Two good French biographies are N.E. Dionne's *Samuel Champlain, fondateur de Québec et père de la Nouvelle France*, 2 vols (Quebec 1891) and Gabriel Gravier's *Vie de Samuel de Champlain, fondateur de Québec et père de la Nouvelle France* (Paris 1900).

Though a prime mover in the colonization of New France, de Monts remains a somewhat shadowy personality. William Inglis Morse in his *Pierre du Gua, sieur de Monts* (London 1939) has put together a collection of interesting documents that deal with his activities, but it is not really a biography.

The only biography of Poutrincourt is Adrien Huguet's *Jean de Poutrincourt, fondateur de Port Royal en Acadie, viceroi du Canada, 1557–1615. Campagnes, voyages et aventures d'un colonisateur sous Henri IV* (Amiens and Paris 1932). Huguet has done a good deal of very useful research and has reprinted in full a number of important documents that relate to the Biencourt family. Unfortunately, Huguet's style is high-flown and flowery, and in his determination to portray Poutrincourt as a hero palpitating with soul, spirit, and high endeavour, he renders him less interesting as a man. And Poutrincourt was never viceroy of Canada as the title claims.

Again, I have read and consulted a number of other secondary sources. These will be mentioned in the notes.

NOTES AND REFERENCES

PART I: AN ENTERPRISE THE MOST VALIANT AND
LEAST ASSISTED

Title of this part taken from the opening sentence of Lescarbot's
Fourth Book HNF II 209

CHAPTER ONE: TOWARDS THE COUNTRIES AND CONFINES
OF LA CADIE (3–14)

3 Of the three ships that sailed from Le Havre for Acadie on de
Monts' voyage we know the name of only one. This is *La Bonne
Renommée*. In secondary accounts there is some confusion as to
whether this was the ship commanded by de Monts and captained
by Timothée or the one commanded by Gravé and captained by
Morel. The question is resolved by doc 50 of ND (86). In this, dated
20th February 1604, it is expressly stated that Gravé will be sailing to 'the place of the Mine on the coast of Canada' on the *Bonne
Renommée* of approximately one hundred tons. The master, too, is
mentioned: Nicolas Morel of Dieppe.

  Visitors to the replica of Cartier's *Grande Hermine* in Quebec, a
120-tonner, will have some idea of the size and general design of
these ships, even though the seventy years between Cartier and de
Monts had wrought some changes in marine architecture.

  For rhyme HNF III 511 (my translation)
4 For Coton's observations MNF I 5
5 For Henri II's patent to de Monts NF 1–6

5-6   For drawing of Champlain plate v in wsc ii

6   Champlain's exotic voyage to the West Indies and Central America has been questioned, particularly in connection with the authorship of the *Brief Discours*, which describes such a voyage. For a discussion of this, see Marcel Trudel's *Histoire de la Nouvelle-France*, vol i (Montreal 1963) 257-8.
For 'pleasure' wsc iii 309

7   For Poutrincourt's height NF 193
For Lescarbot on Poutrincourt NF 7
The "larger ship," the one captained by Timothée, was the *Don de Dieu*. This is made clear by Jean Liebel in his *Pierre Dugua sieur de Mons, fondateur de Québec* (Paris 1999), see in particular pp. 95-108. Liebel has drawn on documents in the Departmental Archives in Calvados.

8   For the state of religion in France during the sixteenth century see two books by Roland Mousnier: *Les Institutions de la France sous la monarchie absolue*, vol i (Paris 1974); and *Les XVIe et XVIIe siècles: la grande mutation intellectuelle de l'humanité...* (Paris 1961).
For Lescarbot on Aubry NF 12

9   For de Monts as a 'heretic' MNF i 18

10   All knowledge we have of d'Acosta is based on documentation of lawsuits between this Rouen merchant, Nicolas de Bauquemare, on one hand, and de Monts and Ralluau on the other. Docs 105, 106, 117, 168 in ND give some information about the complex sequence of business dealings that led to these lawsuits. A few interesting facts emerge.

On the 28th May 1608, Bauquemare signed a contract with d'Acosta engaging him for three years as an interpreter and to peform 'other services' on the voyage to 'Canada, Acadia and elsewhere.' He was to receive 60 crowns (180 livres) a year when on a voyage, and in the meantime 3 florins a week. We can see that his services were highly valued. The best-paid artisan at Port Royal in the year 1606-7 received 150 livres, and Louis Hébert, the apothecary, 100 livres. (See 72.) About five years later, in 1613, Jesuit missionaries engaging an interpreter, Jean-Jacques Simon, advanced him 100 livres. (See 221 and note.)

On the 2nd December 1609, eighteen months after this contract was signed, Bauquemare had d'Acosta confined in the royal prison of Le Havre for his 'insolences,' and sent word of this to de Monts.

On the 11th December 1609 de Monts signed a document recognizing that Bauquemare, in all his dealings relating to d'Acosta, had been acting on his, de Monts', behalf. On the same day he signed another document requesting the civil and criminal lieutenant of Le Havre to release d'Acosta and hand him over to de Monts' representative—probably Ralluau.

There is no indication of what became of d'Acosta after this. But lawsuits dragged on until 1619. It is clear that Bauquemare felt that he had been insufficiently compensated for the expenses he had incurred in restoring d'Acosta to de Monts. One also senses in d'Acosta a certain feistiness.

Some secondary sources tend to confuse d'Acosta with another black man who was out on the 1606-7 voyage with Poutrincourt and who died of scurvy. Lescarbot writes that Poutrincourt 'made a negro to be opened that died of that sickness in our voyage' (NF 36). As we have just seen, d'Acosta was very much alive and kicking in December 1609. So he could not possibly have been the man Poutrincourt had dissected two years earlier.

In the celebrations held in August 1980 at the reconstructed Habitation to commemorate the 375th anniversary of the founding of Port Royal, much was made of the fact that blacks too had made an early contribution to exploration and settlement. Pierre Trudeau, who was then Prime Minister, remarked that it was 'moving to realize that the black man came with the white man to meet the red man 375 years ago.' We cannot be absolutely sure that d'Acosta was there then. But there was certainly a black presence in those early years.

As regards Mathieu d'Acosta, in "Looking for Mathieu Da Costa," an unpublished piece written for Parks Canada, the historian Hilary Russell points out that Da Costa "could have been in de Monts' employ in North America in 1600 and/or 1604." More information on this intriguing figure can be found in an article, "Quelques aspects de la dissolution de la compagnie de M. de Monts, 1607" by T. K. Kupp in *Revue d'histoire de l'Amérique française*, December 1970. Peter Bakker deals not only with Mathieu Da Costa but also with other black interpreters in "First African into New Netherland" in *de Halve Maen* (68, 3) published in the fall of 1995.

For Maître Jacques WSC I 375. Sclavonia was that area of today's Yugoslavia between the Drava and Sava rivers.

It is not absolutely certain what are the dates of birth of Gravé and Champlain. As S.E. Morison has pointed out, in his *Samuel de Champlain* 276, doc I in ND (1) reprints a baptismal certificate that seems to be Gravé's and that gives his date of birth as 27 November 1560. If this is so, both Gravé and Champlain, who thought of Gravé as old enough to be his father, were younger than is usually stated. Like Morison, however, I have kept in line with Trudel and the *Dictionary of Canadian Biography*, where Gravé's date of birth is set c 1554.

For Brother Sagard's comments on the Gravés, both François and his son, Robert, see Gabriel-Théodat Sagard's *Histoire du Canada et Voyages que les Freres Récollets y ont fait pour la conversion des infidelles*...ed Edwin Tross (Paris 1866). For quotation see 891.

11–12 For meeting with the Montagnais at Tadoussac see wsc i 99–103.
For books and articles that deal with the enormous cultural
differences between Europeans and Indians and the attitudes of both
groups towards these differences see Alfred G. Bailey's *The Conflict
of European and Eastern Algonkian cultures, 1504–1700* (2nd ed,
Toronto 1969); Olive P. Dickason's 'The concept of l'homme sauvage
and early French colonialism in the Americas' in *Revue d'histoire
d'outre-mer* 64 (1977) 5–32; Cornelius J. Jaenen's article 'Amerindian
Views of French Culture in the Seventeenth Century,' *Canadian
Historical Review* 55 (1974); and his book *Friend and Foe: Aspects of
French-Amerindian Cultural Contacts in the Sixteenth and Seventeenth
Centuries* (Toronto 1976); Calvin Martin's *Keepers of the Game: Indian-
Animal Relationships and the Fur Trade* (Berkeley 1978); L.F.S.
Upton's *Micmacs and Colonists* (Vancouver 1979).

14 Henri iv's life, character, and policies are the subject of numerous
works. The ones on which I have chiefly drawn when presenting
this most energetic and engaging of French monarchs are Maurice
Andrieux's *Henri IV dans ses années pacifiques* (Paris 1954) and his
Henri IV (Paris 1955); Jean-Pierre Babelon's *Henri IV* (Paris 1982);
the duc de Lévis-Mirepoix's *Henri IV, roi de France et de Navarre*
(Paris 1971); Desmond Seward's *The First Bourbon: Henri IV, King of
France and Navarre* (Boston 1971); Pierre de Vassière's *Henri IV*
(Paris 1928).

17 For Sully's comment see Marcel Trudel's *Histoire de La Nouvelle-
France* ii 14.

CHAPTER TWO: EXPLORING THE COASTS (19–34)

19 For Arcadie to Acadie see Trudel ii 21.
For quotation from Champlain wsc iii 320
For his comment on Tadoussac wsc iii 308

19–20 For Chauvin's colony wsc iii 310

20 For some details of the early career of the Marquis de la Roche and
his attempts to set up French colonies in North America see H.P.
Biggar, *The Early Trading Companies of New France* (Toronto 1901).
Biggar's mention of the outbreak of violence among the people left
on Sable Island is, however, not as up-to-date as the spirited account
to be found in appendix C of the original edition of Morris

Bishop's *Champlain*, 347–9. Bishop's account is based on an article
by Gustave Lanctot, 'L'Etablissement du Marquis de la Roche à L'île
de Sable,' in *Annual Report of the Canadian Historical Association*
(1933) 33–42.

Doc 63 in ND (109–12) consists of part of a memorandum written
by the Marquis de la Roche himself and addressed to Henri IV.
The reprinted section concerns his Sable Island venture.

Doc 46 ND (78–9) names the eleven survivors. The Parlement of
Rouen ruled that they were to be given two-thirds of the skins
brought back from Sable Island. Their confiscated possessions and
clothing were also to be restored to them.

20–1 For joiner NF 8

22 Champlain, Lescarbot, and Biard all gave accounts of the Souriquois, now called the Micmacs. Lescarbot's account (HNF III 77–288)
is fuller than Champlain's, Father Biard's (JR III 69–135) more
systematic than Lescarbot's.

In 1631 Nicolas Denys, a merchant from La Rochelle, arrived in
Acadia as representative for the One Hundred Associates, and
spent many years in Acadia. It is he who gives the most detailed
account of all in his *Description géographique et historique des costes de
l'Amérique septentrionale avec l'histoire naturelle du païs*, 2 vols (Paris
1672), translated and edited by William F. Ganong as *The Description and Natural History of the Coasts of North America (Acadia)* (Toronto
1908) For Micmacs see 398–452. Though he observed and wrote
some decades later than the others, there was little alteration in the
Micmac way of life. Any that Denys heard of, he noted.

Another later observer who still had interesting descriptions to
give was the Récollet missionary Father Chrestien Le Clerq in his
*Nouvelle Relation de la Gaspésie, qui contient les mœurs et la religion des
sauvages gaspésiens porte-croix, adorateurs du soleil, et d'autres peuples
de l'Amérique Septentrionale, dite le Canada* (Paris 1691); of which
the English version is W.F. Ganong's edition, *New Relation of
Gaspesia, with the Customs and Religion of the Gaspesian Indians* (Toronto
1910).

Secondary sources which deal with the Micmacs or in which they
are described are Elizabeth A. Hutton's *The Micmac Indians of
Nova Scotia to 1834*, an unpublished thesis for Dalhousie University
(1961); Diamond Jenness' *The Indians of Canada* (Ottawa 1955); P.

André Sevigny's *Les Abénaquis: habitat et migrations (17e et 18e siècles)* (Montreal 1976); Bruce G. Trigger's edition of *Handbook of North American Indians*, vol 15 (Washington 1978); Wilson D. Wallis and Ruth Satwell's *The Micmac Indians of Eastern Canada* (Minneapolis 1955).

For useful descriptions and illustrations of Micmac clothing and artifacts for this and later periods see Ruth Holmes Whitehead's *Elitekey: Micmac Material Culture from 1600 A.D. to the Present* (Halifax 1980). In the Nova Scotia Museum in Halifax one can view videotapes (made by the Nova Scotia Department of Education working with CBC) which reconstruct, quite vividly, Micmac life before the coming of the white man – in so far as it is possible to do so.

It is likely that in the sixteenth century the Micmac population was larger than three thousand. See Virginia Miller, 'Aboriginal Micmac Population: A Review of the Evidence,' *Ethnohistory* 23 (1976) 117–27.

24–5 For Champlain's comment on religious disputes WSC III 327

25 For good brief descriptions of the pinnace (*patache*, *barque*) and the shallop or long-boat (*chaloupe*) see S.E. Morison, *Samuel de Champlain: Father of New France* 278. The pinnace, about six to eighteen tons, was the vessel favoured for exploration. Champlain wrote that for this purpose he preferred it to a larger ship because it 'draws little water, ferrets everywhere and finds suitable places for settlements' (WSC I 390). A pinnace had two masts, was not completely decked over, and was usually assembled on shore after the Atlantic crossing. The shallop or long-boat was small enough to be lodged on the deck of a ship and was basically a rowing boat that might have a mast or two. It could also be towed behind a large ship or pinnace.

26 For quotation from Champlain WSC I 251

27 For Champlain as hunter WSC I 244
For 'silver mine' WSC I 246 and for 'soil' WSC I 248
For Lescarbot on Poutrincourt NF 9

29 For the origins of the name 'Fundy' see Trudel's *Histoire de la Nouvelle France* II 19.
For Champlain on Port Royal WSC I 256–9

30 For Lescarbot on Spanish cruelty NF 15

31 For river WSC I 269
32 For Champlain on the site of Ste Croix Island WSC I 271–2
33 For Lescarbot on Aubry NF 23

CHAPTER THREE: SETTLING IN (35–46)

35 For an extensive description of Ste Croix Island see article by
     William F. Ganong, 'Dochet (Ste Croix Island),' in Royal Society
     of Canada, *Proceedings and Transactions*, 2nd series VIII (1902) 126–231.
37–8 For de Monts on Bituani NF 25 and HNF II 509
38 For Lescarbot on the Indians NF 24
39 For de Monts' reception of the Basques WSC I 277
40 For the caribou ND 90, 106
41 For danger near the Casquets NF 30
     For complaints against de Monts WSC III 323–4
42 For the King's hopes HNF II 225
     For the 'isle des Monts-deserts' WSC I 283
43 For the 'broader river' WSC I 284
     For Norumbega see S.E. Morison's *European Discovery of America*
     464–70; quotation, 467.
45 For Champlain's message to the Indians, their response, and Cham-
     plain's comment on the encounter WSC I 295–6

CHAPTER FOUR: DEATHS AND DISCOVERIES (47–60)

48 For Biard's description JR III 53
49 For Champlain on scurvy WSC I 303–4
49–50 For 'Annedda' see Trudel's *Histoire de la Nouvelle-France* I 104.
50 For the 'deadly season' NF 34
52 For loans to men on this voyage ND 97
54 For Champlain's comment on superstition WSC I 317
     For a critical view of Champlain's attitudes to the Indians see Bruce
     Trigger's 'Champlain Judged by His Indian Policy: A Different
     View of Early Canadian History' in *Anthropologica* 13 (1971) 85–114.
     For chief Aneda WSC I 322
55 For the little island WSC I 330
58 For Champlain's near-accident WSC 354
     Though Champlain uses the term 'coups de mousquet' (musket shots),

he also states specifically that the weapon that exploded in his hands was an arquebus (a handgun). As the arquebus was much shorter and lighter than the musket, which at that period was so heavy that it had to be supported on a rest, it seems likely that the weapons that the French carried on these voyages were arquebuses, not muskets. But Lescarbot as well as Champlain uses both terms, arquebus and musket, almost as though they were interchangeable. As was mentioned in chapter 1, it is in the act of firing an arquebus that Champlain is depicted at the battle of Lake Champlain (1609). For a detailed description and illustration of arquebus and powder flask see S.E. Morison's *Samuel de Champlain* 282–3. For Lescarbot's comment NF 53

59 For Weymouth's voyage see Rosier's fascinating *A True Relation of the Voyage of Captaine George Waymouth, 1605*, reprinted in *Early English and French Voyages*, ed H.S. Burrage (New York 1906) 353–94. For the 'sole intent' see 388.

60 A brief mention of this voyage and the praise of the captured Indians for their 'great civility' are found in Sir Ferdinando Gorges' *A Briefe Narration of the Original Undertakings of the Advancement of Plantations*. This narration by the 'Father of English Colonization in America' has been reprinted in the Massachusetts History Collection, 3rd series VI, 45–93. For appreciation of Indians see 51.

CHAPTER FIVE: FIRST WINTER AT STE CROIX (61–78)

62 For an account of the planning of this replica see Charles W. Jefferys' article 'The Reconstruction of Port Royal' in the *Canadian Historical Review* 20 (1939) 369–77. Someone who would undoubtedly find the reconstructed Habitation more solid and splendid than the original is Father Biard, who arrived at Port Royal in May 1611. His comments on the lack of comfort and convenience at the Habitation will be found in chapters 12 and 13. For cellar WSC I 373

63–6 For Peiresc's account of the exhibits see ND 102–6. Readers of *Tristram Shandy* will recognize that this is the same 'learned Peireskius' about whom Dr Slop feels a pang of petty resentment when Uncle Toby mentions that Peireskius 'walked a matter of five hundred miles' in order to see Stevinus' 'cclebrated sailing chariot.'

Dr Slop had put himself out by only four miles to view the same wonder. As we can see, Peiresc's reputation as scientist and antiquarian far outlasted his lifetime.

66 For the Dauphin's viewing of the canoe see extracts taken from the diary of Jean Hérouard, the prince's personal physician for the first seventeen years of his life. Edited by A.-Léo Leymarie in 'Le Canada pendant la jeunesse de Louis XIII' in *Nova Francia* I (Paris 1925) 161–70. For quotation see 170.
For 'summer-house' WSC I 371–3

66–7 In Lescarbot's writings Secoudun is called Chkoudun.

67 For comments on Membertou WSC I 384 and NF 129

68 For quotation Sagard's *Histoire du Canada* I 26

69–70 For quotations concerning the attempted voyage to Florida WSC I 379–83

71–2 For contracts with artisans ND 114–25

72 Madame de Poutrincourt, née Claude Pajot, and Louis Hébert were first cousins. Claude's father, Isaac Pajot, was the brother of Louis' mother, Jacqueline, who had married Nicolas Hébert, an apothecary and dealer in spices. For detailed information on the Pajot and Hébert families, see articles by M. Jurgens, 'Recherches sur Louis Hébert et sa famille' in *Mémoires de la Société Généalogique Canadienne-Française* 8:2 (April 1957); 8:3 (July 1957); 11:1 and 11:2 (January and April 1960).

The monument raised to Louis Hébert in the old quarter of Quebec mentions his first sojourn at Port Royal. In fact, if it had not been for Poutrincourt, Hébert might never have come to New France. As we shall see, he was associated with Acadia and the Biencourt family until 1615.

73 For Lescarbot's letter to his mother HNF III 516
For Lescarbot's 'Adieu ...' see HNF II 532–5

74 For the La Tour family see M.A. MacDonald's very interesting *Fortune and La Tour: The Civil War in Acadia* (Toronto and New York 1983); also Azarie Couillard-Després' *Charles de Saint-Etienne de la Tour, gouverneur, lieutenant-général en Acadie, et son temps 1593–1666* (Arthabaska and Quebec 1930).

75 For Daniel Hay HNF II 330
For the 'common people' HNF II 289

76 For priests NF 67

For euphemism NF 70
For porpoise NF 73
For Membertou's watchfulness NF 88
78 For Poutrincourt's largesse NF 90

CHAPTER SIX: BEYOND MALLEBARRE (79–91)

79 For resettlement NF 95
80 For the 'necessaries of life' NF 93
For the 'Adieu ...' HNF III 470–2
Translation by F.R. Scott, *Collected Works* (Toronto 1981) 300–3
81 For quotations on wine HNF II 320. Could Lescarbot be right in thinking that 'good wine' prevented scurvy? It would be pleasant to think that it did indeed contain enough vitamin c to justify Lescarbot's claim. Expert dietitians, however, are not quite sure. Recent food composition tables state that vitamin c is thought to be present in wine but that there is still a lack of reliable data. But they do know that 169g of European grapes contain 6mg vitamin c. As vitamin c is water-soluble, it would be found in the juices of the grape too. But what about wine processing methods? Heat, oxidation, and alkaline medium destroy vitamin c. Wine, however, has an acidic medium which would help preserve the vitamin. But if exposed to heat and/or air, the vitamin content would be lost. Much then would depend on the methods of processing.
　Still, Lescarbot might have a point. The men at Ste Croix had only dirty water, frozen cider, and poor Spanish wine to drink and there were many deaths from scurvy. Over the 1606–7 winter at Port Royal good wine was in plentiful supply and very few men died.
82 For Paradise HNF III 526 and for Promised Land NF 91
For Champdoré WSC I 393
83 For grapes WSC I 395
87 For quotations dealing with attack NF 110–11
90 For Champlain's complaint WSC I 431
The three ships were the *Susan Constant*, the *Godspeed*, and the *Discovery*. Replicas of these can be seen at Jamestown, where there is also a reconstruction of the first rough settlement, a triangular palisaded fort.
91 For Popham-Gilbert settlement see notes to 116.

CHAPTER SEVEN: A WINTER OF GOOD CHEER (92–106)

92 For 'Théâtre de Neptune' HNF III 473–9
The two translations from which I have quoted are Marc Lescarbot's
Theatre of Neptune, tr R. Keith Hicks (Abenaki Press, Nova Scotia
nd), and *The Theatre of Neptune in New France*, tr Harriette Taber
Richardson (Boston 1927). Mrs Richardson was one of the prime
movers responsible for the reconstruction of the Habitation at Port
Royal.

92–4 Translations by R. Keith Hicks

94 Translation by Harriette Taber Richardson

95 For echoes and other quotations on this 'jollity' HNF III 479
For quotation from Trudel see his *Histoire de la Nouvelle France* II 63.

96 For soil HNF III 246

97 For Lescarbot's comment HNF III 279
For Champlain's description WSC I 444–5

98 For Lescarbot on bear and beaver meat III 224–5, on moose meat NF
118 and on daily fare NF 96
For cranberries HNF III 257. 100g of cranberries contain 11mg vitamin C. This fruit then has a considerably higher vitamin C content
than grapes.
For participants NF 118

99 For Ouagimou's daughter HNF II 360
For the Dauphin and his 'Canada' see extracts from Hérouard's
journal (168–9) mentioned in note to 66.

100 For Membertou HNF II 355

101 For moose feast HNF III 221–2
For artifacts HNF III 201

102 For nobility HNF III 229–30; for lack of greed HNF III 157
For women executioners HNF III 216
For Poutrincourt HNF III 213
For feasts HNF III 182

103 For songs HNF III 106
For lack of religion HNF III 92
For the Aoutem HNF III 110

103–4 For Poutrincourt's zeal HNF III 486

104 For Lescarbot as lay preacher HNF II 267
For 'pantoffles' NF 46

105 For 'honest company' NF 47
For verse see HNF III 481. (My translation)

CHAPTER EIGHT: FAREWELL TO NEW FRANCE (107–20)

107 For Lescarbot as gardener HNF II 266
108 For 'Niridau' see HNF III 484–5
110 For orations and mock battle HNF III 264
111 For bribery WSC III 324
111–12 For Poutrincourt and men HNF II 351–3
112 For Gutter Lane NF 128
113 For Chevalier HNF II 356 and HNF III 213
For Secoudun HNF III 94
114 For Ste Croix HNF II 358–9
115 For cod HNF II 362
116 For an account of Raleigh Gilbert's expedition and settlement on the
Kennebec see *A Relation of a Voyage to Sagadohoc 1607–1608* in H.
Burrage's *Early English and French Voyages* (New York 1906) 399–419.
A shorter account appears in Sir Ferdinando Gorges' *A Brief Narration*, reprinted in *Massachusetts History Collection*, 3rd series VI 45–93.
Both accounts mention that with the colonizers went Skidwarres (or
Skicowaros), one of the Indians kidnapped by Weymouth in the
summer of 1605. The English hoped that he would serve them as
intermediary and interpreter. His aid proved somewhat erratic,
though he did arrange for the English to meet Bessabez' brother.
Bessabez, it will be remembered, was the great chief of the
Penobscot area, the one with whom Champlain had made that first
important alliance.
For Savalette HNF II 362–3, called 'Savalet' by Lescarbot
117 For Lescarbot's epic HNF III 497–508
119 For refrain HNF III 489, 513 (my translation)
For Mont Saint-Michel HNF II 366

PART II: THE MISERIES OF THESE PARTS

CHAPTER NINE: WESTWARDS ONCE MORE (123–37)

123–4 The hostility between Champlain and Lescarbot has often been
commented upon. See in particular WSC I 452. Champlain, it seems,

was irritated with Lescarbot for stealing his thunder by publishing in 1609 his *Histoire de la Nouvelle France* with *his* account of French settlement in Acadia and exploration south. Champlain's version in his *Voyages* did not appear until 1613, and yet it was Champlain, not Lescarbot, who had been a principal participant in these ventures and adventures. So he gets in a dry little dig at Lescarbot, landlubber, by deliberately pointing out that once Lescarbot had arrived at Port Royal, he journeyed only fourteen to fifteen leagues beyond it. This, of course, was on the occasion of Lescarbot's visit to Secoudun on the Saint John River and then to Ste Croix. Lescarbot was annoyed at this and showed his annoyance by saying, somewhat huffily, in the 1617 edition of his *History* that he had never claimed anything to the contrary, so why should Champlain seize on this? (HNF II 359). And in Ganong's words he 'also removed or modified certain complimentary references to Champlain, and altered other passages in a way to lessen Champlain's prominence.'

It is interesting to note that it is immediately after his little dig at Lescarbot that Champlain describes with almost malicious dispassionateness Poutrincourt's foolhardy attempt at climbing Cape Split. WSC I 453

In his account of hostilities between the Jesuits and the Biencourts, Champlain sides firmly with the Jesuits. In fact his account (WSC IV 1–22) is really only a bald précis of Father Biard's extended version in his *Relation*.

125 A very brief account of the building of Fort St George can be found in *A Relation of a Voyage to Sagadohoc 1607–1608*, in H. Burrage's edition mentioned in note to 116. Another very thorough edition is that by Henry O. Thayer, *The Sagadohoc Colony* (Portland, Maine 1892). Secondary sources that deal with this settlement are J. Windsor's *Narrative and Critical History of America* III 175–7 and A. Brown's *Genesis of the United States* I 191–4. Brown reprints a plan of the fort as sent to Philip of Spain by Zúñiga, the Spanish ambassador in England, for the Spaniards were keenly suspicious of English voyages to and settlements in the New World. Visitors to today's popular Popham Beach can see the Fort Popham memorial erected there to commemorate this attempt at settlement.

126 For Poutrincourt's reason for settling HNF II 234

For Biencourt background see Huguet 33–137. A photograph of the

Poutrincourt keep, and also one of a nearby sixteenth-century farmhouse and outbuildings which Poutrincourt and his family must have known and visited, can be found in a pamphlet, *En Picardie: Cayeux et les Bas-champs* by Jean Estienne, archivist of the Somme.

129 For Biard in Bordeaux JR III 163

130 For letter to Pope HNF II 369–72

133 For an account of Madame de Guercheville's encounter with the King see Parkman's *Pioneers of France in the New World* II 106–9. See also Eugène Thoison's *Madame de Guercheville, esquisse historique* (Fontaine-bleau 1891). By one of the ironies of history, the Marquise's portrait can be found in the Cabinet des Estampes at the Bibliothèque Nationale only by looking for it under the name of Madame de Liancourt.

Information on Father Massé for this chapter and for chapter 4 is taken from the obituary written for him by a fellow Jesuit and reprinted in JR XXIX 29–43.

133–4 For Coton and de Monts WSC IV 28

134 For Coton on de Monts MNF I 18 and on Poutrincourt MNF I 22 Much has been written about the Jesuits. I have consulted the entry on the Society in the *Catholic Encyclopedia* (New York 1914); also R. Fülop-Miller's *Power and Secret of the Jesuits*, translated by F.S. Flint and D.F. Tait (London 1930); Christopher Hollis' *History of the Jesuits* (London 1968) and Father Thomas J. Campbell's *The Jesuits 1534–1921* vol I. Charles Kingsley's *Westward Ho!* presents an extremely crude nineteenth-century travesty of sixteenth-century Jesuits, interesting in that it brings together so many of the popular prejudices against the Society and its members.

136 L'Estoile's comments on the Jesuits appear throughout his *Journaux-Mémoires*, ed Brunet et al (Paris 1875–96). For the Fuzy-Lescarbot incident see X 87–8.

CHAPTER TEN: FIRST CONVERTS (138–52)

139 For Henri's praise of Poutrincourt JR II 125
For the King's anger at Poutrincourt see Biard's *Relation* in JR III 162–3; Campeau (MNF I 170) suggests that the Poutrincourt who held Beaumont-sur-Oise against Henri was Jean's older brother, Jacques. A reference quoted by Huguet 62 upholds Lescarbot's claim

that it was Jean, mentioned as 'le sieur de Pouttraincourt le jeune.'
Lescarbot, it is true, is often over-enthusiastic when singing his
friend's praises, but there would have been too many contemporaries
who knew the story (not least among the Biencourts themselves)
for Poutrincourt to claim his brother's exploit as his.
For Poutrincourt's response JR III 163
On the question of a gentleman's honour see Arlette Jouanna's
'Recherches sur la notion d'honneur au XVI siècle,' in the *Revue
d'histoire moderne et contemporaine* 15 (1968) 597–623.

140 For voyagers HNF III 35
Lescarbot has a sieur de Jouy wintering at Port Royal (JR II 167),
but the furrier Louis de Jouy was in Paris on 4 October 1610
(ND 207).

141 For Jessé Fleché HNF III 41

145 For 'masterpiece' HNF III 41
For Bertrand's impression and letter quoted below JR I 121–3

145–6 For Poutrincourt's letter to Lescarbot see HNF III 73.

146 For garden JR II 165

148–9 For Martin's death JR II 149

150 For complaints JR II 169

151 For Lescarbot's comment and Membertou's recovery JR II 151–3
For 'sweet land ...' JR I 159

CHAPTER ELEVEN: NO REWARDS AND A NEW ALLIANCE (153–64)

154 For background to life at court and in Paris at this time see two books
by Louis Battifol: *La Vie intime d'une reine de France* (Paris 1906),
translated by Mary King as *Marie de Médicis and the French Court in the
XVIIth Century* (London 1908); and *La Vie de Paris sous Louis XIII*
(Montreal 1936). For Coton's alleged exclamation see L'Estoile's
Journaux-Mémoires X 227.

155 For meeting between Robin and Mme de Guercheville JR III 167

155–6 For Coton on Massé MNF I 330

157 For royal letters MNF I 326–7

157–8 For Lescarbot on the Jesuits JR I 81–3 and on necessity to colonize
first JR II 175

158 For Lescarbot on Church and State JR II 147

158–9 For the King's letter MNF I 327

159 For Coton's recommendation MNF I 329
For Madame de Guercheville's MNF I 328–9

160 For Biard on readiness of ship JR III 171

161 For gifts JR III 169

162 For Huguenot merchants HNF III 48
For relic MNF I 101
St. Lawrence O'Toole. Readers of Proust might remember that in his discourse on etymologies Bichot makes the point that patriotism should not prevent Frenchmen from recognizing that Saint-Laurent-en-Bray is named not after the well-known Roman martyr but after 'Saint Lawrence 'Toot [sic] archêveque de Dublin,' the Irish archbishop who died in Normandy when in pursuit of an interview with Henry II of England.

163 For 'peddlers' JR III 175

164 For loan ND 274. With this and the 737 livres they owed the Jesuits, combined debts were 1,937 livres.
For contract HNF III 49–52. Here it should be noted that Father Lucien Campeau puts forward an interesting plot theory that has Robin stage-managing this complex series of events from beginning to end. For he sees Robin as planning this outcome right from the first interview he and Biencourt had with the two priests. According to this theory, Robin was responsible for prompting the Huguenot merchants to refuse to have anything to do with a venture that included Jesuits. The court, Robin assured the merchants, would eventually buy them out. But this 'plot' seems both too complex and too pat. Could Robin really have been sure of manipulating so many people from the merchants to Madame de Guercheville with quite such ease? Were these Huguenot merchants quite so conscienceless? And in the long run his friend, Biencourt, did *not* get what he really wanted: funds, with no Jesuits attached.

CHAPTER TWELVE: SWORD AND BREVIARY (165–78)

165 For Massé's marginal notes MNF I 456–7; for 'sarcasmes non nécesaires' 474

167 For Massé's 'dear Canadas' JR XXIX 33

168 For living 'as in France' MNF I 334

168–9 For passage from *Factum* MNF I 335–6

170–1 For meeting with baptized Indians JR I 163–5. For site on eastern shore of Nova Scotia see MNF I 134 note 34.

173 For Biard on Gravé JR I 171

174 For sword versus breviary statement MNF I 343; also in HNF III 53

175 Quotation from lines 2–3 of E.J. Pratt's 'Brébeuf and His Brethren'; reprinted by permission of University of Toronto Press
For cramped quarters JR II 89
For servant JR I 189
For chapel JR I 169

175–6 For Biard on Fleché JR I 161–3

176 For Membertou's objection JR I 165–6

176–7 For Biard on the Indians JR I 173

177 For modification of Biard's views JR III 73
For praise of Biencourts JR I 181

178 For comments on Jesuits HNF III 53 and 67

CHAPTER THIRTEEN: CONFLICTS (179–93)

179 Principal works by the remarkable Rand are his *Dictionary of the Language of the Micmac Indians* (Halifax 1888) and *Legends of the Micmacs* (reprinted New York 1971).

180 For 'stupid natives' JR II 219
For ribaldries JR III 197

181 For difficulties in translation JR II 11
For Biard on Biencourt JR III 197

182 For English account, probably written by Sir William Alexander, the founder of Nova Scotia, see Samuel Purchas' *Purchas his pilgrimes* ... (Glasgow 1905–7) XIX 207–17.

185 For Membertou's grave and funeral MNF I 350–1
For Biard's aid JR II 99

187–8 In his account of this incident in the *Relation* of 1616 (JR III 210–17), Biard makes a special point of emphasizing that he was stationed at the *door* (217), thus obliquely defending himself against a particularly nasty innuendo that appeared in the 1614 *Factum* (MNF 347)

188 For Biard's appreciation JR II 31

189 For infertile soil JR II 35
For the singing JR II 37

190 For hair-raising experience JR II 41

191 For flattery JR III 223
For speechmaking JR II 45
The name Eméténic seems to indicate that this island is today's
Metenic or Matinicus, but the distance Biard gives – eight leagues
from Fort St George – points to Monhegan, as Campeau has
observed (MNF I 240 note 57).

192 For commendation of Biencourt JR II 47
For virtues of Indians JR II 49

CHAPTER FOURTEEN: EXCOMMUNICATION (194–209)

194 For quotation from Hérouard see extracts in *Nova Francia* (165)
mentioned in note to 66.
For quotations from Lescarbot JR II 181, 187

195 For lands HNF III 58

196 For Biard's comment JR III 235
For rations JR III 227

197 For the Indian Antoinette JR II 15
For 'sign of friendship' JR III 147

198 For Lescarbot's comment HNF II 267
For 'saving waters' JR II 225

199 For Biard's suggestion JR III 229
For Massé's commendation MNF I 387

200 For Biencourt's annoyance MNF I 362

201 For Imbert on Jesuit hypocrisy MNF I 363
For Imbert's claim MNF I 356–7

203 For quotation from *Factum* MNF I 363–4
For Imbert drunk JR II 237

203–4 For passage from *Factum* MNF I 364–5

204 For Biencourt's letter MNF I 372

205 For 'rebellion' and comments on Jesuits MNF I 388
For quotations from Massé's letters MNF I 384–7
For comment on Jesuits MNF I 385

207 For Biard, and Biencourt's account of interview with Massé, MNF I 376

208 For 'thunderbolt' MNF I 371
For Louis Membertou MNF I 371–2

209 For Biencourt on Biard MNF I 377
For quotations from letter MNF I 378

CHAPTER FIFTEEN: ALARMS, EXCURSIONS AND EXPEDITIONS
(210–23)

210 For 'clothes' sold MNF I 388
211 For complaints to prelates and illness MNF I 389 and HNF III 61
For 'attic' MNF I 401
212 For Massé's note MNF I 554
213 For Biard on the devil MNF I 381
214–15 For Queen's letter MNF I 259–60
215 For contract between Poutrincourt and La Saussaie, which gives
their places of residence, ND 228–9
216 For 'borrowed name' and 'secret enterprise' HNF III 62–3
217 For debt to Imbert ND 232
218 For court condemnation of Poutrincourt ND 242–4
220 For Jesuits' wretched life JR III 259
For Aquaviva's concern MNF I 270
221 For Simon MNF I 274–6
For Brother Gilbert's prayer JR IV 13
221–2 For legal separation of property Huguet 396
222 For negotiations between Poutrincourt and the Bishops of Verdun
ND 298–302
223 For Poutrincourt's exclamation HNF III 62

CHAPTER SIXTEEN: VIRGINIA TRIUMPHANT (224–40)

224 For Queen's command JR III 263
225 For Biard's despondency JR III 267
226 For site of St Sauveur MNF I 568 note 11. David Quinn disagrees. He
thinks that the first landfall was on Frenchman Bay and that then
the expedition moved to Somes Sound. See David Quinn's *North
America from Earliest Discovery to First Settlements* (New York 1977) 412.
For 'very evident' sign JR IV 93–7
227 Works consulted on Virginia are Charles M. Andrews' *The Colonial
Period of American History* (Newhaven 1934–49); W.F. Craven's *The
Southern Colonies in the Seventeenth Century* (Louisiana 1949); Richard
L. Morton's *Colonial Virginia* (North Carolina 1960).
231 For Argall on 'marauders' and missing letters and for Biard on Argall
JR IV 15

232 For Indians' concern JR III 71
    For Biard's praise of them JR IV 17
    For Argall's terms and Biard's reaction JR IV 21
233 For Biard's comment JR IV 27
234 For loot see a contemporary account: Ralph Hamor's *A True Discourse of the Present State of Virginia* (London 1615; reprinted Richmond Virginia 1957).
    For feared fate JR IV 33
236 For Biard on Argall JR IV 39
    For Poutrincourt's new expedition Huguet 424–5
239–40 For Biencourt on Biard and Biard on Biencourt JR IV 45–9
240 For Biard's elegiac exclamation JR IV 45

EPILOGUE: STAYING ON (241–51)

242 For Jesuits MNF I 397–404
    For Poutrincourt's aim MNF I 396
    The *Factum* was printed probably quite early in 1614 (MNF I 320–1), for though mention is made of the destruction of St Sauveur by Argall, there is none at all of the destruction of Port Royal. No lawsuit ensued and it is, in fact, much more of an anti-Jesuit pamphlet than a genuine *factum*. As for its probable author, the unsavoury Imbert, we last catch a brief glimpse of him in 1618 trying to obtain from Poutrincourt's heirs the wages he was owed (ND 232 note 1).
    Father Biard obviously read the *Factum*. As we have seen, he answered its crude charges obliquely and with dignity by giving his own version of events. As well as this long *Relation*, written in French and printed in 1616, he also wrote a Latin version for his fellow priests of all nationalities. In 1618/19 Lescarbot's third edition of his *History of New France* appeared. In this Lescarbot fairly politely, but unmistakably, espoused the Biencourt side and put forward Poutrincourt's accusation that it was Father Biard who had set the Virginians upon Port Royal. Father Biard was outraged. He asked permission of the new General in Rome, Father Vitelleschi, to spend some months in drawing up an answer to Lescarbot. Permission was granted, since, from the Jesuit point of view, it was necessary to defend the good name of the order. But in 1622 the

General wrote to Father Biard's superior in Lyons to say that the censors had advised against publication of this document. In vindicating himself Father Biard had obviously given full rein to his acrimony. The censors found the Apologia too full of digressions that had nothing to do with the Society of Jesus. The author had used too many unusual and old-fashioned expressions; and certain things did not 'savour sufficiently of the moderation and gravity befitting a priest.' L. Campeau's *Monumenta Novae Franciae* II: *Etablissement à Québec* (46–7) No doubt for those very reasons it made excellent reading!

244 For Poutrincourt's deposition to the Admiralty HNF III 68–71

244–5 For documents relating to Biencourt-Gravé agreements and quarrels ND 366–70 and 377–87; France, Archives départementales de la Seine-Maritime (Rouen), Série B, Fonds du Parlement, Arrêts civils. Registre juin-juillet 1633. PAC, MG 6, A9, 17 pages, transcripts, arrêt du Parlement de Rouen rejetant un appel des héritiers de Legendre contre une sentence de l'Amirauté (27 août 1632) rendue en faveur de Samuel Georges et associés.

245 For Poutrincourt's self-imposed title ND 381

246 For the *Fortune* see document drawn up by a notary, Chesneau, on 5th January 1616: France, Archives départementales de la Charente-Maritime (La Rochelle), Série E, Titres de famille, état civil, notaires. Minutes Chesneau, 1616–23, f° 1–1v. PAC, MG 6, A2, 5 pages, transcripts, charte-partie entre David Lomeron, secrétaire de Charles de Biencourt, et François Soreau, maître de la *Fortune* (180 tonneaux), 5 janvier 1616.

246–7 For Poutrincourt's death HNF III 538

The civil disturbances in France were caused by the Prince de Condé, the new Viceroy of Canada. As a Prince of the Blood, next in line to the throne after the King's brother, Gaston, he wanted to wrest power from the hands of the Queen Regent and her clever, greedy favourite, the Italian adventurer Concini. In August 1814 Condé declared himself champion of the King, ready to fight for the freedom of the realm. In September the fourteen-year-old King, on his way south to marry the Spanish Infanta, Anne of Austria, pronounced his champion a rebel. Condé proceeded to occupy towns and fortresses. One of the places captured was Méry-sur-Seine in Champagne, a town of which Poutrincourt had once been governor.

For epitaph HNF III 74–5. 'Sagamos' (sic) in this translation.

248 For Biencourt's self-imposed title see France, Archives départementales de la Charente-Maritime (La Rochelle), Série E, Titres de
famille, état civil, notaires. Minutes Chesneau, 1616–23, f° 24–6.
PAC, MG 6, A2, 5 pages, transcripts, obligation par Lomeron au
nom de C. Biencourt, 20 janvier 1618.

For quotations from letter Huguet 463–4. At the end of this Charles
signs himself 'Poutrincourt.'

249 For Scottish settlement see John G. Reid's 'The Scots Crown and
the Restitution of Port Royal, 1629–1632' in *Acadiensis* (spring 1977)
39–63.

For Biencourt in Acadia see Robert Le Blant, 'L'avitaillement du
Port Royal d'Acadie par Charles de Biencourt et les marchands
rochelais, 1615–1618' in *Revue d'histoire des colonies* 44 (1958) 138–64;
also H. Leander d'Entremont, *The Forts of Cape Sable of the Seventeenth Century* (Halifax 1938)

For Biencourt's 'repentance' JR XXIX 31

250 For Biard's verdict on the Biencourts JR III 137–9

INDEX